State in Society

The essays in this book trace the development of Joel S. Migdal's "state-in-society" approach. His process-oriented analysis illuminates how power is exercised around the world, and how and when patterns of power change.

Despite the triumph of the concept of state in social science literature, actual states have demonstrated less coherence than their theoretical counterparts, and, despite their apparent resources, have had great difficulty in transforming public policies into successful social change. The state-in-society approach demonstrates both that states are fragmented and that they face a multitude of social organizations – families, clans, multinational corporations, domestic businesses, tribes, political parties, and patron-client dyads – that maintain and vie for the power to set the rules guiding people's behavior.

These ongoing and overlapping struggles ally parts of the state with groups in society against other such coalitions. In the process, they determine how societies and states create and maintain distinct ways of structuring day-to-day life, including the nature of the rules that govern people's behavior, whom they benefit and whom they disadvantage, which sorts of elements unite people and which divide them, and what shared meanings people hold about their relations with others and their place in the world.

Joel S. Migdal is the Robert F. Philip Professor of International Studies in the University of Washington's Henry M. Jackson School of International Studies. His books include *Palestinian Society and Politics*, *Peasants, Politics, and Revolution*, *Strong Societies and Weak States*, *Through the Lens of Israel*, and (with Baruch Kimmerling of the Hebrew University of Jerusalem) *Palestinians: The Making of a People*.

Cambridge Studies in Comparative Politics

General Editor
Margaret Levi   *University of Washington, Seattle*

Associate Editors
Robert H. Bates   *Harvard University*
Peter Hall   *Harvard University*
Stephen Hanson   *University of Washington, Seattle*
Peter Lange   *Duke University*
Helen Milner   *Columbia University*
Frances Rosenbluth   *Yale University*
Susan Stokes   *University of Chicago*
Sidney Tarrow   *Cornell University*

Other Books in the Series

Continued on the page following the index

State in Society

STUDYING HOW STATES AND SOCIETIES TRANSFORM AND CONSTITUTE ONE ANOTHER

JOEL S. MIGDAL

University of Washington

CAMBRIDGE UNIVERSITY PRESS
Cambridge, New York, Melbourne, Madrid, Cape Town, Singapore, São Paulo

Cambridge University Press
40 West 20th Street, New York, NY 10011–4211, USA
www.cambridge.org
Information on this title:www.cambridge.org/9780521792868

First published 2001
Reprinted 2003, 2006

Printed in the United States of America

A catalogue record for this book is available from the British Library.

Library of Congress Cataloguing in Publication Data
Migdal, Joel S.
State in society : studying how states and societies transform and constitute one another
/ Joel S. Migdal.
p. cm. – (Cambridge studies in comparative politics)
Includes bibliographical references and index.
ISBN 0-521-79286-X (hb) – ISBN 0-521-79706-3 (pb.)
1. State, The. 2. Social control. 3. Power (Social sciences) I. Title. II. Series.
JC131.M54   2001
306.2–dc21   2001025468

ISBN-13   978-0-521-79286-8 hardback
ISBN-10   0-521-79286-X hardback

ISBN-13   978-0-521-79706-1 paperback
ISBN-10   0-521-79706-3 paperback

Dedicated to sisters and brothers

Ayala and Yudi
Penina and Mickey
Steve and Nancy

For their never-ending love and support

Contents

Acknowledgments

The ideas in this book have been battered by merciless criticism from colleagues and students at Tel-Aviv University, Harvard University, and the University of Washington over the last three decades. Colleagues from other universities also weighed in at various times with their own brands of dissatisfaction. I suppose that only the hard-edged nature of their critiques forced me to work over these ideas countless times. The book, I think, is the better for it. A number of colleagues deserve special thanks: Myron Aronoff, Mickey Glazer, Penina Migdal Glazer, Reşat Kasaba, Atul Kohli, Ben Smith, Robert Vitalis, and Patricia Woods. Chandni Gupta, Kammerle Schneider, Tina Smith, Cathy Vuong, and Zoë Stemm provided selfless hours of research assistance and preparation time. And Jane Meyerding helped in final preparation of the manuscript. Support for work on the book came from the Robert F. Philip Professorship at the University of Washington. Nothing has been more important to me than the warm, supportive environment my sprawling clan has given me over the years. It is with warm affection that I dedicate this book to my sisters and brothers, by birth and by marriage (the latter known in our family as the *zugekommeners*).

PART I

Introduction

1

The State-in-Society Approach

A NEW DEFINITION OF THE
STATE AND TRANSCENDING
THE NARROWLY CONSTRUCTED
WORLD OF RIGOR

This introductory chapter frames the ideas that have preoccupied me over the past two decades, when the remaining essays in this book were written. I have four primary goals here. First, I want to present a concise statement of the state-in-society approach that is the centerpiece of the book, especially in light of the literature that I have drawn on – and have found wanting. My second aim is the principal one for this chapter: I present a new definition of the state in place of Max Weber's widely used one, which I believe has led scholars down sterile paths. My hope is that the new definition will offer social scientists a better, more grounded way to conceive of the state and will suggest new, innovative lines of inquiry to them. Third, implicitly these essays reject what has become standard method in political science and related social science disciplines. I want to spell out the point of how better to approach comparative research and state why I think political scientists should abandon the blinders that have limited their work. And, finally, I want to show how a state-in-society perspective can provide new and exciting answers to well-studied issues in comparative studies by recounting the work of several young scholars who have used the approach.

State-in-Society as an Approach to Studying Domination and Change

The themes explored in the essays in this book, domination and change, are by no means original. Identifying and analyzing patterns of domination – the recurring ways in which some use violence, threats, and other means to make others behave in ways they would not have otherwise chosen – and when and why those patterns change have preoccupied thinkers in every period and in practically every culture. They have been at the center of modern social science for the last two centuries.

As for me, these issues first began to enter my consciousness when I was still a college student in the tumultuous 1960s, as I viewed the topsy-turvy world around me. I and thousands of other college students like me hooted, sat-in, and marched in the hope of bringing about change in U.S. Vietnam policy and, eventually, to transform the way authority was exercised both in the United States and in the international arena. I do not think that I can underestimate the lasting impact of the Vietnam War on me, especially in cultivating what would become my life-long preoccupation with how authority and power are established, maintained, and transformed.

From a far more distant perch, I witnessed during my high school and college years an epic revolution in the world map. The crumbling of the great European empires led to the appearance of dozens of new states in Africa and Asia. New political leaders made all sorts of bold claims about the prospects for social change inside their borders as well as their intention to break the stranglehold of outmoded forms of authority internationally. It was a moment of great optimism. Even in the midst of the never-ending background noise of the Cold War, with its own not-so-subtle messages about world power – about governmental mastery and personal vulnerability – the Vietnam War and the larger process of decolonization of which it was a part made me acutely aware of patterns of domination and gave me confidence that the more pernicious forms of it could be upended.

The books that I consumed in those years grappled – sometimes explicitly, more often implicitly – with the question of who makes the rules for how others behave, who forces his or her will on others, and when such patterns are transformed. The social science works I read fell into several camps as authors tried to put their finger on the heartbeat of the new postwar world. By far the most popular, and probably the most unsatisfying, was the literature drawing from Talcott Parsons's social-systems theory.[1] Parsons's approach subsumed both state and society in a broad conception of the so-called social system, whose various parts are bound together by an overarching and unified set of values. Ultimately, according to the social-system approach, it is that package of values that takes center stage in the analysis of power, structure, and change. Parsons

---

[1] Talcott Parsons, *The Social System* (Glencoe, IL: Free Press, 1951).

stressed that the study of political structure and process was "in the context of a general theoretical analysis of the total society as a social system."[2] He noted that "the core of a society, as a system, is the patterned normative order through which the life of a population is collectively organized."[3] His analysis relied on the concept of a singular set of social values and norms, which he argued were internalized by society's members.[4] Following his lead and using a somewhat tendentious reading of Weber, other scholars saw norms and values weaving together elites and institutions from the social, political, religious, and economic realms.

In the United States and sometimes in Europe, scholars characterized the operation of these forces – the controlling values and their ties to elites and social institutions – as pluralism, a harmonious operation of competing interest and status groups. Again, Parsons explains the rationale for pluralist theories of the period: "No society can maintain stability in the face of varying exigencies and strains unless interest constellations of its members are grounded in solidarity and internalized loyalties and obligations."[5]

For other parts of the world, especially the newly formed countries in Asia and Africa where such normative solidarity was presumed to be absent, the focus was on the development of an ethic powerful enough to transform divergent (unharmonious) norms and institutions (often seen as traditional and inferior). The key in effecting (desirable) change, then, was to knit together a normative consensus that would be the center or engine for a functioning social system. While that would seem a daunting task – after all, which of all the dissenting normative sets would win out? – the problem was wished away by assuming teleologically that modern, Western values would inevitably triumph in the end.

Parsons was the leading sociologist of his era, but his influence extended beyond his discipline to other social scientists, as well. As a political science major in college, I initially engaged the problems of domination and change through variants of social-systems, or simply "systems," theory. Among the most prominent political science authors

---

[2] Talcott Parsons, "The Political Aspect of Social Structure and Process," in David Easton (ed.), *Varieties of Political Theory* (Englewood Cliffs, NJ: Prentice-Hall, 1966), p. 71.

[3] Talcott Parsons, *Societies: Evolutionary and Comparative Perspectives* (Englewood Cliffs, NJ: Prentice-Hall, 1966), p. 10.

[4] Parsons, *Societies*, p. 14.

[5] Ibid.

in this stream were Gabriel A. Almond and David Easton.[6] To me, the clearest and deepest thinker promoting this view of domination and change in new states was Edward Shils, an important collaborator of Parsons and a person whose work I continue to find endlessly fascinating and largely relevant.[7] For all his extraordinary insights, Shils also slipped into teleological traps, repeatedly writing of the "not-yet" developed centers outside the West.

Shils seemed to have an intuitive feel for both the material and ethereal sources of authority that eluded many other writers. He grasped the elusive point that societies are not, and cannot be bound only through material and instrumental relations. People's connection to one another rests just as fundamentally on a transcendental notion: they seek and create powerful common understandings or meaning in their relationships, forming a strong relational glue that binds them together. For him, a "community is not just a group of concrete and particular persons; it is, more fundamentally, a group of persons acquiring their significance by their embodiment of values which transcend them and by their conformity with standards and rules from which they derive their dignity."[8] I admired the way Shils, as an academic engaged in secular analysis, did not shy away from the difficult issue of the transcendental, absorbing into the core of his analysis how people seek larger meaning in their lives and in their relations with others. I began to think that social connections go beyond the cognitive to affective factors, beyond the instrumental to emotional dimensions.[9] And I continue to feel that social science has erred badly in ignoring phenomena such as revelation and redemption, which have played such a central role in human history. Only a handful of major scholars, such as the brilliant legal scholar Robert Cover, have made revelation a pivotal part of their thinking.[10] Weber made some

---

[6] Gabriel A. Almond and G. Bingham Powell, Jr., *Comparative Politics: System, Process, and Policy* (Boston: Little, Brown, and Company, 1978); David Easton, *The Political System: An Inquiry into the State of Political Science* (Chicago: University of Chicago Press, 1981).

[7] Edward Shils, *Center and Periphery: Essays in Macrosociology* (Chicago: University of Chicago Press, 1975); Talcott Parsons and Edward Shils, *Toward a General Theory of Action* (Cambridge, MA: Harvard University Press, 1951).

[8] Shils, *Center and Periphery*, 138.

[9] On the role of emotion in analysis (in this case, the analysis of nationalism), see Kenneth Gregory Lawson, "War at the Grassroots: The Great War and the Nationalization of Civic Life," Ph.D. dissertation, University of Washington, 2000.

[10] Robert Cover, "Nomos and Narrative" in Martha Minow, Michael Ryan, and Austin Sarat (eds.), *Narrative, Violence, and the Law: The Essays of Robert Cover* (Ann Arbor: University

references to the centrality of redemption but did not pursue its importance in the modern state. For Shils and others dealing with such issues as the creation of shared meaning, including people's feelings about the purpose of society and their place in it, there was an understanding that the forging of social bonds through non-instrumental means excludes as well as includes, setting demarcation lines of who is part of society and who is outside it.

One difficulty that I had with Shils and others was the way in which their use of the systems approach and its cognates blurred the locus of authority. In his celebrated essays on center and periphery, for example, Shils saw the source of authority and change as inhering in a witch's brew of elites, institutions, and shared values.[11] But the source and coherence of this brew, particularly of the shared values, seemed mysterious. Somehow it came together and then used its powerful ideas, resources, and people to seep outward, incorporating in its path less powerful others who operated according to different sets of rules. It all seemed so elusive to me.

When I went to graduate school in 1967, I came into contact with a different school led by the person who was to become my dissertation advisor, Samuel Huntington. Huntington, along with a few others in the 1960s such as J. P. Nettles, insisted that the place to look for the sources of power to enforce order is in political institutions specifically. After a detour into dependency and world-systems theory, both of which properly insisted on the importance of taking into account international power relationships for the purpose of understanding domination and change in any single society, social science theory returned to Huntington's insight in the late 1970s and 1980s. Authors began to insist that the state should be seen as an organization maintaining a special, autonomous status; it has been, in fact, the locus of change.[12] Indeed, that premise has remained a powerful part of social and political theories right up to the present, expressed in statism, structuralism, rational choice theories, neorealism, and more. Domination and change have frequently been analyzed as part of a process in which the state is the fulcrum. Through law, bureaucracy, violence, and other means, the argument goes, the

---

of Michigan Press, 1993), p. 108. Cover writes intriguingly about the "*imagined* instant of unified meaning."

[11] Shils, *Center and Periphery*, p. 4.

[12] Peter B. Evans, Dietrich Rueschemeyer, and Theda Skocpol, *Bringing the State Back In* (New York: Cambridge University Press, 1985).

modern state has reshaped people's behavior and, by extension, their sense of who they are.

The most important line of criticism the new statist literature aimed at the social systems models and Marxist theories was their inability to distinguish analytically between the state – with its seemingly central role in shaping social relations and personal identity – and other sectors of society. The critics, instead, posited the power and autonomy of the state in determining patterns of behavior and stratification.[13] The argument of state theorists was that states do not simply blend into an array of elite-run institutions – as Parsons had described it, the political "must systematically articulate with the other sub-systems"[14] – but stand out as autonomous, highly powerful organizations in their own right. The call was for researchers to shift their focus from the general social system to the unique place of the state in rule making and in effecting social change. In so doing, state theorists aimed to move from the emphasis on the harmony or consensus at the center to the conflicts between a headstrong state and other groupings in society. Like the systems theorists, the state-oriented scholars drew heavily from Max Weber. But the Weber they followed was the one who stressed the conceptualization of the state as an autonomous organization with extraordinary means to dominate.

In 1974, a couple of years after I had finished my dissertation, I led a seminar of five masters students at Tel-Aviv University in Israel, where I held my first teaching post. The course examined the city and its role in larger societal and political change through history. We looked into the centrality of the city in popular imagination and, directly or indirectly, in the various social science theories of change and domination. I think that my years in Israel itself, including the traumatic three weeks of the Yom Kippur War and its long, painful aftermath, as well as the months I spent in the villages of the occupied West Bank researching a book,[15] unconsciously brought into doubt many of my assumptions about how authority is exercised and how it changes.

---

[13] Ibid. State-centered theory aimed its general critique at another type of literature, though one far less popular in the United States, which was the home of much of social science writing in the decades after World War II. That was neo-Marxism. As with the systems approach, the state theorists faulted the neo-Marxist literature for failing to account for the state's autonomy from social forces, in this case, from the dominant social class.

[14] Parsons, "The Political Aspect of Social Structure and Process," p. 104.

[15] Joel S. Migdal, *et al.*, *Palestinian Society and Politics* (Princeton, NJ: Princeton University Press, 1980).

Despite the almost mythical power of the Israeli state, especially after its resounding six-day victory against three Arab states in 1967, I found that the situation in the Palestinian villages that it occupied bore only slight resemblance to its carefully designed policies. The same impression of a disjunction between state leaders' will and the actual outcomes of their policies came through strongly during and after the 1973 war, as I sat in Tel Aviv glued to the radio and then visited both fronts, the Golan Heights and Suez Canal. Nor did the United States fare any better with its policies in Vietnam. At about that time, too, I heard a lecture by a visitor in the department, Seymour Mann, arguing that, while the Model Cities program in the United States had indeed initiated substantial social and political change in inner cities, the results were a far cry from what policymakers had planned or anticipated.

I began to grow increasingly uncomfortable with what I was teaching in that seminar in the wake of the Yom Kippur War. During one of the class sessions, it struck me that the various schools of social science literature may have been posing their questions in an unhelpful way. They implicitly asked where they could find that center or state or distinctive set of institutions that could have its way with the population, that could effectively make and enforce the rules for daily life and, in so doing, mold people's understanding of themselves. Once that magical site was discovered, it would unlock the secrets, whether material or cultural, depending on the theory, that could tell us how patterns of domination are established and how they change. The assumption was that the city or center or core or state or dominant social class – some integrated locus of authority – held superior resources and ideas that it could use in order to extend its will throughout an entire society.

Those acted upon, the objects of control, played little role in the theories; they were the ones who changed, the passive recipients of others' rules. More often than not, they were assumed to be a supine mass. Only later would subaltern theories from South Asia and works by scholars such as James C. Scott challenge those views. In 1974, Western social scientists seemed nearly unanimous in the mechanics of domination and change that discounted the active role of the masses. Beyond that, they variously asked why some loci of authority succeeded more and others less?;[16]

---

[16] For example, Samuel P. Huntington, *Political Order in Changing Societies* (New Haven, CT: Yale University Press, 1968); a more recent example is David Waldner, *State Building and Late Development* (Ithaca, NY: Cornell University Press, 1999).

why some states took on particular forms, such as democracy, and others not?;[17] and so on. Even various shades of Marxists seemed to reserve a role for lower classes only in fiery revolutions, not in day-to-day patterns of domination.

Possibly, I suggested to the participants in the seminar, domination and change were not best understood in terms of the outcomes of purposeful, goal-oriented loci with overpowering resources and ideas at hand, such as the state, as we found in prevailing theories. Perhaps, we should look at multiple sites to understand domination and change – and at results that did not fit any of the parties' designed policies. I submitted to the students that the unintended outcomes of multiple conflicts in society – over whose rules should prevail, over which ideas should predominate – may explain more about domination and change than did existing theories.[18] States (or any other integrated site of resources and ideas) engage in pitched battles with other powerful figures and groups with entrenched ways of doing things. Sometimes, the power of these other social formations is obvious, as in the ability to withhold badly needed credit; sometimes, it is veiled, as in ostracism in a small community. In either case, the struggles over revenues, other goodies, and which ideas should prevail are fierce and real.

In Israel in the wake of the 1967 and 1973 wars, these conflicts were intense and pervasive. The students witnessed them daily in the form of wildcat strikes, the overnight establishment of illegal settlements in the West Bank, resistance of numerous couples to state-mandated religious weddings, marches by so-called Black Panthers protesting Ashkenazi domination, scattered acts of resistance by Palestinians in the occupied territories, and much more. Israel was in turmoil, and the sorts of conflicts that were hard to detect prior to these two wars were now out in the open and impossible to overlook. I asked if the conflicts that underlay these acts, as well as the coalitions that formed around them, might not tell us far more

---

[17] Barrington Moore, Jr., *Social Origins of Dictatorship and Democracy: Lord and Peasant in the Making of the Modern World* (Boston: Beacon Press, 1966); Guillermo O'Donnell and Philippe C. Schmitter, *Transitions from Authoritarian Rule* (Baltimore, MD: Johns Hopkins University Press, 1986); Samuel P. Huntington, *The Third Wave: Democratization in the Late Twentieth Century* (Norman: University of Oklahoma Press, 1991).

[18] Recently, a scholar made this point by noting that any "attempt to preserve particular hegemonic representations of class, gender, and community . . . are interrupted by moments of contestation." Leela Fernandes, *Producing Workers: The Politics of Gender, Class, and Culture in the Calcutta Jute Mills* (Philadelphia: University of Pennsylvania Press, 1997), p. xiii.

about patterns of domination and change than the designs and goals of single, admittedly powerful sites or actors. Indeed, could the apparently rock-hard Israeli state remain fundamentally the same after engaging in these difficult domestic battles? (The answer was soon to be clear; it could not.[19])

Of course, I could not imagine during the seminar that my questions to the students back then would lead me to think and write about these issues for the next quarter of a century. In fact, the ideas generated in that class turned out to be the seed of the "state-in-society" approach developed in the following essays, as well as the origin of a revised definition of the state, which I will offer later in this introductory essay. Throughout the book, my emphasis will be on process – on the ongoing struggles among shifting coalitions over the rules for daily behavior. These processes determine how societies and states create and maintain distinct ways of structuring day-to-day life – the nature of the rules that govern people's behavior, whom they benefit and whom they disadvantage, which sorts of elements unite people and which divide them, what shared meaning people hold about their relations with others and about their place in the world. And these processes also ordain the ways that rules and patterns of domination and subordination are challenged and change.

My view of the inner workings of domination and change starts with the axiom that no single, integrated set of rules, whether encoded in state law or sanctified as religious scriptures or enshrined as the rules of etiquette for daily behavior, exists anywhere. Quite simply, there is no uncontested universal code – in law, religion, or any other institution – in any society for guiding people's lives. The state-in-society model used here zeroes in on the conflict-laden interactions of multiple sets of formal and informal guideposts for how to behave that are promoted by different groupings in society.[20] These multiple groupings, all of which use subtle and not-so-subtle rewards and sanctions – including, at times, out-and-out violence – to try and get their way, comprise loose-knit informal collections of people as well as highly structured organizations with manifold

---

[19] See Joel S. Migdal, *Through the Lens of Israel: Explorations in State and Society* (Albany: State University of New York Press, 2001).

[20] Yoav Peled and Gershon Shafir, "The Roots of Peacemaking: The Dynamics of Citizenship in Israel, 1948–93," *International Journal of Middle East Studies* 28 (1996): 391–413. They describe this axiom as a "conceptual framework that deconstructs the multiple and competing conceptions of citizenship" (p. 392).

resources at their disposal. In short, all societies have ongoing battles among groups pushing different versions of how people should behave. The nature and outcomes of these struggles give societies their distinctive structure and character.

States are no different from any other formal organizations or informal social groupings in this regard. Their laws and regulations must contend with other, very different types of sanctioned behavior, often with utterly unexpected results for the societies that states purport to govern – and for the states themselves. Michel de Certeau captures this dynamic in the hidden struggle of indigenous peoples in South America against the Spanish colonizers. "Submissive, and even consenting to their subjection, the Indians nevertheless often *made* of the rituals, representations, and laws imposed on them something quite different from what their conquerors had in mind; they subverted them not by rejecting or altering them, but by using them with respect to ends and references foreign to the system they had no choice but to accept."[21]

It is not simply poorly designed policies or incompetent officials or insufficient resources that explain the failures or mixed results of state policies. States must contend with opposing groupings, some of which are quietly and indirectly subversive, such as the Indians that de Certeau cites, others of which are openly confrontational. These multiple groupings of opposition have created coalitions to strengthen their stance, and these have cut right into the very structure of states themselves. The resulting coalitional struggles have taken their toll: state policy implementation and the outcomes in society have ended up quite different from the state's original blueprints. Even the boldest state plans, as Scott has demonstrated in his discussion of the designs of modernism, can turn into disastrous follies.[22]

Some of the difficulties in recognizing the limitations of states come from popular ideas about them and from the conventional ways that social science has understood what they are. In the press and in everyday speech, the state has been represented as if it were a coherent, integrated, and goal-oriented body. In anthropomorphic tones, news stories have emphasized the overall coherence of the state, its singular mind-set ("China denied

---

[21] Michel de Certeau, *The Practice of Everyday Life* (Berkeley: University of California Press, 1984), p. xiii.

[22] James C. Scott, *Seeing Like a State: How Certain Schemes to Improve the Human Condition Have Failed* (New Haven: Yale University Press, 1998).

today . . ."). More than that, state leaders have relentlessly pushed the idea that the state, as a purposeful and coherent entity, is a representation of the transcendental meaning that Shils referred to in his essays: the state is the embodiment of *the* nation or *the* people, and its rules – The Law – hold a special sanctity.[23] As one activist in Egypt, criticizing the arrest of a sociologist who supposedly "defamed" Egypt by referring in a documentary to election fraud, noted, "The government has convinced the people that Egypt and the government are one and the same thing."[24] And, while that notion has been regularly contested (*e.g.*, people's proclamation of fidelity to a *higher* law), it has had a considerable effect on popular thinking. Indeed, people characterize others by their overall orientation to that singular Law, as in, "She is a *law-abiding* citizen, but he is a *law-breaker*." The Law's transcendental quality, then, is represented not only in its role in connecting people, making them The People, but also in its fundamental moral quality as the right way to behave.

Many of the same elements found in popular thinking have also appeared in social science literature with a slightly different twist. Weber, who cast such a large shadow over twentieth-century social science, offered what has become a now-classic definition of the state. It still maintains wide currency as the way to understand today's states. First, he wrote, "the modern state is a compulsory association which organizes domination."[25] For him, "the state is a relation of men dominating men, a relation supported by means of legitimate (i.e., considered to be legitimate) violence."[26] In his most widely quoted statement, "A state is a human community that (successfully) claims the *monopoly of the legitimate use of physical* force within a given territory."[27] Weber assumed that states are *goal-oriented* associations, but because they can hold such disparate goals he chose to define them in terms of their *means* (the use of force) instead. For him states are purposeful associations with varied purposes but similar means.

---

[23] Shils, *Center and Periphery*, pp. 75–6, recognizes that the center does not hold a monopoly of authority and that there are multiple sources of competing authority. But an imposing center, he notes, integrates society through "the image of the society which it precipitates" (p. 74).

[24] Gasser Abdel Razik quoted in *The New York Times*, July 10, 2000, p. A10.

[25] *From Max Weber: Essays in Sociology*, translated and edited by H. H. Gerth and C. Wright Mills (New York: Oxford University Press, 1958), p. 82.

[26] Ibid., p. 78.

[27] Ibid., p. 78.

13

Even though Weber carefully placed the word "successfully" in parentheses in the last quote above, in practice all sorts of states, both successful in monopolizing violence and not, have appeared in social science scholarship as if they were tight-knit, purposeful organizations, with autonomous goals, using violence and legitimacy as successful tools in maintaining social control and implementing policy. Weber was much more exact than many who followed him in his assumptions. He was careful to note how limited the experience of states *successfully* centralizing and monopolizing violent means actually was. Others unfortunately stretched the basic assumption that with extraordinary resources at its disposal, all sorts of states manage to use violence, the threat of violence, and other means to induce the people in their claimed territory to submit to, or even embrace, a near-endless array of laws and regulations.[28] These rules are given a singularity (again, The Law), and the state's role is to construct a Rule of Law.[29]

When one attempts to analyze individual states and particular patterns of domination, several serious problems crop up in how scholars have used Weber's definition. The emphasis on monopoly masks situations where authority is fragmented and contentious. Even a word such as "legitimate" diverts attention from contending forms of authority or disgruntlement with dominant forms of authority. Scholars pay lip service to the fact that Weber was certainly not referring to all states but was attempting only to create a heuristic, ideal type state. But Weber's use of an ideal type state monopolizing legitimate force and ruling through rational law gives scholars precious few ways to talk about real-life states that do not meet this ideal. Actual states are deviations from the ideal or corrupted versions of the ideal.

Weber's definition has the state firing on all cylinders, and, while he certainly did not mean the ideal type to be taken as the normal type, that is precisely what has happened in subsequent scholarship. Of course, in real human society, no state can do all that an ideal-type state can, as Weber

---

[28] "Law exists when there is a probability that an order will be upheld by a specific staff of men who will use physical or psychical compulsion with the intention of obtaining conformity with the order, or of inflicting sanctions for infringement of it." *From Max Weber*, p. 180.

[29] "Only bureaucracy has established the foundation for the administration of a rational law conceptually systematized on the basis of such enactments as the latter Roman imperial period first created with a high degree of technical perfection. . . . The 'rational' interpretation of law on the basis of strictly formal conceptions stands opposite the kind of adjudication that is primarily bound to sacred traditions." *From Max Weber*, p. 216.

makes perfectly clear. Tremendous variation has existed among states in the levers that their leaders and officials have controlled in order to garner resources and to accomplish a skewed distribution of economic (and other) opportunities; in the sheer quantity of resources they could mobilize through taxation, aid, plunder, conscription, and so on; in their effectiveness in making sure the resources ended up in the hands they intended; in the inner coherence they exhibited in deciding and acting upon whom to favor; and in the means they used to achieve the selective distribution of rewards. Those differences among states are extremely important (for scholars of the state, these variations have been the stuff of comparative politics).

But, with Weber's definition as the starting point, variation can be conceptualized and measured only as distance from the ideal type. As long as the *idea* of the state is uniform and constant, the variation of states, even the failure of some states, can be expressed only in terms of deviation from the standard. If real states fell short of the standard, as they were bound to do, all sorts of words had to be invented to express the gap between actual practice and the ideal. Terms such as corruption, weakness, and relative capacity implied that the ways things really worked were somehow exogenous to the normative model of what the state and its relations to society are, or should be. Comparison comes in specifying and measuring deviation from the norm or the ideal. State capacity is gauged against a measuring stick whose endpoint is a variant of Weber's ideal-type state.

The assumption that only the state does, or should, create rules and that only it does, or should, maintain the violent means to bend people to obey those rules minimizes and trivializes the rich negotiation, interaction, and resistance that occur in every human society among multiple systems of rules. It posits a human society where one incredibly coherent and complex organization exercises an extraordinary hegemony of thought and action over all other social formations intersecting that territory. It provides no way to theorize about arenas of competing sets of rules, other than to cast these in the negative, as failures or weak states or even as non-states. In short, Weber's ideal state when taken as the normal state obscures as much as it illuminates by continually measuring actual states against an ideal version of what states are or should be.

A New Definition of the State

The state-in-society approach offered here and in the following essays suggests a different definition of the state from Weber's. The state is a field of power marked by the use and threat of violence and shaped by (1) *the image of a coherent, controlling organization in a territory, which is a representation of the people bounded by that territory*, and (2) *the actual practices of its multiple parts.*

Actual states are shaped by two elements, *image* and *practices*.[30] These can be overlapping and reinforcing, or contradictory and mutually destructive. Image has tended to be homologous from state to state, especially the image of the modern state that has its origins in the fifteenth through seventeenth centuries in northwest Europe and came to encompass the entire globe in the last half of the twentieth century. Conversely, practices have tended to be diverse, and, while there are certainly recognizable comparative patterns, they have defied neat categorization.

First is the image. I adapt this from Shils, who used the term to describe the "center," not the state. "The image," he explained, "amalgamates the numerous institutions of which the performers are members and on behalf of which they exercise authority, into an *image* of a dominant and single center of society."[31] In the definition here, the image of the *state* is of a dominant, integrated, autonomous entity that controls, in a given territory, all rule making, either directly through its own agencies or indirectly by sanctioning other authorized organizations – businesses, families, clubs, and the like – to make certain circumscribed rules.[32]

Image implies perception. Here, perception of the state is by those inside and outside its claimed territory as the chief and appropriate rule maker within its territorial boundaries. In that regard, the perception assumes a single entity that is fairly autonomous, unified, and centralized. While everyone recognizes the complexity and sheer sprawl of this organization – that its parts will not always work in pure harmony, that "image"

---

[30] Akhil Gupta, "Blurred Boundaries: The Discourse of Corruption, the Culture of Politics, and the Imagined State," *American Ethnologist* 22 (May 1995): 375–402. In this brilliant article, Gupta attempts an ethnography of the state by looking both at its "everyday practices" and its "discursive construction." I first read a draft of the article in the late 1980s, and I think subconsciously it had a major effect in my working toward the present definition of the state. While his "discursive construction" differs from my understanding of image, the article makes clear the need "to take into account [the state's] constitution through a complex set of *spatially* intersecting representations and practices" (p. 377). These ideas will be echoed below.

[31] Shils, *Center and Periphery*, p. 74 (my emphasis).

[32] Weber writes, "The right to use physical force is ascribed to other institutions or to individuals only to the extent to which the state permits it. The state is considered the sole source of the 'right' to use violence." *From Max Weber*, p. 78.

16

is a likeness that does not display every wart – still, the image of the state induces people to perceive its agencies as generically integrated and acting in conjunction with one another.

The image posits an entity having two sorts of boundaries: (1) territorial boundaries between the state and other states, and (2) social boundaries between the state – its (public) actors and agencies – and those subject to its rules (private). While for some limited groups, such as certain nomadic tribes, territorial borders may appear not to exist, for most others, from travelers to importers, the lines on school maps represent clearly defined images of how the world is structured geographically. Weber got it right in saying, " 'Territory' is one of the characteristics of the state."[33]

More than that, the image of territorial borders separating spaces of control by different states is augmented by the common notion that those states somehow embody the people inside their lines; this is what I referred to as representation in the definition at the beginning of this section. Thus, it does not seem incongruous to read in the newspaper about a chief executive speaking for the "people," as if the state's boundaries manifest some underlying unity among those in the territory. In the image, the state, although separated from the general population of the territory, as will be discussed momentarily, is the avatar of that population, as seen in UN votes, interstate diplomacy, or any number of other daily venues. Such representation signifies that territorial boundaries serve both as limits of state control and the circumscribing of a connected people. I will return to the issue of the connection of the people shortly.

Besides territorial boundaries, the second sort of boundary that the image of the state includes is a social boundary, separating the state from other non-state, or private, actors and social forces. Weber noted that the separation of public and private – he was looking particularly at public and private law – is a hallmark of the modern, bureaucratized state. The conceptual separation of public and private law "presupposes the conceptual separation of the 'state,' as abstract bearer of sovereign prerogatives and the creator of 'legal norms,' from all personal 'authorizations' of individuals."[34]

The state is not only separated, it is elevated. That is, its representation of the people distinguishes it from all other entities, which in the image can signify only particular interests. Only the state is the general

---

[33] Ibid., p. 78. [34] Ibid., p. 239.

representation of the commonality of the people, deriving from their underlying connection.

After image, the second key aspect of the definition of state is practices. The routine performance of state actors and agencies, their practices, may reinforce the image of the state or weaken it; they may bolster the notion of the territorial and public-private boundaries or neutralize them.

Endless numbers of practices have fortified the image that the territorial markers on maps are real and effective. State leaders have employed visas, passports, border markers, barbed wire and electronic fences, border police, armies, official maps, school textbooks, and more to mark off the territory that the state purports to govern. This list makes clear that the threat or use of violence stands behind many of its practices. Additionally, practices by those outside the state entity can also reinforce and validate the image of map lines being real. The United Nations, for example, has given states claiming control over specified territory a "seat" among the world's other states.

Likewise, practices may serve to recognize, reinforce, and validate, not only the territorial element of state control, but also the social separation between the state and other social formations (the public-private divide) in numerous ways. Ceremonies, such as a coronation or inauguration, for example, have solemnly affirmed the separation. So, too, have the consignment of state work to special spaces, such as courthouses or city halls or federal buildings. In these and other countless ways, the image of the state as a distinct, even elevated, social body has been sharpened.

Foucault, I think, tried to probe the often anomalous relationship between image and practice, even when practices tend to reinforce the image or myth of the state:

But the state, no more probably today than at any other time in its history, does not have this unity, this individuality, this rigorous functionality, nor, to speak frankly, this importance; maybe, after all, the state is no more than a composite reality and a mythicized abstraction, whose importance is a lot more limited than many of us think.... It is the tactics of government which make possible the continual definition and redefinition of what is within the competence of the state and what is not, the public versus the private, and so on; thus the state can only be understood in its survival and its limits on the basis of the general tactics of governmentality.[35]

---

[35] *The Foucault Effect: Studies in Governmentality*, edited by Graham Burchell, Colin Gordon, and Peter Miller (Chicago: University of Chicago Press, 1991), p. 103.

While Foucault separates practices, or what he calls the tactics of governmentality, from image, he still tends to see those practices as reinforcing the mythicized abstraction, the accepted definition of what the state can do, and the perceived distinction between public and private. But practices may also work against these myths and perceptions. What my definition of the state captures, allowing new theoretical lines to emerge, is precisely those practices – those routinized performative acts – that batter the image of a coherent, controlling state and neutralize the territorial and public-private boundaries. Practices are often pitted against image. Bertrand Russell caught the distinction between image and practice beautifully: "We have, in fact, two kinds of morality side by side; one which we preach but do not practise, and another which we practise but seldom preach."[36] Russell pointed to the breach between image and practices in his emphasis on morality. While the image of the state implies a singular morality, one standard way, indeed *right* way, of doing things, practices denote multiple types of performance and, possibly, some contention over what is *the* right way to act.

These practices have not simply been the deviations from normative – good – behavior as set out in state codes. They have been moral codes in their own right, contending with that expressed in the state's image for predominance in recruitment of officials into state offices, distribution of state resources, discretion in the application of regulations, and much, much more. Jean-François Bayart, Stephen Ellis, and Béatrice Hibou singled out many of these practices in a recent, innovative book on Africa, *The Criminalization of the State in Africa*.[37] Although the authors gave a technically narrow definition of what they meant by criminal, I think it is an unfortunate word to use in this context, since it implies behavior that is not only unlawful but also morally wrong. From an analytic point of view, it privileges the laws and codes of the image of the state in question (or of states generally), making them the researcher's *analytic* standard, over what are often conflicting standards expressed in the practices of its parts. What may be easily labeled as corruption or criminality, such as nepotism or smuggling, can also be looked at, for instance, as a morality favoring kinship ties over meritocracy or one expressing the right of

---

[36] Bertrand Russell, "Eastern and Western Ideals of Happiness" in *Sceptical Essays* (New York: W. W. Norton, 1928).

[37] Jean-François Bayart, Stephen Ellis, and Béatrice Hibou, *The Criminalization of the State in Africa* (Bloomington: Indiana University Press, 1999).

movement of people and goods across the boundaries arbitrarily imposed by state law.[38]

How can one understand the appearance of multiple sets of practices, many of which might be at odds with the dictates of the image (and morality) of the state? The sheer unwieldy character of states' far-flung parts, the many fronts on which they fight battles with groupings with conflicting standards of behavior, and the lure for their officials of alternative sets of rules that might, for example, empower or enrich them personally or privilege the group to which they are most loyal, all have led to diverse practices by states' parts or fragments.

Various parts or fragments of the state have allied with one another, as well as with groups outside, to further their goals. Those practices and alliances have acted to promote a variety of sets of rules, often quite distinct from those set out in the state's own official laws and regulations. These alliances, coalitions, or networks have neutralized the sharp territorial and social boundary that the first portrayal of the state has acted to establish, as well as the sharp demarcation between the state as preeminent rule maker and society as the recipient of those rules.

Examples of such practices neutralizing boundaries associated with the image of the state start with state officials using their office space to conduct private business, thus quietly hammering away at the public-private divide. In one wonderful case recounted to me, an African official brought his cow to graze on the lawn of the state building in which he worked. Gupta's article on "blurred boundaries" analyzes the opposite, where private space was used for public business. He recounts the case of Sharmaji, an Indian land official who kept the records for about five thousand plots of land. In the lower part of Sharmaji's home was a room that he used as his "office." "That is where he was usually to be found, surrounded by clients, sycophants, and colleagues."[39] One of his aides helped mediate between Sharmaji and people coming to change or register land titles, making clear how much it would take to "get the job done." Another assisted with official tasks as well as those for Sharmaji's household. The distinction between private and public space, private and public work, and private and public fees was all but lost.

---

[38] "Instead of treating corruption as a dysfunctional aspect of state organizations, I see it as a mechanism through which 'the state' itself is discursively constituted." Gupta, "Blurred Boundaries," p. 376.

[39] Gupta, "Blurred Boundaries," p. 379.

Ellis's account of apartheid (and post-apartheid) South Africa presents more complex instances of neutralizing the state-society divide.

> Some explicitly criminal gangs have developed close relations with the security forces. This has produced within some sections of the security forces a highly ambiguous attitude towards certain types of crime. During the last phase of the guerrilla war some police and army officers even developed criminal enterprises of their own, such as in the weapons, gems, ivory and marijuana trades, partly for their own profit and partly as a covert means of providing arms and funds for informal militias opposed to the ANC [African National Congress] and SACP [South African Communist Party]. The range of state-sanctioned law-breaking included sophisticated smuggling operations and currency frauds which brought the government's own secret services into business relationships with major smuggling syndicates, Italian Mafia money-launderers and other operators in the international criminal underworld.[40]

Territorial boundaries, too, face the onslaught of contrary practices. Nicole Watts has shown how key alliances between liberal Turkish officials and Kurdish activists weakened the territorial image of the Turkish state, opening the door to a competing image, that of Kurdistan.[41] In fact, Watts argues, transnational alliances between those promoting Kurdish rights and European human rights activists have created a new imagined entity altogether.

> [In] Virtual Kurdistan West, which encompasses parts of Germany, France, Sweden, Britain and other European countries, . . . information technology and cheap airfares have permitted a new nomadism fostering the re-invention of a Kurdish community. Existing . . . without the benefit of codified territorial maps or formal recognition, Virtual Kurdistan West nonetheless plays a concrete part in the affairs of Turkey, its Kurdish populations, and their relations with Europe.[42]

The coalitions inside Turkey and into the European countries contested the image of Turkish state morality and representation. İsmail Beşikçi, who spent years in prison for his writing on Kurds, challenged the exclusivity of state morality: "Sociological realities are denied by means of an official ideology [i.e., morality]. Official ideology is not just any ideology. Official ideology implies legal sanction. Those who stray outside the

---

[40] Bayart, Ellis, and Hibou, *The Criminalization of the State in Africa*, pp. 61–2.

[41] Nicole Watts, "Virtual Kurdistan West: States and Supra-territorial Communities in the Late 20th and Early 21st Centuries," Ph.D. dissertation, University of Washington, forthcoming.

[42] Nicole Watts, "Kurdish Rights, Human Rights: Boundaries of Transnational Activism," paper presented to the Workshop on Boundaries and Belonging, July 1999, p. 2.

boundaries of official ideology are shown the way to prison."[43] Despite the risks, both state officials and private actors in Turkey forged alliances challenging the morality and representation contained in the state's image, adopting practices that denied the moral rightness and exclusivity of state ideology.

In encapsulating both image and practices, the definition of state here uses the concept of "field," adopting it (and adapting it) from Bourdieu.[44] He notes that the "field" highlights relationships in a multidimensional space, one in which the symbolic element is as important as the material (what he calls "substances"). "What is at stake," writes Bourdieu, "is the very representation of the social world."[45] The central phenomenon is struggle. "Every field is the site of a more or less overt struggle over the definition of the legitimate principles of division of the field."[46] In describing the state as a field of power, I want to emphasize what Bourdieu calls the "multi-dimensional space of positions," using the word "power" to denote the struggles over who dominates.

In brief, the state is a contradictory entity that acts against itself. To understand domination, then, demands two levels of analysis, one that recognizes the corporate, unified dimension of the state – its wholeness – expressed in its image, and one that dismantles this wholeness in favor of examining the reinforcing and contradictory practices and alliances of its disparate parts. The state-in-society model focuses on this paradoxical quality of the state; it demands that students of domination and change view the state in dual terms. It must be thought of at once (1) as the powerful image of a clearly bounded, unified organization that can be spoken of in singular terms (e.g., a headline stating, "Israel accepts Palestinian demands"), as if it were a single, centrally motivated actor performing in an integrated manner to rule a clearly defined territory; and (2) as the practices of a heap of loosely connected parts or fragments, frequently with ill-defined boundaries between them and other groupings inside and outside the official state borders and often promoting conflicting sets of rules with one another and with "official" Law. Theories that do not incorporate the two sides of the paradoxical state end up either overidealizing its ability to

---

[43] Cited in Nader Entessar, *Kurdish Ethnonationalism* (Boulder: Lynne Rienner, 1992), p. 105.

[44] Pierre Bourdieu, "The Social Space and the Genesis of Groups," *Theory and Society* 14 (November 1985): 723–44. I am also indebted to Zubaida's development of the concept of "political field." Sami Zubaida, *Islam, the People and the State: Essays on Political Ideas and Movements in the Middle East* (New York: Routledge, 1989), pp. 145–52.

[45] Ibid., p. 723.

[46] Ibid., p. 734.

turn rhetoric into effective policy or dismissing it as a grab-bag of every-man-out-for-himself, corrupt officials.

Method in Comparative Studies

Another important dimension of the state-in-society approach is its approach to comparative research, or method broadly conceived. The model developed in this book does not focus on a static picture of multiple groups and their fixed sets of goals and rules producing definitive results. The approach here is one that focuses on process rather than on conclusive outcomes. This is not a prize-fighter model in which each combatant remains unchanged throughout the bout and holds unswervingly to the goal of knocking out the other. Instead, the state-in-society approach points researchers to the *process* of interaction of groupings with one another and with those whose actual behavior they are vying to control or influence. This is an important distinction. The dynamic process changes the groupings themselves, their goals, and, ultimately, the rules they are promoting. This portrayal is akin to Woody Allen's Zelig, who constantly changes form as he interacts with others. Like any other group or organization, the state is constructed and reconstructed, invented and reinvented, through its interaction as a whole and of its parts with others. It is not a fixed entity; its organization, goals, means, partners, and operative rules change as it allies with and opposes others inside and outside its territory. The state continually morphs.

Norbert Elias, the great twentieth-century sociologist, made this point. He noted that our way of conceiving of human phenomena "makes us feel that one cannot come to grips with observed happenings as flowing events in speaking and thinking." Elias decried seeing change, or something dynamic, only in relationship to something static, and he labeled this phenomenon *Zustandsreduktion*. He argued that rather than seeing society as it *is*, one must view it "as it *becomes* – *has become* in the past, *is becoming* in the present, and *may become* in the future."[47]

The essays in this book reflect my own move from the hard causality associated with Elias's *Zustandsreduktion* toward a method that takes into account a continuing process, "becoming." While I have drawn

---

[47] This statement comes from an interview that he gave in Amsterdam in 1969. Johan Goudsblom and Stephen Mennell (eds.), *The Norbert Elias Reader* (Oxford: Blackwell, 1998), p. 143.

readily from much of hard political science and other social science disciplines, I have also grown increasingly impatient with limitations built into their standard methods. Much has been made of the rigor of the methods used in rational-choice, empirical/quantitative, structural, and other fashionable approaches in the social sciences. But this rigor, I have found, is as limiting as it is illuminating. The presentation of highly stylized pictures in which the action is frozen, in which we are presented with static independent variables (such as fixed preferences or structures or institutional arrangements) bearing the weight of causality, places far too restrictive blinders on students of comparative domination and change.

Such approaches can trap social and political life within a narrowly constructed world of rigor. One way that is done is through the search for what might be called *the moment of original sin* – the event or condition or crossroads that one can read back to from the present to see how the current state of affairs came to be. It is the quest for that frozen moment in time that determines what is to follow. In Waldner's language, it is a "critical juncture."[48] Geoffrey Eley and David Blackburn brilliantly criticized this sort of historiography, which, they claim, fruitlessly attempts to pinpoint the momentous turning point that explains the rise of Nazism in Germany.[49] And here, too, the explanation for development, or lack of it, is, in Elias's terms, in relation to the static – the decisive structural condition of elite conflict – at the outset.

The problem is that this sort of hard causality overdetermines the present state of affairs and forces history into the holding pen of its hypotheses. Fashionable rigor may force-feed overly constraining hypotheses on readers by searching for one-way causality that starts at a key moment. Existing methods popularly found in political economy, rational-choice, and structural analyses can overemphasize the explanatory power of independent variables, such as distinctive institutional arrangements. By fixing those variables in time, they ignore how the effects that they spawn may, in turn, transform them.

Existing understanding of rigor may divert the observer from the continuing dynamic that Cover called narrative – the unexpected, the unstable, the reactive to daily life. Cover did not rule out the hard variables –

[48] Waldner, *State Building and Late Development*.
[49] Geoffrey Eley and David Blackburn, *Reshaping the German Right: Radical Nationalism and Political Change after Bismarck* (New Haven, CT: Yale University Press, 1980).

what he called *nomos*, that is, the structure of the normative world – but at the same time he noted that *nomos* is continually transformed by how "it enables us to submit, rejoice, struggle, pervert, mock, disgrace, humiliate, or dignify. . . . The very imposition of a normative force [e.g., the inclination to court lower classes due to elite conflict or a particular set of preferences by powerful actors] upon a state of affairs, real or imagined, is the act of creating narrative."[50] Countries' stories do not end with the original sin or the critical juncture where there is the imposition of a powerful normative force; they only begin, for those forces call into being resistance and struggle, cooperation and coalitions, that transform the original impulse.

To put it a bit differently, social scientists need to understand the effects, not only of revelation, but also of the quest for redemption. Revelation is an act fixed in time, in which Truth is collectively discovered and assimilated. It creates the founding principles that inspire people to act within a shared framework of meaning, displacing their own material desires in favor of those hallowed principles, even to the point of martyrdom or dying for one's country. But the quest for redemption is ongoing. It holds out the hope for deliverance from the ills and decline that are part of the human condition – pain, sickness, poverty, decadence, decline, corruption, selfishness, and the like. Redemption offers the promise of collective deliverance and restoration. It prompts ongoing reactions to the world in which people find themselves, continually motivating responses to the failed human condition, to the failed promise of revelation.

The sort of method implied by Elias and Cover extends even to territorial dimensions of states. Social scientists have tended to treat the territorial configurations of states as constants in their inquiries, as nearly invariable and largely uncontested. They have been inclined to see world space as carved up into static blocks called states, which can periodically go through an eruptive change, as in the dissolution of the Soviet Union, but for long periods in between stay constant. Ian Lustick was one of the first theorists in recent years to challenge this perspective, urging scholars to see states as entities with often fundamentally contested, changing boundaries.[51]

---

[50] Cover, "Nomos and Narrative," pp. 100, 102.
[51] Ian Lustick, *Unsettled States, Disputed Lands: Britain and Ireland, France and Algeria, Israel and the West Bank-Gaza* (Ithaca, NY: Cornell University Press, 1993).

As noted above, the image of the state rests on the notion of two stable boundaries, territorial borders and the separation between state and other social actors. But, as the definition of state offered here makes clear, a focus on image alone can be quite misleading. Both sorts of boundaries have acted not only as simple social separators, dividing one people or nation from another and state actors from private ones in the territory. Boundaries have also suggested realms of meaning, in the sense suggested by Shils. Practices that have neutralized these boundaries have done more than destroy the image; they have created their own new spatial configurations of meaning, as Watts made clear in the Turkish-Kurdish case. De Certeau made this point, stating that resistance to the image (what he called the historical laws of a state of affairs) and its "dogmatic legitimations" ends up "redistributing its space."[52] Whereas Lustick urged scholars to see variability in territorial boundaries both physically and in terms of public debate over their physical placement, I am suggesting that, even when physical boundaries are static, their effect as lines encompassing a people connected through shared meaning may vary considerably.

Smuggling rings, clan and tribal relationships that have spanned territorial and/or public-private boundaries, regional and secessionist movements, certain sorts of religious solidarities, and numerous other social formations have quietly put forth systems of meaning that imply boundaries quite different from those represented in the image of the state. Some have sought to change the lines on maps; others act only to minimize the importance of those lines. In both cases, they have openly or surreptitiously challenged a key element in the image of the state: its claim to be the avatar of the people bounded by that territory and its assumption of the connection of those people encompassed by state borders as a (or *the*) primary social bond. In short, the ongoing contestation of rules has implied, as well, a continuing struggle over systems of meaning and the territorial and social divisions marking off a "group of persons acquiring their significance by their embodiment of values which transcend them."[53] Territorial boundaries may vary even though the formal lines on maps remain unchanged; the meaning attached to those boundaries in the image of the state may be challenged in a variety of ways.

---

[52] de Certeau, *The Practice of Everyday Life*, p. 18.
[53] Shils, *Center and Periphery*, p. 138.

New Answers to Old Questions: Research Using the State-in-Society Approach

I have tried to demonstrate that the state-in-society approach suggests a different definition of the state and an alternative way of conceiving and doing comparative research. The approach should also lead to new sorts of answers and explanations for perennial issues that have engaged scholars of comparative studies. In order to demonstrate that it can do just that, I will summarize three studies consciously using the approach, all coming out of my home institution, the University of Washington, that deal with such central issues: ethnic or communal conflict, the relationship between social movements and the state (in particular, the state's judiciary), and drawing the lines of the nation.

Issue 1: Growing Ethnic Violence

Niall Ó Murchú inquires into the seemingly endless violence between Jews and Palestinian Arabs and between Northern Irish Protestants and Catholics. He asks why the apparently powerful British state was incapable of imposing some sort of satisfactory solution in two small subject territories, Palestine in the 1920s and 1930s and Northern Ireland from 1969 until the 1990s, in order to quell the disorder of rival groups?[54] How can one understand the persistence, even intensification, of ethnic violence in the face of a strong commitment by a powerful state to impose order? Arab-Jewish tensions escalated under the British mandate in Palestine from the beginning until the end, culminating in a war that Israeli Jews call their war of independence and Palestinian Arabs refer to simply as *al-nakbah*, the disaster. In Irish territory absorbed into the United Kingdom, similar tensions festered for decades, with violence spilling over even into cities in Great Britain; only in the last few years have Catholics and Protestants moved toward some sort of resolution of their conflict. Hapless British officials, in both cases, seemed stymied for a couple of decades, at least, in quelling conflict between their subjects or, for that matter, violence directed against them and the broader public of the UK. Punctuated violence in Palestine grew steadily from 1920 to 1948, with

---

[54] Niall Ó. Murchú, "Labor, the State, and Ethnic Conflict: A Comparative Study of British Rule in Palestine (1920–1939) and Northern Ireland (1973–1994)," Ph.D. dissertation, University of Washington, 2000.

each outburst through the end of the 1930s accompanied by yet another White Paper or commission out of London proposing an answer to the interminable ferment and brutality. None worked. In Northern Ireland violence peaked a few years after the beginning of the Troubles in 1969, but the British failed for a quarter of a century beyond that peak to control the violence fully and move toward some sort of long-term solution.

The answer as to why violence grew in the face of the commitment of one of the world's great powers to stamp it out, Ó Murchú argues, starts with skepticism about the image of the powerful British state. Britain's seemingly inexplicable ineptitude leads in his analysis to an initial questioning of the reach and coherence of the state. Despite British leaders' continued call to overseas bureaucracies to impose order, those elements of the state that were supposed to impose a solution found themselves with cripplingly limited knowledge about local groups and woefully insufficient resources to do the job. In both cases, parts of the British state located in the territories tried to overcome these deficiencies by forming quiet coalitions with local agents in society. In fact, they became dependent on the Jews and Protestants for capital, local knowledge, skilled manpower, security personnel, and more. Ó Murchú argues that each of these groups entered into a capital-coercion bargain with the state.

In Palestine, the severe fiscal restraints placed by London on the High Commissioner and his Palestine Government made that government highly dependent on Jewish immigration and capital investments, despite the unending ire these raised among Arab leaders. Britain's failure in Northern Ireland to find some sort of accommodation from 1968 to 1974 led to its emphasis on security. To achieve that, local officials beefed up a number of security agencies, all of which were almost entirely staffed by Protestants. The devolution of a "solution" from London to Ulster fostered a coalition between elements of the UK state with the Protestants.

Those coalitions in Palestine and Northern Ireland intersected and neutralized the lines between the state and other social formations implied in the state's image and emphasized by British state officials in far-off Britain. The quiet trade-off for Jewish capital and Protestant security was both direct and indirect British support for each of these groups to maintain an ethnically divided labor market. The split labor market excluded Arabs and Catholics from certain sectors and industries and kept their wage levels lower than those for Jewish and Protestant workers. In so doing, it was fuel for continuing ethnic conflict.

28

The day-to-day practices of state public expenditures, security policies, and revenue collection, then, actually structured and exacerbated communal divisions, even as London officials continually spoke about and acted to bridge those divisions. British state officials in Palestine and Northern Ireland thus turned out to be complicit in structuring the basis of continued conflict through their effect on the ethnically divided labor market, in direct opposition to the goals of state leaders and ministry officials in London. Their dependence on Jews and Protestants made them turn a blind eye to the exclusivism that the two dominant groups exercised in the labor market, economically and politically marginalizing Arabs and Catholics. The ability of Jews and Protestants to divide the labor market enabled them to preserve their economic and political advantage.

The story, though, does not end with the political economy of a split labor market and the dominant coalitions that explain so much about how and why communal conflict became so intense in the two territories. Arabs and Catholics continued to influence the unfolding of events through violent resistance precisely because they did not simply accept with equanimity the dominant coalition the state had entered into with the Jews and Protestants. And their resistance had profound effects. In Palestine, the Arab Revolt in the late 1930s effected a resurgence of interest in London and a final White Paper that largely accepted Arab demands (although by that time the Arab leadership had a hard time itself accepting Britain's acceptance). That reversal in policy, though, was made moot by the entry of Britain into World War II. It suspended all policy initiatives until after the War, when Britain's primary action was directed toward getting out of Palestine altogether.

In Northern Ireland, the Catholics' success in dramatizing their plight led to compensatory policies to bolster Catholic education and employment rates. The successful conciliation of most Catholic economic grievances, argues Ó Murchú, was a necessary precursor to the IRA's 1994 ceasefire and the beginnings of today's peace process. In fact, the Catholics managed to unravel the state-Protestant alliance and the practices that came out of it, opening a new chapter in Northern Ireland's history.

Issue 2: The Growing Power of the Judiciary

Like Ó Murchú, Patricia Woods researches state-society relations, particularly how societal conflict is played out by interest groups and social movements aligning with parts of the state, in her case, Israel's judiciary.

By bringing the judiciary into her analysis, Woods extends state-society analysis and also places her work in a growing body of research asking how and why judiciaries from the European Union to Argentina to Pakistan have succeeded in dramatically expanding the power of courts, starting in the last quarter of the twentieth century.[55] Her case is the Israeli High Court of Justice, Israel's Supreme Court. Without fanfare, the High Court assumed the power of judicial review, eased rules of standing to allow individuals and groups easier access to the court, and began to introduce new principles of legal reasoning. And, in much more high-profile fashion, it rendered controversial decisions on some of the most sensitive issues in the country: who is a Jew, Arab-Jewish relations, and the use of torture by state security agencies, to name a few. In the course of the 1990s, the High Court occupied a dazzling new building in Jerusalem, tipped the balance of power among the branches of the Israeli state in favor of itself, and gained unprecedented visibility in Israeli society. The actions of the High Court have constituted little less than a revolution in Israeli state and society.

Woods focused her research on a key element of this process of empowerment, the High Court's displacement of both state rabbinical courts and the parliament, the Knesset, in issues of personal-status (family) law and religious authority through a series of rulings involving religion and other related questions. In 1987, for the first time, the High Court of Justice began repeatedly to challenge the rulings of the rabbinical authorities. This decision to stand up to the rabbinical establishment, which in Israel is an integral, if controversial, part of the state, could not have been taken lightly by the justices. Indeed, in the next decade, the breach provoked huge public demonstrations against the court, harsh denunciations in the Orthodox and ulta-Orthodox press, and even death threats against the chief justice, Aharon Barak. What emboldened the justices to take this fateful step? An earlier foray into these waters had led to the Knesset's reversal of the ruling less than three weeks after the court's

---

[55] Patricia Woods, "Courting the Court: Social Visions, State Authority, and the Religious Law Debates in Israel," Ph.D. dissertation, University of Washington, forthcoming 2001; also see Paula R. Newberg, *Judging the State: Courts and Constitutional Politics in Pakistan* (New York: Cambridge University Press, 1995), Mark J. Osiel, "Dialogue with Dictators: Judicial Resistance in Argentina and Brazil" in *Law and Social Inquiry* 20 (Spring 1995): 481–560, Martin Shapiro and Alec Stone, "The New Constitutional Politics of Europe" in *Comparative Political Studies, Special Issue: The New Constitutional Politics in Europe*, 26 (January 1994): 397–420.

decision. Why once again risk parliamentary retribution that could set back the High Court's other apparent gains, such as the power of judicial review?

Woods argues that crucial "implicit alliances" between the court and social forces inside and outside Israel gave the justices the motivation and strength to challenge other parts of the state. In so doing, they upset the existing balance of power among the key institutions of the state. Three sets of social groups turned to the court in the 1980s after being repeatedly rebuffed by the Knesset: the women's movement, the religious pluralism movement, and the civil rights movement. The mere existence of social movements in Israel is a relatively new phenomenon, and the court seemed to sense this change and jump to take advantage of it. Still, none of these movements was much more than a blip on the radar screen in Israeli society – small, marginal, often fractious, their causes certainly did not resonate with the larger Israeli population. Nonetheless, the most successful of these, the women's movement, ended up effecting far-reaching changes in Israeli society by turning to the High Court in a series of what turned out to be pivotal cases.

The High Court, in turn, seized on the increased demand the movement generated for court decisions through its suits and appeals, as well as on the arguments of law that the movement put forth in its briefs. Using general Israeli law (particularly basic laws promising gender equality) and natural law suggested by the movement's leaders, the justices weighed into some of the most contentious boundary issues imaginable: who is a Jew (and who not) and who is an Israeli (and who not)? These issues went to the heart of questions of group boundaries, of who is in and who is out of the nation or society. Precisely who are the people of which the state is a representation?

In time, the court itself was transformed by the implicit alliance with the women's movement and the new sorts of cases that this alliance thrust upon it. Early on, it used the women's cases to make narrow judgments, arguing that state religious decisions and practices needed be overturned because they trod on legal guarantees of gender equality articulated in general Israeli law. But the natural law language found in the decisions, while not the basis for those decisions, expressed a vision of society involving rights, personal freedoms, and the state's responsibility in defending the individual, even at the expense of deeply entrenched communal, and, later, even security, values and issues. The new language implied too that it was the High Court, among all the institutions of the state, that was properly positioned to guard the state image contained in general Israeli law and in Israel's acceptance of natural law. In short, the implicit alliance with the women's movement emboldened the court, shifted the bases of its legal reasoning, and eventually raised its strength within the Israeli state significantly.

At the same time, the jurists of the High Court of Justice found other trade-offs outside the boundaries of the country, moving them, too, toward a more activist stance. Woods's interviews indicate that the justices have been very involved in broader transnational legal communities and have been very concerned about their reputations in those circles. A number of them have taught in leading U.S. law schools on a regular basis, for example. These ties have subtly and not-so-subtly put pressure on the justices to put their actions to the test of natural and international human rights law, even when they have not used those laws as the strict criteria upon which decisions have been made. These outside forces have also been brought to bear on the struggles in which the justices have sought to expand the power of the High Court against parliament, the intelligence services, rabbinical courts, and other state institutions. In one recent case that gained world-wide attention, the court clearly tipped its hat to its outside juridical allies in banning the use of severe and even moderate force (torture). Attempts by the Knesset to overturn that ruling quickly fell apart because of the fear of the strength of those outside allies and their ability to mobilize world opinion.[56]

Woods, in sum, sets out to explain how social movements – even ones that are fairly small – could interact with a part of the state, the judiciary, and bring about a change in the balance of power among state institutions involving the expansion of the judiciary's power in Israel. She inquires about the High Court's success in struggles over what the image of the state should be, and the answer turns on her understanding of a state whose parts often operate at cross-purposes. Her central argument is that implicit alliances by the jurists that intersect the public-private boundary implied by the established image of the state, alliances with social forces inside and outside Israel, have strengthened the justices' sway. Beyond that, these implicit alliances have transformed the domestic groups, as well as the court itself, leading it to new forms of legal reasoning and into new areas of contestation, such as the rights of Arabs to buy land in exclusivist Jewish

---

[56] Speech by Yossi Beillin, Israel's Minister of Justice, to the Association of Israel Studies Annual Meeting, Tel Aviv, June 26, 2000.

settlements and the ability of the security services to use physical force to interrogate terrorist suspects.

Issue 3: State and Nation

Probably no phenomenon has had as profound an effect on the establishment of social boundaries as war. Kenneth Lawson's wonderful study, "War at the Grassroots," looks at how the state's engagement in war, in this instance World War I, had ripple effects even in small towns far, far from where its leaders took the fateful decisions to enter the war.[57]

In Park City, Utah, and Rossland, British Columbia, the state's far-off war seemed to charge the air, invigorating people's sense of national purpose and resulting in markedly higher levels of civic participation. It was not simply that people strengthened their bonds to one another and to the state in order to further the war effort. To be sure, that occurred. In Park City's newspaper, the *Park Record*, the editor wrote at the close of the Great War that the town's citizens could "always be depended upon for doing their full share for the public good."[58] They planted "war plots," raised money for the "Liberty Loans," volunteered to fight, organized public expressions of support, and much more. Rossland's population signed up volunteers to help cover the fifty thousand men whom the Canadian government had promised to Britain. The Rossland Rifle Association offered its shooting range to prepare contingents for the front. And the Rossland Farmers' Institute donated flour to alleviate the "want and suffering" caused by the war. All these acts fortified the image of the state at a moment when public support and unity were crucial for success.

But the citizens' response to the war went beyond a calculation of what was needed for victory. It included, too, an outpouring of emotion that constricted the definition of "the people," or "the nation," redrawing social boundaries in a way that defined some citizens as outside the nation. At the same time that they expressed unswerving support for the state, local citizens acted to challenge the image of the state's representation of the population by redefining who really belonged to "the people." A third town in the study, Boyle, in County Roscommon, Ireland, launched a challenge to the state that was even stiffer. Most of the population there

---

[57] Kenneth Gregory Lawson, "War at the Grassroots: The Great War and the Nationalization of Civic Life," Ph.D. dissertation, University of Washington, 2000.

[58] Ibid., p. 90.

displayed not enthusiasm but horror or indifference to war mobilization. Citizens sat on their hands, denying the British state the representation official leaders claimed and, with that, the mobilization the state was attempting to effect.

Lawson's study uses the far corners of society to study the relationship between the state and the people it purports to govern. This subject has been a central concern in the social sciences, especially in the fields of civil society and nationalism studies. His contribution in looking at these three remote towns is to see how actions by social forces, even when they are fairly marginal and ostensibly in full support of the state, can redraw social boundaries. In so doing, they transform society, redefining insiders and outsiders, and they transform the state in terms of its representation, or, as Lawson puts it, who properly belongs in civic life.

In Park City, attendants of a patriotic meeting held shortly after the United States entered the war asked immigrant groups, especially those the local newspaper called the "Austrian element," those from the Austro-Hungarian Empire, to affirm their loyalty. Already lines were being drawn. That was followed by a series of violent acts against immigrants whose commitment was questioned. As one historian wrote about actions taken throughout the country, "People were whipped, beaten, tarred and feathered, humiliated and lynched at will."[59] One Park City "foreigner" had his name mistakenly appear on a list of slackers during the Fourth Liberty Loan drive. Despite the man's assurance that he had bought a bond and could prove it, he was abused and practically run out of town.

Lawson looks at the treatment not only of "alien citizens" (as the local newspaper referred to them) but also of those who consciously battled U.S. participation in the war or the new understanding of the nation that was emerging at the local level. Dissenters resented pleas to the general citizens, such as the following: "You couldn't take off your hat to the flag with half the sense of *ownership* if you didn't [buy Liberty Bonds]."[60] Lawson comments,

Ownership points to the possibility that the flag and the nation-state it represents are merely an extension of oneself. . . . This suggests, if you will, a kind of transcendence of the separation between the individual, the nation, and the state, as the state is itself seen simply as an expression of one's self and collective national identity. . . . The flip-side of all this was that those relatively few who did not closely identify with either the nation or the state, or who may have for whatever

---

[59] Thomas Lawrence quoted in ibid., p. 119.   [60] Ibid., p. 125.

reason resented being drawn into war, took great risks for letting their feelings be known or for refusing to share in the sacrifice.[61]

"Enforced Americanism," as Lawson calls it, was directed in Park City first at those deemed disloyal but spread to "alien citizens" and, eventually, to labor radicals in the International Workers of the World (IWW). In Rossland, the situation was not much better. "Enemy aliens, shirkers, slackers, conscientious objectors, and radical labor agitators were chief among [excluded] groups."[62] "Foreigners" faced some of the same enmity as immigrants in Park City. And, in Boyle, Ireland, the war reflected a much more radical redrawing of social boundaries, dooming the British state as a representation of the people of Ireland. There, the war resulted in "mass political conversion and civic reconfiguration. The war accentuated differences existing within Irish society about the meaning, conditions, and content of Irish nationalism."[63]

In short, World War I prompted states to mobilize the home front by emphasizing their embodiment of the people, what Lawson referred to above as the transcendence of the separation among the individual, the nation, and the state. They called on people to act upon the feeling that the state in its hour of travail expressed their collective identity and needed their collective effort. Those calls resonated in society, but they also had unintended effects on the notion of exactly whom the state was a representation. In all three countries that he studied, Lawson found that "in order to create, shape, and enforce the social boundaries that define the nation, those groups and individuals who are perceived as outside these national boundaries tend to be excluded from civic participation on equal terms."[64] And that exclusion occurred both in cases where the bulk of society responded positively to the state's entreaties, the United States and Canada, and where it responded to the state's pleas by opposing the state, Ireland.

Conclusion

The central issues in the three pieces of research that I have recapitulated – ethnic conflict, the growing power of judiciaries, and the complex relationship between nation and state – have received considerable attention in many other social science works, as well. Yet, Ó Murchú, Woods, and

---

[61] Ibid., pp. 126–7.   [62] Ibid., p. 174.   [63] Ibid., p. 258.   [64] Ibid., pp. 263–4.

Lawson have brought fresh, illuminating perspectives to their topics. They have treated the state as a much more tentative, limited entity than many standard works have. Ó Murchú and Woods found practices that had parts of the state working in opposing directions. In both works, there were key coalitions between social groups and parts of the state. The practices of those alliances neutralized the public-private separation that was trumpeted by state leaders, including the very same officials, Britain's overseas civil servants and Israel's judges, who were engaging in those neutralizing practices. Lawson's three cases each demonstrated how problematic it is to take the territorial boundaries of the state as a simple representation of the people or nation, even as the reigning image of the state induces people to do just that in their everyday language. Even when people acted to reinforce the unitary, heroic image of the state, they ended up engaging in practices that drew new lines of inclusion and exclusion. Funny things happened to boundaries of meaning, often quite at odds with what state officials intent on war mobilization had in mind.

Each of these works used the state-in-society approach to great effect. The essays that follow in this book trace the development of the approach, especially in light of important literature in the social sciences. The two chapters in Part 2, "Rethinking Political and Social Change," elaborate the idea of thinking about society as a web or mélange, rather than a pyramidal structure with the state's rule-making mechanisms at the apex. The metaphor of the web, set out in Chapter 2, allows one to think about society in terms of multiple rule-making loci and the hidden and open conflict among these multiple centers seeking to exercise domination. Chapter 3 places the state in a broad context of international and domestic constraining forces. This environment helps explain the odd behavior of state leaders who frequently undermine the very state agencies they have built as, what they hoped would be, the foundation for strong states.

Part 3, "A Process-Oriented Approach – Constituting States and Societies," begins by laying out the state-in-society model in Chapter 4. It differentiates the concept of domination, looking at both "integrated" and "dispersed" domination. And it analyzes how the interaction of parts of society and parts of the state, especially through implicit alliances, transforms both in an ongoing fashion. Chapter 5 examines how states' images are produced and maintained (even though I did not use the word "image" when I wrote that essay). It focuses on the use of ritual, the role of law, and the creation of a public space with rules not legislated or enforced by the state as means that state leaders use to reinforce the image of the state and keep them intact.

In the following section, "Linking Micro- and Macro-Level Change," I deal with what social scientists today fashionably call the micro-foundations of theory. Much of contemporary theory has become trapped, as the title here emphasizes, within its narrowly constructed world of rigor. Part of the problem, I believe, rests on standard theories' micro-foundations, on the view of the individual as an integrated personality, with clear preferences that are hierarchically ordered and that motivate one to act. This understanding of the individual originates in established American psychology, which rests on unspoken liberal assumptions and sees personality development coming from the anxiety generated by conflicts that threaten the unity of the personality, dissonance. In Chapter 6, I critique assumptions about the individual – particularly the unity and integrity of personality – found in some of the most important early works on the Third World. It is important to add that these same limiting assumptions are still very much a part of today's literature, particularly rational-choice works. The chapter presents an alternative conception of the individual, one that I believe allows researchers to escape the assumptions of standard positivistic theories and move toward a process-based method. Rejecting a simple material or methodological-individualist approach to human change, the article presents a model based on inconsistency in individual behavior, depending on the context of action – what I call the syncretic personality. Such a model points to the conflicting sets of principles and values that individuals call upon in an environment of conflict among states and other social organizations.

Finally, the last part of the book, "Studying the State," takes aim at how scholars have conceived the state. The two essays in this section set the stage for the new definition of the state that I presented above. The first, Chapter 7, demonstrates how assumptions about European states were extended by social scientists to the new states that emerged after World War II. It argues that the ontological status that states had in this Europe-based view needs to give way to a perspective in which states are not treated as "omnipotent givens" but as variable in their ability to effect social policy and reshape society. The final chapter deals with the issues of meaning that I referred to earlier. Here, I advocate modifying the strong structural emphasis in institutional analyses to incorporate cultural variables. Through their practices, states lay claim to the collective consciousness of their population. Institutions *and* symbols have been at the core of the continuing reinvention of society. But tremendous contestation prevails over who – the state as a whole, parts of the state, other social organizations – defines and taps into the forms of collective consciousness in society.

PART II

Rethinking Social and Political Change

2

A Model of State-Society Relations

Introduction: Images of the Impact of State on Society

The incredibly quick unraveling of empire in Asia and Africa following World War II suggested to many the hidden political strength of poor, subjugated peoples. Daring leadership, such as that of Mohandas Gandhi, Kwame Nkrumah, and Gamal Abdul Nasser, together with imaginative political organization, such as that found in India's Congress, Algeria's National Liberation Front (FLN), and the Vietnamese Communist party, could topple the rich and powerful. An imperial state could be reduced to a Gulliver among the Lilliputians. Even to third-world leaders who eluded fiery anticolonial struggles, events in distant India or Algeria lent confidence about the important role that centralized, mobilizing politics could play in their countries after independence.

Western imperial powers were not only the bêtes noires in the transition from colony to statehood; they were models to be emulated as well. The aims of the founders of new states were taken largely from already successful states and the dominant European nationalist ideologies of the nineteenth century.[1] New political leaders of Asia and Africa came to believe, like leaders in the West and the socialist bloc, in their states' potential to shape their societies – to move their economies from agriculture to industry, to create a skilled workforce, and to induce the population to abandon outmoded beliefs. Even in Latin America, where many

---

[1] See, for example, two articles by Benjamin Neuberger: "The Western Nation-State in African Perceptions of Nation-Building," *Asian and African Studies* 11 (1976): 241–61; and "State and Nation in African Thought," *Journal of African Studies* 4 (Summer 1977): 198–205.

state organizations were exceedingly weak and corrupt throughout the 1950s, a new "can-do" spirit gripped many who aspired to state leadership and to the creation of an effective bureaucratic state organization. In fact, the organization of the state became the focal point for their hopes of achieving a new social order, a unified channel for people's passions that until now had run in countless different directions. The state was to be the chisel in the hands of the new sculptors.

Great expectations in third-world countries about what the state organization could create were reinforced by another cultural artifact of their former masters, Western social science of the 1950s and 1960s. Images in scholarly works of integrated centers swallowing hapless peripheries, of Great Traditions subsuming little traditions, of modern states and allied organizations shaping heretofore traditional societies, all had reverberating effects. In the 1980s, another wave of social science literature – bringing the state back in – generated a new wave of confidence that the autonomous state could generate independence from powerful social groups in order to realize its own goals for social and economic change. Over and over again, articles, books, and lectures in the second half of the twentieth century bolstered the belief that the impact of policies upon populations would be fairly close to what the policymakers had in mind as they devised their new laws, programs, and organizations. The notions of Western thinkers helped generate anticipation about the capabilities of new and renewed states in Africa, Asia, and Latin America.

The state-in-society approach discussed in this chapter brought that confidence about the power of the state in the Third World, and elsewhere, into question. It led social scientists to reassess the character and capabilities of states, such as China, India, Egypt, Russia, and the United States. Scholars have noted how infrequently potential strength has been translated into effective action.

True, even weak states have had continuing and profound effects on numerous aspects of social life, but few have been able to channel that influence to create centralized polities and highly integrated societies. The character of social fragmentation into tribes, linguistic groups, ethnic communities, and religious blocs has changed in character in countries such as India, the former Yugoslavia, and Mexico, but the actions of state leaders notwithstanding, the net result has often been only heightened communal tension and violence. The political issue is not simply one of political instability – in fact, some leaders of weak states have discovered wily methods that have kept them in office for years on end – but of the severely limited capability of states to regulate and transform their societies as had been expected.

The earlier images of modern states shaping formerly traditional societies were based on presuppositions about the overall role of politics in the organization of society and the dynamics of social and political change. The next section will examine some of these important premises about order and change – many of, which have survived in contemporary research in one way or another. The chapter will then present an alternative understanding of the role of politics in society and a model for how to approach the question of overall societal change.

Explaining Order and Change through Dichotomous Models of Society

Oddly, the earliest theories in the 1950s and 1960s that addressed state-society relations rarely mentioned the state at all. The state was more assumed than explained. Social scientists subsumed it within a broader array of organizations linked by similar ideas – the Great Tradition, urban society, the modern sector, or the center. Whether the state is truly autonomous – seeking its own course rather than the goals of another social group or mix of groups – was not a meaningful question. It was generally assumed that the members of a modernizing leadership (political, economic, social, and religious elites) share values and aims. Differences between the modern and traditional sectors (or between the components of similar dichotomies used by social scientists, such as center-periphery or elite-mass) represented the major contour in the landscape for theorists. Societal change many assumed, comes in the gathering strength of the modern sector: enabling it to overcome stubborn beliefs and structures in the traditional sector. The images suggested a beachhead from which the center's modern elites would move outward to transform the hostile terrain of the traditional periphery. The political institutions would meld with churches and industries to form the advance force, the imposing modern center.

The Center-Periphery Model

Given the unassuming role of the state in most writings, it is not surprising that a sociologist, rather than a political scientist, carefully laid out many of the premises dealing with order and change in such a model. Drawing on Max Weber and Talcott Parsons, during the course of thirty years Edward Shils penned a large number of essays on aspects of this model.[2] These are worth looking at not only because of Shils's own impact upon the social sciences, but also because in them he spelled out what were for others implicit assumptions about the relations between center and periphery, modern and traditional, and other dichotomous models. What did Shils mean by center and periphery? In fact, he never gave a precise definition, but from several scattered statements we can sketch a picture of the modern center. Three primary components constitute the center: values and beliefs, institutions, and elites, and these combine in a seamless weave.

Values and beliefs – what Shils called the central value system – form the core of what people in society hold sacred and the foundation that the elites act upon. Shils saw the center not simply as a random collection of stated and unstated preferences, but in regularized and harmonious terms as the "*order* of symbols, of values and beliefs, which govern the society."[3] Thus, besides giving society a recognizable configuration by differentiating center from periphery, Shils was eager to set forth the internal structure of centers, making them comparable in form if not in content. It is this form, this order, that is irreducible, connecting the center's values and beliefs.

A second component of the center is institutional. This is the critical realm of action. The offices, roles, and organizations express the order inherent in the central value system. No group of people has completely homogeneous values; the institutional component implements the values of the center throughout society. Its authority is the motor of social change. Shils's center is activist and aggressive; its institutional network both embodies and propounds the center's values and beliefs. "The center," he wrote, "consists of those institutions (and roles) which exercise authority, whether it be economic, governmental, political, military, and of those which create and diffuse cultural symbols (religious, literary, etc.) through churches, schools, publishing houses, etc."[4]

---

[2] Many of those essays are collected in Edward Shils, *Center and Periphery* (Chicago: University of Chicago Press, 1975). Also, see his *Political Development in the New States* (Paris: Moution, 1966).

[3] Shils, *Center and Periphery*, p. 3 (my emphasis); see also 48–9.

[4] Ibid., p. 39.

Besides the components of values and institutions (or symbols and offices, as Shils would have put it), those who fill the offices and play the roles act as elite custodians of the central value system. The standards of the elites form their authoritative decisions. The elites are thus intimately connected to the central values (their standards) and the institutions (their means). At one point, Shils simply equated an elite (or a single member of an elite) with authority; at other times, he spoke more broadly of the center as a repository of society's authority. A center must have the all-important ingredient of authority; it must be able to enforce its decisions despite differing tendencies and preferences in other parts of society. The activism of the center, its unrelenting drive to spread its values and beliefs, and its overpowering strength, which derives from the integration of its elites and their organizations, combine to mold the periphery. Indeed, the need for authority implies that the center's values are not universally shared. The periphery contains dissenting habits, values, and beliefs. Authority expands the center into the periphery. Through its institutions, the center uses a smorgasbord of rewards and sanctions to facilitate the acceptance of its decisions and values.

The periphery plays a dutifully peripheral role in Shils's analysis. Although he described the periphery as highly differentiated, these differentiations were of little interest to him. It never occurred to him that change generated in the periphery might affect the very nature and capabilities of the center. Shils's understanding of society rests upon the dynamism and activism of the center; the periphery remains a passive recipient. There is an implied sameness, then, to processes of social change; the nature of structures and beliefs in the periphery seems to matter very little. Centers are of primary interest to social scientists because they have a coherence, a unity, an agenda-setting capability that peripheries lack.

Although the degree of consensus varies from society to society, the essential point for understanding a stable society is the center that brings together elites from disparate sectors, each with its own organizations and rules. Only a consensus on the essential order of values among these elites can result in united sufficient authority to bind the society together, and it is the integration of society that concerned Shils. The center integrates the society through a consensual pattern among the elites that assimilates the diverse persons, rules, and roles into a center. The elites constitute a ruling class, and the state is the political arm of this class.

The element of consensus or affinity is a powerful assumption on Shils's part, for it explains to us not only how society is held together but also how the entire society changes. The rules spewed out by the political institutions and the norms demanded by other center organizations constitute the limits of acceptable behavior; habits and ways that lie outside those boundaries must be altered by judicious use of the rewards and sanctions available to the center's institutions.

Problems with the Model   The center-periphery models of society and macro sociological change proposed by Shils and others were accepted by social scientists from a variety of disciplines. These models have a parsimony and elegance that continue to attract numerous researchers, though scattered writings have meanwhile made thrusts at various aspects of the models. Many authors have questioned some deep-rooted Western biases in the dichotomous models. Shils was more direct in his biases than many others: For him, the course of "historical development or evolution" is toward modernity. "Modernity," wrote Shils, "entails democracy and democracy in the new states must above all be equalitarian. . . . To be modern is to be scientific. . . . Modernity requires national sovereignty. . . . Modern means being Western."[5] Modern values form the consensual basis for the center, which is the modern sector. Increasingly, students have become uneasy with such notions, which ultimately equate macro-level change with a necessary move toward Western ways. They have faulted Shils and others for a myopic view of social and political change.

Scholars have also questioned whether accepted images of strong, modernizing centers depict third-world and other countries accurately. Shils recognized the paradox of virile centers in applying his model to societies in which things fall apart. It is true, he admitted, that many states in Asia and Africa "have *not yet* become societies in a modern sense because they do *not yet* have effective centers."[6] Besides introducing an unwarranted teleology, which provides final answers before the questions are fully posed, an emphasis on the "not yet" grants that the center-periphery model is inadequate to depict the here and now. We are left with a tool, the center, which assumes a situation that, Shils tells us, is inapplicable to the societies being studied. The consensus and integration so important to the modernizing model were often lacking in third-world societies,

[5] Shils, *Political Development*, pp. 8–10.
[6] Shils, *Center and Periphery*, p. 44 (my emphasis).

which, according to Shils, were not real societies at all but only protosocieties. Others have added that even in contemporary Western Europe, a jumble of different value systems continue to survive, suggesting that centers may not be that effective and dominant in modern societies either.[7] Historically, Charles Tilly wrote, "the Europeans of 1500 and later did not ordinarily expand from a highly organized center into a weakly organized periphery."[8]

By the 1970s and 1980s, criticism of the center-periphery or modern-traditional models also mounted over their supercilious treatment of the state. Social scientists pointed to the special, perhaps even autonomous, role that the state organization plays in making and enforcing rules and in influencing the very structure of society. Differing components do not mesh into a center as effortlessly as Shils and others had suggested. Indeed, there was a stealthy reemergence of the state in Shils's work. Unexpectedly, and only after his three major essays on center and periphery, he referred to the "prominence of the governmental center."[9]

States and Societies: Organizations in a Melange

In the cautious move away from modern-traditional and center-periphery models, political scientists gave renewed attention to the state, focusing not on its formal legal mode but on its actions in society. They noted the leading role the state tried to take in numerous areas relating to national development. Yet writings in the last couple of decades of the twentieth century produced a Janus-faced image in confronting the reality of the state. Those writing on corporatism and bureaucratic authoritarianism, for example, portrayed states as autonomous and effective, even as creating major social groupings in the society,[10] while others portrayed the activist state as more illusory than real. The latter remarked on the hapless, bumbling nature of states, emphasizing their instability and their

---

[7] Suzanne Berger and Michael J. Piore, *Dualism and Discontinuity in Industrial Societies* (Cambridge, MA: Cambridge University Press, 1980).

[8] Charles Tilly, "Reflections on the History of European State-Making," in Charles Tilly (ed.), *The Formation of National States in Western Europe* (Princeton, NJ: Princeton University Press, 1975), p. 24.

[9] Shils, *Center and Periphery*, p. 74.

[10] See, for example, Frederick B. Pike and Thomas Stritch, eds., *The New Corporatism: Social-Political Structures in the Iberian World* (Notre Dame, IN: University of Notre Dame Press, 1974); and David Collier, ed., *The New Authoritarianism in Latin America* (Princeton, NJ: Princeton University Press, 1979).

ineffectiveness in carrying out their grand designs.[11] Detailed case studies more concerned with events and trends at ground level than with speculation about what has "not yet" occurred harped on the disorganization and weakness of many states. To examine the role that states actually play requires an overall approach to the maintenance of particular types of order and the process of change in society as a whole. Following Shils's example, we must build a new model, while avoiding, of course, the pitfalls he encountered. An understanding of how societies persist and change must start with the organizations that exercise social control, that subordinate individual inclinations to the behavior these organizations prescribe.[12] These informal and formal organizations, ranging from families and neighborhood groups to mammoth foreign-owned companies, use a variety of sanctions, rewards, and symbols to induce people to behave according to the rules of the game. These are the norms and laws that define the boundaries of what is acceptable behavior, and they may include at what age to marry, what crop to grow, what language to speak, and much more.

At the top of the list of critical changes in human affairs during the last half-millenium has been a radical change in many societies' distribution of social control. The diversity of norms within areas – one set for this tribe and another for a neighboring tribe, one for this region and another for that – has been attacked by the state. Those running (or seeking to run) the state organization have striven to have it provide the predominant, often exclusive, set of rules. Indeed, we can say that the "idea of the state" is, through its law and regulations, to impose a single standard of behavior in a given territory, one that is legislated, executed, and adjudicated by the various parts of the state organization. To be sure, the goal of uniform rules is not totally novel; one need only think of the monism of certain city-states. The difference in the modern era has been how state leaders have tried to impose one set of rules over so large a territory, and how

---

[11] See, for example, Samuel P. Huntington, *Political Order in Changing Societies* (New Haven, CT: Yale University Press, 1968); and Gerald A. Heeger, *The Politics of Underdevelopment* (New York: St. Martin's Press, 1974).

[12] "Social control" is used in a broad sense and is interchangeable with a concept such as "power." It refers to "situations in which A gets B to do something he would not otherwise do." David A. Baldwin, "Power Analysis and World Politics: New Trends Versus Old Tendencies," *World Politics* 31 (January 1979): 162–3. Baldwin notes that it is important to denote both the scope and domain of such concepts. The issue of domain (who is influencing whom) is at the heart of the rest of the discussion. The domain (influence in respect to what) involves the social behavior of individuals in a given society.

universal this goal has become. There have been few universals in the processes of social change, yet on this issue one can generalize very broadly. By the middle of the twentieth century, in practically every society on earth, political leaders asserted the "idea of the state" as right and proper – to create a state organization that would itself either make the rules that govern the details of people's lives or determine which other organizations might establish these rules (and then monitor those organizations).

But success in achieving this goal has been elusive. Political leaders have faced tremendous obstacles in their drive to assert such control, obstacles that they have often failed to overcome. Leaders of other social organizations have been unwilling to relinquish their prerogatives, their ability to devise rules governing some aspects of people's lives, without a fierce struggle. These other formal and informal social organizations have joined forces with parts of the state, sometimes even with the beleaguered heads of states themselves, and developed practices contradicting the official laws and regulations of the state. The participation of fragments of the state in such coalitions that intersect the state-society divide are practices of the state, and "practices of the state" may directly contradict the "idea of the state." Indeed, the central political and social drama of recent history has been the battle between the idea of the state and the often-implicit agendas of other social formations (which may very well include parts of the state itself) for how society should be organized. The dispute is over who makes the rules, who grants the property rights that define the use of assets and resources in the society, whose system of meaning people will adopt to explain to themselves their place on this earth.

Scholars dealing with the maintenance of order and change in society as a whole need an approach that brings this struggle for social control into stark relief. The model I am suggesting, what I call state-in-society, depicts society as a mélange of social organizations rather than a dichotomous structure. Various formations, including the idea of the state as well as many others (which may or may not include parts of the state) singly or in tandem offer individuals strategies of personal survival and, for some, strategies of upward mobility. Individual choice among strategies is based on the material incentives and coercion organizations can bring to bear and on the organizations' use of symbols and values concerning how social life should be ordered. These symbols and values either reinforce the forms of social control in the society or propose new forms of social life.

Indeed, this struggle is ongoing in every society. Societies are not static formations but are constantly *becoming* as a result of these struggles over social control.

To be sure, in some instances, the idea-state may make and enforce many rules in the society or may choose to delegate some of that authority to other mechanisms, such as the church or market. There are other societies, however, where social organizations actively vie with one another in offering strategies and in proposing different rules of the game. Here, the mélange of social organizations is marked by an environment of conflict, an active struggle for social control of the population. The state is part of the environment of conflict in which its own parts struggle with one another. The battles may be with families over the rules of education and socialization; they may be with ethnic groups over territoriality; they may be with religious organizations over daily habits. In the early twentieth century, Mustafa Kemal of Turkey locked horns with religious organizations over whether men should wear hats with brims or without. As with so many other skirmishes, the issue was not as inconsequential as it may appear; the conflict was over who had the right and ability to make rules in that society.

In many third-world societies, where these struggles are most evident in the 1980s, states face a multitude of social organizations that maintain and vie for the power to set rules. Families, clans, multinational corporations, domestic businesses, tribes, political parties, and patron-client dyads may be among those actively engaged in the environment of conflict. Why have state leaders taken on all these foes, in rhetoric and often in direct action, to struggle for the ultimate rule-making capability? After all, central political organizations have not always taken such an aggressive stance. This sort of multi-front war can easily sap the state's strength and eventually topple it.

The answer can be found by considering the special character of the world system that has been the backdrop for these struggles, forming a second tier of relationships for each state. Each state is not only one organization in a domestic mélange but is also one among many states globally. Its role on one tier, the society, is highly interdependent with its place in the other, the system of states. Since the fifteenth and sixteenth centuries, when modern states began to appear in Western Europe, they have presented dire threats to all other existing political forms. Their fantastic comparative advantage in mobilizing and organizing resources for war and other purposes brought the survival of other political entities into question. Only societies that developed state organizations themselves had a chance to resist being conquered and swallowed up by other states. A prime motivation in expanding the state's rule-making domain at the expense of other social organizations within its boundaries – even with all the risks that entails – has been to build sufficient clout to survive the dangers posed by those outside its boundaries.

How does increased social control by the state improve its prospects in the international arena? A state's ability to survive rests on a number of factors, including the organizational capabilities of its leaders, population size, available and potential material resources, and the larger international configuration. Probably none is more important in marshaling strength for the state, though, than the ability to mobilize the population.[13] Mobilization is the channeling of people into specialized organizational frameworks that enable state leaders to build stronger armies, collect more taxes, and complete any number of other complicated tasks.

It is not surprising that the growth of the very first modern states in Europe involved building three essential tentacles of the state – a standing army, a vastly improved tax-collecting mechanism, and an expanded set of courts. The imposition of state law in place of customary or feudal law through the extension of the court system was the essential ingredient in inducing people to behave as state leaders wanted them to behave and not according to dictates of local lords or others. In other words, the courts along with the police and all others who fed into the workings of the courts, were an essential mechanism for shifting social control to the state. For the ambitious state leaders to succeed, they had to build an organization in which officers of the court, police, and other agencies followed the top leadership's dictates, rather than using their positions as sinecures operating under different rules. Mobilization of the population to serve in and financially support a standing army (or for other tasks) could grow only out of the increasing social control by the state made possible by the expanded domain of the courts. Social control, then, is the currency for which social organizations compete. With high levels

---

[13] Krasner has made the point quite well. A state's strength in external relations rests on its strength in relation to its own society. Stephen D. Krasner, "Domestic Constraints on International Economic Leverage," in Klaus Knorr and Frank N. Trager, eds., *Economic Issues and National Security* (Kansas City: Regents Press of Kansas, 1977). To be sure, the state is dealing in two different domains, and internal social control is not totally and immediately fungible to power in the world of states. Nonetheless, such social control is a necessary, if not sufficient, condition to exercise power internationally.

of social control, states can mobilize their populations effectively, gaining tremendous strength in facing external foes. Internally, state personnel can gain autonomy from other social groups in determining their own preferred rules for society; they can build complex, coordinated bureaus to establish these rules; and they can monopolize coercive means in the society to ensure that other groups do not prevent the enforcement of state rules. Increasing levels of social control are reflected in a scale of three indicators.

Compliance At the most elementary level, the strength of the state rests on the degree to which the population conforms with its demands. Compliance is often compelled by the most basic of sanctions, force. Who controls the local police is often one of the most important questions one can ask about the distribution of social control in a society. The ability to control the dispersal of a broad scope of other resources and services also determines the degree to which the state can demand compliance.

Participation Leaders of the state organization seek more than compliance. They also gain strength by organizing the population for specialized tasks in the institutional components of the state organization. In practical terms, leaders may want peasants to sell produce to the state cooperative or to frequent state-licensed clinics instead of unauthorized healers.

Legitimacy The most potent factor determining the strength of the state, legitimacy is more inclusive than either compliance or participation. Legitimacy involves an acceptance of the state's rules of the game, its social control, as true and right. It means the acceptance of the symbolic order associated with the idea of the state as people's own system of meaning. Whereas compliance and participation may be a practical response by individuals to an array of rewards and sanctions, legitimacy means accepting the symbolic component that the rewards and sanctions embody. It is the popular acknowledgment of a particular social order.

The strength of the idea of the state in an environment of conflict depends, in large part, on the social control the state organization exercises. The greater the social control, the more currency – compliance, participation, and legitimacy – is available to state leaders to achieve their goals. Leaders of other social organizations reject the state's claim to predominance, and they too desperately seek social control. They can use the same currency of compliance, participation, and legitimacy to protect and strengthen their enclaves, in which they will try to determine how social life should be ordered, what the rules of the game should be. They can also be officials of the state themselves or be allied with such officials. There is no guarantee that states will act as totally coherent organizations, as the idea of the state suggests. Actual state practices may support conflicting forms of social control.

The Constraints on States

Many current students of macro-level political and social change have been mesmerized by the power of the state, much as earlier scholars were taken with capabilities of modern sectors or centers. Where threats to state dominance have been woven into analyses, there has been a tendency to focus on the constraints imposed by the rivals to central power, those who constitute an alternative state leadership.

With the tremendous comparative advantage that states have, it is little wonder that many social scientists have assumed the predominance of the state without carefully analyzing the outcomes of struggles with other organizations, even those in a nook of society whose leaders harbor no hope for central power. The state leaders, after all, can draw succor from norms in the international environment (led by those set forth by the UN) that exalt the role of the state in setting the rules on the status of women, treatment of children, issues of health, questions of reproduction, and much more. Also, the state is almost invariably the largest employer and accounts for a greater share of the gross national product (GNP) than any other organization in society. Not only are the rewards at its disposal many, but the portion of its budget devoted to maintaining armies and police is substantial.

Survival of Local Control

Yet the very character of the state and the substance of its policies can be shaped by a vicious cycle created by an environment of conflict. To enhance their strength and autonomy, states must increase their social control. But without the ability to mobilize human and material resources into specialized, task-oriented frameworks that come with already-existing social control, states encounter grave difficulties in offering viable strategies of social survival to individuals throughout the country. Using a potpourri of sanctions and rewards, other social formations may organize resources into selective incentives constituting alternative strategies. In brief, state leaders may find that despite all the seeming riches at their disposal, their organization, the state, lacks the wherewithal to dislodge people from the existing strategies offered by organizations with rules different from the state's. The "periphery" is far more important in shaping the future of a society than either Shils or later writers on the state imagined. And, with the resources they mobilize and the legitimacy they garner, these other social formations may use parts of the state, from single positions to whole bureaus, to further their own sets of rules and meaning.

The bounty of state resources and personnel does have a tremendous impact on the rest of society, but often in ways unintended and unanticipated by state leaders. Social control by other organizations, gained from their mobilization of portions of the population, gives them a strength that can be very threatening even to the state's local political representatives or bureaucrats inclined to follow official laws and regulations. The state official is caught in a vise, with clear instructions from state superiors on how to use resources but with counterpressures from other social groups to employ different priorities. To avoid the damage local authorities might inflict upon their chances for advancement or even their political survival, many strategically placed state employees accommodate these local figures. State resources in many cases have had a deep impact on local society but in ways that have strengthened local social organizations at the state's expense.

Whole portions of states have been captured by people enforcing guidelines on how to use state resources that differ from those advanced by state leaders. State leaders' rules are contained in the official policies designed to regulate and monitor strictly the flow of state resources. It is tempting to see any deviation from these rules as corruption, as if the problem involved only a deficiency in monitoring distribution. In fact, much of what is commonly called corruption is not simply a single individual stuffing his or her pockets with state resources. It is behavior according to dissenting rules, established by organizations other than the state. Nepotism, for example, though against state law, may be a cardinal norm within the family or clan. How people are recruited into state jobs is an indication of whose rules of the game are being followed. The issue goes beyond technical monitoring of state functionaries to guard against nepotism or other infringements of state rules. Such transgressions reflect pockets of social control outside of the domain of state leaders, which have been able to shape how the state acts or, at least, how one tentacle of the state acts.

A Model of State-Society Relations

Even in the most remote parts of a country, states have had a huge impact. At times, it is difficult to imagine how a given place might have evolved without state penetration. Remote villages have state-financed police, roads, potable water, state tax collectors, credit, marketing cooperatives, schools, subsidized contraceptives, electricity, health care, and more. The distribution of state "goodies," collection of taxes, and application of force, however, may not be at all what state leaders had in mind – not to mention the resulting social structure, the effective rulers in the village, or the distribution of social control.

Lack of a Strong Political Base

Without the strength provided by the mobilization of the population in villages and towns across the country, the state faces two additional difficulties. First, it may lack a sufficiently strong political base to pursue, even at a gross level, policies that run counter to the existing distribution of power among sectors in the society.[14] State policies on taxing, pricing, capital investment, and welfare favor the most powerful sector, and without sufficient social control the state has insufficient autonomy to break this pattern. Second, an inadequate power base for the state makes it a tempting prize for those who do have some organizational backing, either in society at large or even within one of the state's many tentacles. But the prize is often chimerical, for what aspiring leaders seize is not the capability to transform their societies in accordance with their goals, but simply seats coveted by others. Just to preserve their seats, they must adopt means that foreclose the use of power to fulfill their original purposes. Instead, substantive policy issues are pushed to the back burner. Lacking the means to mobilize sustained and organized internal support, leaders of weak states must increasingly turn their attention to staying in power, lest others develop the means to displace them. In these circumstances the political life of leaders, though not necessarily short, is certainly nasty and brutish. When the head of state does not attend to the course of policy, it is little wonder that the tail, the state functionary assigned far from the state capital, may find the most compelling pressures coming from strong local figures and organizations with rules very different from those of the state.

---

[14] Michael Lipton, *Why Poor People Stay Poor: Urban Bias in World Development* (Cambridge, MA: Harvard University Press, 1977), p. 13.

Conclusion: New Directions for Research

Even in societies where other social organizations exercise significant social control, the state is still a major presence. In certain areas, such as negotiating with other states, dealing with transnational actors, and maintaining peace among different sectors of society, the state usually has a built-in set of advantages for playing a major role. Other tasks, such as taxing exports or making particular kinds of transfer payments, may be possible without achieving predominance. Social scientists focusing on these sorts of issues have stressed the state's prowess, pointing to its growing bureaucracy, its role in funneling private foreign capital to local entrepreneurs, and its ability to maintain social peace through corporatist measures. When social policy demands changes in behavior among broad segments of the population, however, states can be far less effective.[15] The same Mexican government that had considerable success in regulating the share of equity and the operations of foreign-owned firms repeatedly failed to execute a fair-price-for-the-poor policy in rural areas in the 1970s.

In brief, states are not always the unfettered prime movers of macro-level societal change they are sometimes portrayed to be. To be sure, the strength they draw from an international environment that continuously thrusts them into critical roles and offers resources to play those roles bolsters their position, particularly on issues such as diplomacy, war making, and transfer payments. At the same time, states are often severely constrained by their domestic environments from achieving an independent reordering of society. The autonomy of states, the slant of their policies, the preoccupying issues for their leaders, and their coherence are greatly influenced by the societies in which they operate.

Social organizations in a mélange, including the state, coexist symbiotically. In an environment of conflict, especially, the social control exercised even by small social organizations tucked away in remote areas constrains the state tremendously. The state is hemmed in – indeed transformed – by these internal forces, just as it is by international forces. But society is also transformed by the state. Social organizations, and the structure of

---

[15] Baldwin makes a point that should lead those writing on corporatism and bureaucratic authoritarianism to exercise some caution. "The so-called 'paradox of unrealized power' results from the mistaken belief that power resources in one policy-contingent framework will be equally useful in a different one. . . . The theme of such explanations is not 'he had the cards but played them poorly,' but rather 'he had a great bridge hand but happened to be playing poker.'" Baldwin, "Power Analysis," p. 164.

society as a whole, are molded by the opportunities and impediments that the state presents, just as they are affected by other social organizations and by the openings and limitations posed by the world economy. In short, the interaction of states and other social formations is a continuing process of transformation. States are not fixed entities, nor are societies; they both change structure, goals, constituencies, rules, and social control in their process of interaction. They are constantly *becoming*.

The model presented here – a mélange in which multiple sets of rules struggle for predominance and the state is seen both as an idea and as diverse practices that may be at loggerheads – focuses attention on the crucial battle for social control. In the modern world system, the idea of the state is at center stage in this struggle. Yet this position in the lime-light does not necessarily spell victory. Many societies remain in an environment of conflict in which order and macro-level change must be understood in terms of two tiers of forces. The first includes the effects of society on the state and vice versa. The second involves the impact on state and society of other states and of the world economy. A partial research agenda based on this approach might include the following issues:

1. Under what circumstances has the distribution of social control in an environment of conflict altered? How can one explain variations in social control from society to society?
2. Can one generalize about the impact of transnational forces on the distribution of social control? How have these forces affected the role played by domestic social organizations in maintaining a particular order or in fostering certain types of societal change?
3. How has the form of politics – democracy, single party authoritarianism, and so on – been affected by the distribution of social control?
4. When social organizations besides the state exercise significant social control, how has the state's ability in different issue areas been affected?
5. What has been the nature of the struggle between state and other social organizations in the post–World War II period? Which social organizations have been the most successful in maintaining and extending social control? Has this pattern changed over time? Does the pattern hold across cultures?
6. How have states and other social organizations interacted in societies in which states have not achieved predominance?

3

Strong States, Weak States

POWER AND ACCOMMODATION

Two Images of the State

It has been a generation since decolonization abruptly transformed the world map. But we still do not have a very clear picture of the relationship between politics and social change in former colonies, let alone effective theories to explain why things are as they are. An odd duality, or even contradiction, has marked the social science literature. One portrait gleaned from scholarly works has set politics – especially the state – at center stage, kneading society into new forms and shapes, adapting it to the exigencies created by industrialization or other stimuli. This is the image of the strong state. A second perspective portrays the state as nearly hapless in the swirl of dizzying social changes that have overtaken these societies, changes largely independent of any impetus from the state itself. Some scholars view the dynamics of these changes within the country's borders while others see these uncontrollable forces coming from large powers and the world economy. In both instances, the image is of a weak state.

The word "state" itself, ironically, at first did not figure prominently in either of these two images. In fact, it has become an almost commonplace criticism in recent years that the state was a neglected variable in theories of social and political change for most of the postwar era.[1] That criticism, however, may be somewhat overstated. In third-world

---

[1] See, for example, Theda Skocpol, "Bringing the State Back In," *Social Science Research Council Items* 36 (June 1982): 1–8, Eric Nordlinger, *On the Autonomy of the Democratic State* (Cambridge, MA: Harvard University Press, 1981), Stephen D. Krasner, "Approaches to the State: Alternative Conceptions and Historical Dynamics," *Comparative Politics* 16 (January 1984): 223.

studies, at least, one could probably better say that the state was more assumed or taken for granted than neglected during the 1950s and 1960s. Many social scientists writing about non-Western societies saw the conscious manipulation of social life – public policy – as a central ingredient of the social histories and futures of newly independent societies. Such manipulation, of course, lies at the heart of politics. The concept of the state came to be assumed, rather than dealt with in more explicit terms, only because politics was often viewed as the outgrowth of other sorts of more fundamental processes (for example, those in economic life or in communications). Or politics and states were subsumed within larger constructs, such as "centers" and "modern sectors," which were portrayed as the movers (or potential movers) in shaping new social habits, a new national consciousness, and new politics in formerly intractable peripheries.

It was not until Samuel P. Huntington's well-known article in the 1965 volume of *World Politics*, "Political Development and Political Decay," that politics as an independent and autonomous enterprise became a widely accepted notion.[2] Even then, however, the acceptance of the centrality of politics (and the notion of the state itself) did not lead to unanimity about the capabilities of states. One still finds projected in the literature of the 1970s and 1980s the two images of states – sometimes the very same state – as both strong and weak. Many scholars tended to dismiss existing third-world states as ineffective manipulators of social life. Huntington himself began his book *Political Order in Changing Societies* by noting that the major distinction between states lies not in their type of government but in the degree to which the government really governs.[3] Or as Aristide R. Zolberg put it with respect to African states, "The major problem is not too much authority, but too little."[4] While holding out hope and even giving prescriptions for political institutionalization, consolidation, and centralization of states, many authors found third-world states to be disorganized, confused conglomerates of people and agencies. Instability and ineptness stood out as primary subjects of inquiry.

[2] Samuel P. Huntington, "Political Development and Political Decay," *World Politics* 17 (April 1965): 386–430.
[3] Samuel P. Huntington, *Political Order in Changing Societies* (New Haven, Yale University Press, 1968), pp. 1–2.
[4] Aristide R. Zolberg, *One-Party Government in the Ivory Coast*, revised edition (Princeton, NJ: Princeton University Press, 1969), p. x.

At the same time, the image of the strong third-world state managed to hold its own, or even to increase in importance. This perspective was undoubtedly influenced by studies of Western societies. The Western state's autonomy (or at least relative autonomy) and its ability to organize social groups able to penetrate deeply into the fabric of society became major topics of research.[5] And to a considerable degree within the last decade, the presumptions about the Western state have spilled over into the study of non-Western ones. Literature on states, particularly those in Latin America and East Asia, emphasizes how they reshape societies. States promote some groups and classes while repressing others, all the while maintaining autonomy from any single group or class.

The activism and strength of the third-world state in regulating, even shaping, the eruptive conflicts that come from industrialization and the mobilization of new social groups have been emphasized in theories of corporatism and the bureaucratic authoritarian state.[6] The state, wrote James M. Malloy, "is characterized by strong and relatively autonomous governmental structures that seek to impose on the society a system of interest representation based on enforced limited pluralism."[7]

Although this second image of the state in the Third World as robust and capable was influenced by recent works on the West, it had also been inchoate in many of the earlier studies of non-Western societies written in the 1950s and 1960s. Even before the word state became fashionable, Charles W. Anderson noted the attraction to such an image in Latin American studies. "Many contemporary notions about development," he remarked, "seem to posit government as a kind of 'omnipotent given' that could if it would set matters right."[8] Although contemporary corporatist and bureaucratic authoritarian theories are often less sanguine about the

[5] See, for example, the works in Peter J. Katzenstein (ed.), *Between Power and Plenty: Foreign Economic Policies of Advanced Industrial States* (Madison: University of Wisconsin Press, 1978).
[6] See, for example, the chapters by Douglass H. Graham and by Douglass Bennett and Kenneth Sharpe in Sylvia Ann Hewlett and Richard S. Weinert (eds.), *Brazil and Mexico: Patterns in Late Development* (Philadelphia: Institute for the Study of Human Issues, 1982), and by Guillermo O'Donnell and others in David Collier (ed.), *The New Authoritarianism in Latin America* (Princeton, NJ: Princeton University Press, 1979).
[7] James M. Malloy, "Authoritarianism and Corporation in Latin America: The Modal Pattern" in James M. Malloy (ed.), *Authoritarianism and Corporatism in Latin America* (Pittsburgh, PA: University of Pittsburgh Press, 1977), p. 4.
[8] Charles W. Anderson, *Politics and Economic Change in Latin America: The Governing of Restless Nations* (Princeton, NJ: D. Van Nostrand, 1967), p. 5.

state setting matters right, they do continue to attribute great strength to the state, even if they regard those capabilities as malevolent.

Yet a close look at some writings even about a country such as Mexico, which is assumed to house a strong, active state, once again reveals the curious duality of images. Notions of state ineptness still come creeping through. To some field researchers, the "omnipotent, given" appears impotent at times, so much so that some descriptions of so-called bureaucratic authoritarian or other imposing states in Latin America and Asia take on many of the hues of accounts of less-capable African states. Prior to undertaking her work on Mexican state autonomy during the tenure of president Lazaro Cardenas, for example, Nora Hamilton was struck by an odd contradiction. The state played an important role in stimulating Mexico's dramatic economic growth but seemed "unable or unwilling to direct the Mexican economy so that growth benefits of all Mexico's populations."[9] Merilee Serrill Grindle, focusing on the policy process much more carefully, observed the same sort of duality in Mexico. She noted that if political development is thought of as the capacity to govern then the Mexican regime is quite advanced. "Together with the rest of the political class in Mexico, the bureaucratic elite has developed vertical power relationships throughout the society."[10] Despite this power, the bureaucratic elite suffered nasty setbacks in attempting to pursue a redistributive policy in the rural areas. Grindle described in her case study how local-level resistance successfully foiled state leaders from achieving their purposes.

Other authors on Latin America echo this uncertainty about state power. One serious doubter is Linn A. Hammergren:

It is true that constitutions and legislation often accord enormous powers of control to central governments, but the question remains as to whether this control is actually exercised or exists only on paper. The limited success of Latin American governments in enforcing their own legislation suggests that the extent of this control is not great.[11]

---

[9] Nora Hamilton, *The Limits of State Autonomy: Post Revolutionary Mexico* (Princeton, NJ: Princeton University Press, 1982), p. vii.

[10] Merilee Serrill Grindle, *Bureaucrats, Politicians, and Peasants in Mexico: A Case Study in Public Policy* (Berkeley: University of California Press, 1977), p. 178.

[11] Linn A. Hammergren, "Corporatism in Latin American Politics: A Reexamination of the 'Unique' Tradition," *Comparative Politics* 9 (July 1977): 449. A couple of older works on Latin America voiced this refrain as well. See Charles W. Anderson, *Politics and Economic Change in Latin America*, pp. 105–6; and Merle Kling, "Toward a Theory of Power and Political Instability in Latin America," in James Petras and Maurice Zeitlin (eds.), *Latin America: Reform or Revolution* (New York: Fawcett, 1968), p. 93.

Similar statements have come out of Asia. In her chapter of "Failures of Implementation" in India, Francine R. Frankel noted numerous instances of the disjuncture between announced state policies and the actual conformity of society to those policies. One example was state encouragement of cooperative bodies, which were intended to serve as strong "peoples institutions." To that end personnel and resources proliferated in the State Departments of Cooperation:

> This far-reaching administrative apparatus was vested with formidable powers. State acts gave the registrar and his organization extensive regulatory and executive authority over the whole range of operations of cooperative societies. These powers included control over registration of new societies, inspection of finances, arbitration of disputes, supersession of negligent managing committees, annual audit, and even liquidation.... Altogether, these powers provided more than adequate leverage for the implementation of the Planning Commission's policy linking credit to an approval production plan and repayment in kind through crop deliveries to a cooperative marketing society.[12]

The program, however, ended up a failure. The intended clients received little. Local resources were not mobilized as intended. The powers invested in the policy implementors were not sufficient to overcome those bent on changing the policy's purpose.

The Dilemma of State Leaders

How can we account for these conflicting portraits of the state in the Third World? Which image better depicts the real abilities and character of states? To answer these questions, we must place the state back into context. States operate in two intersecting arenas. The first is the world arena in which state officials interact with representatives of other states, large corporations, international organizations, and an assortment of other transnational actors. The second arena is the society that the state seeks to rule.

State leaders face obvious constraints in the sorts of actions they can take in the world arena beyond their borders: war is always a lurking threat. States also face severe, if more subtle, constraints from the world arena in what they can do domestically as a result of the particular niche their society occupies in the world economy. The societies they wish to rule are

---

[12] Francine R. Frankel, *India's Political Economy, 1947–1977: The Gradual Revolution* (Princeton, NJ: Princeton University Press, 1978), p. 196.

part of a larger world social system with established relations and patterns of trade, investment, borrowing, labor migration, and more that have their origins in precolonial days. This social system has created a worldwide pattern of stratification, as well as domestic patterns of stratification. It is only at the greatest peril that state leaders can ignore in domestic policy the power relations generated within the world social system.

It would be a grave mistake to assume (as many writers have) that these power relations determine totally the domestic stratification pattern and the character of state-society relations in third-world countries. The second arena within which states operate, that of the domestic society, allows for important social dynamics and has room for significant state maneuvering. It is here that state leaders seek to maximize their autonomy whenever and wherever possible, even within a context of constraints from world forces. Likewise, leaders of other social groups try to skirt the obstacles placed before them and use as many resources as they can garner, including those from the world arena, to expand their own autonomy. It is this context of domestic state-society relations that needs to be unraveled in order to understand the results of state leaders' efforts to reshape, ignore, or circumvent the strongest groups in their societies. We must move away from a perspective that simply pits state against society. The state is part of society, with many characteristics not very different from those of other social organizations. Officials of the state are members of the larger society. What must be sorted out is any distinctive patterns of their interactions with those in other groups and organizations.

The state is a sprawling organization within society that coexists with many other formal and informal social organizations, from families to tribes to large industrial enterprises. What distinguishes the state, at least in the modern era, is that state officials seek predominance over those myriad other organizations. That is, they aim for the state to make the binding rules guiding people's behavior or, at the very least, to authorize particular other organizations to make those rules in certain realms. By "rules" I mean the laws, regulations, decrees, and the like that state officials indicate they are willing to enforce through the coercive means at their disposal. Rules include everything from living up to contractual commitments to driving on the right side of the road to paying alimony on time. They involve the entire array of property rights and any of the other countless definitions of the boundaries delineating acceptable behavior for people.

In gauging the appropriateness of strong-state or weak-state imageries, the question of "who makes the rules" looms large. It leads us to examine the central elements of the state's domestic capabilities – whether it can get people to do what its laws and other rules prescribe, whether its policies have their intended effect on people's behavior. The analysis in the following pages sets out the argument that social structure, particularly the existence of numerous other social organizations that exercise effective social control, has a decisive effect on the likelihood of the state greatly expanding its capabilities. The strength of these other social organizations influences the priorities of state leaders and ultimately the ability of state agencies to enforce laws and implement policies. In the end, the argument leads to quite unanticipated conclusions: that state leaders may purposely weaken their own state agencies that could apply and enforce rules, and that the state may purposely strengthen those who apply and enforce rules in contradiction to those of the state.

Perhaps because the state's role in making and authorizing rules about public affairs and the intimacies of private life is so much taken for granted in the West, many social scientists have lost sight of the struggles in societies with relatively new states. In many of these societies, state officials have simply not gained the right and ability to make many of the rules that they would like. Families and clans may seek to marry off children at ages quite different from the minimum age of marriage set by law. Landlords and shopkeepers may seek interest rates for loans at variance with those legislated by the state. The major struggles in many societies, especially those with fairly new states, are struggles over who has the right and ability to make the countless rules that guide people's social behavior. Noncompliance here is not simply personal deviance or criminality but an indication of a more fundamental conflict over which organizations in society – the state or other organizations – should make these rules. These struggles are not over precisely which laws the state should enact or how the state's laws or constitution should be interpreted – these, after all, are decided within state organs, legislatures, and courts. No, these struggles are much more fundamental, reaching beyond marginal deviance and beyond the capacities of any existing political institutions in the society. These struggles are over whether the state will be able to displace other organizations in society that make rules against the wishes and goals of state leaders.

Focusing on these struggles within society, between states and other social organizations such as clans, tribes, language groups, and the like, will give new insights into the processes of social and political change, since the very purposes for which leaders employ the state – seeking predominance through binding rules – automatically thrust it into conflict with other organizations over who has the right and ability to make those rules. Many of the existing approaches to understanding social and political change in the Third World either have downplayed conflict altogether (e.g., much of "modernization" theory), or have missed these particular sorts of conflicts, which only on occasion are class based (e.g., much of the Marxist literature), or have skipped the important dynamics within domestic society altogether (e.g., dependency and world system theories).

As we shall see shortly, it is far from inevitable that the efforts of state leaders will achieve predominance for the state. In cases where it is unattainable, at least for the time being, the state does not simply disappear nor does it always continually incur the high costs of battling those who are effectively making the rules in this realm or that, in one locality or another. The most subtle and fascinating patterns of political change and political inertia come in accommodations between states and other powerful organizations in society – accommodations that could not be predicted simply by assuming the autonomy of the state or the determining influences of world forces. The struggle over the state's desire for predominance, the accommodations between states and others, and the maneuvering to gain the best deal possible in any arrived-at accommodation are the real politics of many third-world societies – politics that often take place far from the capital city. These processes can help give a clearer portrait of the state, especially by examining what happens to public policies upon their implementation in the far corners of society, a question rarely asked in the vast literature on postcolonial societies.

Public policy entails the attempt by state leaders to use their organization to make new rules and consequently change the behavior of the public. Sometimes public policy aims to modify the behavior of only a minute fraction of the population, as, for instance, in certain banking regulations. Of course, in cases of policies directed toward large portions of the population, these policy efforts by state leaders represent massive undertakings, often involving the movement of significant resources through the state apparatus and into the society. Such attempts broadly challenge the existing rules in society and, with them, the social organizations that enforce those rules and the leaders of those organizations, who benefit most from them. On the one hand, resistance of one sort or another is nearly inevitable. Such resistance will come in states with relatively modest policy agendas, such as bringing new public health measures to villages, as well as ones with much more radical goals, such as changing places on the status ladder for entire social classes. On the other hand, the resources that come with the policy are prime targets to be used as a basis for accommodation – in ways very different from what was anticipated by state officials in the capital city who drafted the policy.

For state leaders, gaining the upper hand in the struggle engendered by initiation of new policies and the challenge to existing rules depends only partially on creating state agencies that can apply fearsome sanctions against the leaders of those other social organizations and their followers. Just as important is the need for state personnel to wean the population from such organizations and their rules by supplying the rewards that have linked people to those organizations and their leaders in the first place. Even better for state leaders would be to undermine those other organizations and the efficacy of their rules by supplying to people a mix of rewards, sanctions, and symbols that constitutes a more attractive overall strategy of survival than that available through the old social organizations.

In talking about the formulation of conflicting strategies of survival by states and other social organizations, I run the risk of making the ground-level struggles in the Third World sound as if they hinge on voluntaristic impulses. Needless to say, vulnerable workers and peasants are not simply shoppers in a strategy or rules supermarket. It is important, nevertheless, to portray the structural dimensions of the environment in which policy is implemented. New policies are not implemented in a vacuum. They almost certainly generate opposition by those with a stake in the status quo. The conflict over who makes the rules is not decided simply by force, but also by other incentives. It is here that policies are thrust into the state's struggle for predominance.

Fashioning effective strategies of survival demands that state leaders build elaborate institutions to implement their policies. The image of the strong state found in the social science literature stems in great part from the rapid expansion of the state organization in Latin America, Asia, and Africa in the postcolonial era, as state leaders set out to offer viable strategies to the populace and win people over to the state's rules. But one must be extremely cautious before equating a growing state apparatus with state predominance. The bureaus of the state may become little more than arenas for accommodations with other organizations.

The literature on the Third World has paid scant attention to existing rule-making organizations outside the domain of the state and in conflict with the aims of state leaders. Yet, strategies offered to people through these structures may be quite complex and binding.[13] During the last century, there has been a tremendous upsurge in the strength of many such organizations. In a large number of cases, colonial divide-and-rule policies injected vast new resources – most notably, wealth and force – into the hands of local and regional leaders, enabling them to strengthen the strategies of survival they could offer clients and followers. In turn, their ability to make and enforce binding rules of behavior also increased. Even where there was no direct colonialism, the expanding world economy funneled resources into societies quite selectively, allowing for the strengthening of caciques, effendis, caudillos, landlords, kulak-type rich peasants, moneylenders, and others. Through credit, access to land and water, protection, bullying, and numerous other means, these leaders or strongmen (for want of a better general term) fashioned viable strategies of survival for numerous peasants and workers.

Although their rules and systems of justice have been quite different from the state's (and, often, from one another's), these strongmen have, nonetheless, enforced those rules and thus ensured a modicum of social stability – if not the same social justice state leaders would like. Challenging these leaders and their organizations, then, threatens social stability unless viable strategies of survival offered by state agencies or organizations allied with the state, such as a political party, are at hand, ready to be substituted. The fear of instability should be a strong motivation for state leaders to build as effective a set of agencies as possible.

There are certainly other inducements as well. When state policy is effectively establishing the rules of behavior, for example, state agencies can better mobilize material resources through tax collection and reorganization of production. "Much of what is traditionally meant by power," writes Alan C. Lamborn, "does involve the government's capacity to mobilize resources."[14] Not only are state revenues enhanced for domestic purposes, but some of the severe pressures state leaders confront from the

---

[13] The main exception is the literature on the clientelism, which was a topic of some interest to social scientists in the late 1960s and early 1970s. Since then relatively little has appeared on the subject.

[14] Alan C. Lamborn, "Power and the Politics of Extraction," *International Studies Quarterly* 27 (June 1983), p. 126.

international economy, stemming from deficits in balance of payments and debt repayment, can be alleviated. In short, building strong states, ones able to set the rules in their societies, is not simply an abstract norm for state leaders; there are clear imperatives coming from within and outside the society to build as strong an apparatus as possible.

State leaders, however, are caught between Scylla and Charybdis, facing a baffling paradox. If domestic and international dangers can be countered through building agencies of the state (which, in turn, can offer effective rules and viable strategies of survival to the population), strengthening those state institutions may at the same time hold out its own perils for state leaders. Agencies of the state – especially those that employ violence, such as the army, but others as well – may themselves pose threats to state leaders who still have only limited ability to marshal widespread public support and resources on their own behalf. The problem is that as long as strongmen continue to offer viable survival strategies to members of their villages, ethnic groups, and so on, there are no channels for state leaders to marshal public support and there is little motivation for the population to lend such support. In other words, state leaders need a set of strong state agencies to be able to make their own strategy of survival acceptable to the peasants and laborers of the Third World. They also need, however, to be able to mobilize support among these peasants and workers so that these same state agencies will not themselves overthrow the state rulers through an army coup or other similar means. Such political mobilization – and here is the catch – cannot be realized without already-established channels to the population that induce mobilization through a viable mix of rewards, sanctions, and symbols – precisely what strong state agencies are needed for in the first place.[15] This paradox is the dilemma of state leaders.

President Gamal Abdul Nasser of Egypt squarely faced this dilemma during the 1950s and 1960s. Bold and extensive land reform measures, begun in the 1950s, had eliminated the class of landowners with huge holdings. Building state agencies to substitute for the policing, lending, marketing, peacekeeping, and other functions that the large landowners

---

[15] J. P. Nettl notes that political mobilization "is the collective and structural expression of commitment and support within society. Such expression may take the form of political parties or quasi-parties – interest groups, movements, etc., anything that has a well-articulated structure." See J. P. Nettl, *Political Mobilization: A Sociological Analysis of Methods and Concepts* (New York: Basic Books, 1967), p. 123.

had overseen, however, was a painstaking process. Nasser and his cohorts fell back on middle peasants (those with holdings large enough so that members of their household need not seek work outside the farm) and rich peasants (those whose holdings were extensive enough to demand extra hired labor on a regular basis) to perform these functions. Some of these rich and middle peasants had played similar roles in earlier years as agents for the owners of large estates. At the same time, Nasser pushed ahead in building state agencies and a single political party. By the mid-1960s, the agencies challenged the strongmen on whom the regime had needed to rely, the middle and rich peasants who had spun out their own strategies of survival for Egypt's vast number of land-poor and landless peasants. Party cadres branded the middle and rich peasants as "feudal" elements.

Nasser's own organizations, however, began to concern him. By the early 1960s, Field Marshal Abdul Hakim Amir had built an officer corps loyal to him, and he withstood attempts by Nasser to bring him under presidential control. To counter Amir's threatening power, Nasser moved in the mid-1960s to build up the Arab Socialist Union (ASU) as the party that could serve as a civilian counter to the military.[16] But, by the late 1960s, even the ASU was a cause for worry. It had clearly moved beyond challenging other social organizations with their "feudal" rules to challenge Nasser's own power within the state. In the end, Nasser attempted to neutralize the ASU itself, going so far as to arrest its powerful first secretary, Ali Sabri, for smuggling. In the countryside, the ASU's Committee of the Liquidation of Feudalism slipped quietly into oblivion. The rich and middle peasants, although a bit worse for wear, remained the most powerful forces in rural Egypt. The Egyptian state had not achieved predominance in large part because its ruler feared his own agencies, the army and the ASU, which were needed to achieve that predominance.

The dilemma of state leaders – this paradox of fearing and undermining the very mechanisms they need in order to reach their own goals – has reverberated throughout the Third World. The degree to which this dilemma has hamstrung state leaders in appropriating power – in having their rules apply throughout the country – has varied from country to country. Where strongmen have been able to maintain a tight grasp on local resources, state mobilization of the population has been all the more

[16] John Waterbury, *The Egypt of Nasser and Sadat: The Political Economy of Two Regimes* (Princeton, NJ: Princeton University Press, 1983), p. 316.

difficult, and the dilemma of state leaders has been acute. On the other hand, where strongmen have been weakened in their control, more opportunities have existed for penetration by state authority. Nasser, for example, did have to his credit the destruction of the most powerful class in rural Egypt. The large landlords had become vulnerable as they moved from the countryside, leaving charge of their affairs to local agents, often rich and middle peasants. The opening that absentee ownership gave Nasser allowed him to build a regime that has now lasted for half a century and to penetrate every village in Egypt through a number of state agencies. The hold of the rich and middle peasants, however, forced unanticipated accommodations (of a sort we shall discuss later) between them and state officials.

Elsewhere, I discuss at some length the causes of variation in state strength from country to country.[17] Briefly, the rapid and deep extension of the world market from the late 1850s through World War I made many of the existing rules in Asian, African, and Latin American societies irrelevant. Colonial administration, in many areas, further undermined the control of strongmen. It was as if a great wind swept through the non-Western world, knocking Humpty Dumpty off the wall. Where colonial rule took hold, Western administrators deeply influenced how Humpty Dumpty was put together again. In some instances, centralizing indigenous groups were promoted. Far more frequently, however, colonial resources were used to reestablish fragmented social control through the promotion of old and new strongmen. Other factors could also influence the hold of strongmen. For example, devastating wars could lead to the flight of landlords and to changing man-land ratios, greatly diminishing the existing social control of strongmen.

The relative control of the state and other social organizations professing other rules vary substantially from country to country. Nonetheless, many third-world countries in the postwar era have witnessed a remarkable further strengthening of local organizations and their strongmen, leaders with rules and agendas in contradiction to those professed by state leaders. The middle and rich peasants of Egypt's four thousand villages have counterparts in many societies of Asia, Africa, and Latin America. Far from being anachronistic relics, such strongmen and their organizations have often thrived during the last generation.

---

[17] Joel S. Migdal, *Strong Societies and Weak States: State-Society Relations and State Capabilities in the Third Word* (Princeton, NJ: Princeton University Press, 1988).

As we shall see, the increased strength of these strongmen contains an ironic note, drawing in many instances from their accommodations with the state itself. Strongmen have carved out protective niches for themselves – invigorated, as it were, by the dilemma of state leaders. In countries where such strongmen have thrived, the dilemma of state leaders has affected the character of the state organization itself. At the apex of the state organization, at the level of the administrative implementor, and at the level of local politics, many states have been deeply influenced by the actions of state leaders who have perceived the dangers in building state agencies and unleashing them against strongmen, who promote different rules and loyalties.

At the Apex: The Politics of Survival

The ability to mobilize broad segments of the population through political parties and state agencies has eluded many leaders in the Third World. Sustained political mobilization demands much more than exhortations, charisma, or ideology, especially where there are fierce battles for loyalty and conflicts over who sets the rules of daily behavior. Mobilization entails conveying to people that the routines, symbols, and ways of behaving represented by the state leadership are essential to their well-being. And it involves providing them with channels to express their support. Without a sense of urgency among broad segments of the population about the dangers of upsetting the routines established by the state and without adequate channels to sustain support, state leaders are forced to fall back on much narrower bases than those provided by mass mobilization – bases such as their organizational prowess and the support of specific social groupings. But because these bases are narrower, they make the position of state leaders precarious, especially in the face of any other significant concentrations of power in the society, which ultimately might be used against them.

Political mobilization is an effective tool for state leaders, then, when there are multitudes of channels of support. No single state agency can provide so much of that support that it can affect the overall amount appreciably. Where such a condition does not hold and a few agencies dominate – a sort of oligopoly of mobilizational capability – the very coherence of the state is diminished. Since the state's leadership in such countries has a limited reservoir of structured support to draw upon, it finds it difficult to check the centrifugal forces that grow as a few, select agencies blossom.

The common, particular views in a given agency that develop over time among its top officials about the purposes and functioning of the entire state apparatus threaten the coherence and, indeed, the stability of the state. Such particular views are created and reinforced in any number of ways, including shared socialization (as in a military academy), the repeated representation of the agency's interests in wider forums (as in the competition for funds), daily personal interaction, the effective allocation of resources and status within the agency, and so on. These factors are found in any complex organization, and the centrifugal forces they generate are familiar to all students of bureaucracy. What is threatening to leaders is abiding loyalties in state organs or allied political parties in the absence of a multitude of effective, opposing centripetal forces. Political mobilization through a large number of channels provides those centripetal forces in many states. In countries in which such support is absent and costly to achieve – where a very few agencies have an oligopoly on mobilizational capabilities – the position of state leaders may be precarious indeed.

The temptation, then, is to "solve" the problem by lessening the centrifugal forces. In other words, where the dilemma of state leaders is acute, a top priority may become a set of actions designed to prevent any large concentrations of power from arising. Like Nasser in his attack against his own agencies – the fast-growing army and ASU – other state leaders have resorted to weakening any group in society that seems to be building extensive mobilizational strength, even agencies of the state itself. Bizarre as it may seem, then, state leaders with limited capacity to mobilize their public have themselves crippled the arms of the state, the very organs that ultimately could have given them that mobilizational ability. We may term their strategies the politics of survival. The actions characteristic of the politics of survival are discussed in the following subsections.

The Big Shuffle

The power of appointment in state leaders' hands can prove to be an important tool in preventing any state agencies or government-sponsored political parties from becoming threatening conglomerates of power. As appointees such as Egypt's Field Marshal Amir or ASU Secretary Sabri settle into their organizational roles, they develop loyal followers. Their own power of appointments within their agencies, along with the patronage and spoils they can dispense, provide them with an important largess. At their disposal is a complex, task-oriented organization staffed by officials, many of whom owe their careers to the person at the top of the agency.

The "big shuffle" is a set of preemptive actions taken by state leaders, using their own power of appointment, to prevent loyalties in potentially strong agencies from developing in the first place. These leaders have frequently replaced ministers of state, commanders of armed forces, party leaders, and top bureaucrats in order to prevent threatening centers of power from coalescing. At the apex of the state, the political style can resemble a dizzying game of musical chairs. In some cases, the same people appear over and over in different key posts. Yesterday, one was the commander-in-chief of the armed forces; today, minister of the interior; tomorrow, ambassador to the United States or chief executive officer of a major state enterprise. In other instances, officials disappear altogether from the political scene.

The *sexenio* in Mexico, for example, has the effect of ensuring that state agencies do not develop deep internal ties over time. Every six-year presidential administration "witnesses a turnover of approximately 18,000 elective offices and 25,000 supportive posts."[18] Those figures were given four decades ago; no doubt they are even higher today. In the dominant party and the bureaucracy, many of those displaced fill new posts, but at the top, many leave public service permanently.

In Egypt, which is probably more representative of a large number of other cases, the falls from the pinnacle have not been as routinized as in Mexico. Field Marshal Amir had "successfully kept control of the promotion process within the officers corps and was able, in addition, to place his people in upper-level management in the growing public sector, as well its the diplomatic corps and the ranks of provincial governors."[19] He was placed under house arrest in September 1967, and several days later his suicide was announced. Amir's demise came after Nasser had "retired" hundreds of officers. Many others were dropped from the high ranks of state agencies by Nasser and his successor, Anwar el-Sadat. Even more extreme are states that experience a permanent purge of top state and party personnel.

---

[18] Frank Brandenburg, *The Making of Modern Mexico* (Englewood Cliffs, NJ: Prentice-Hall, 1964), p. 157.

[19] Waterbury, *Egypt of Nasser and Sadat*, p. 336.

At the core of all these manifestations of the "big shuffle" lies the weakness of state leaders – their inability to use political mobilization as a check to any threatening centers of power within the state organization itself. Sadat, upon assuming leadership in 1970, had no institutional base of support at all. One of his first impressions was that those heading important state agencies and the Arab Socialist Union "never paid any regard to the interests of Egypt and wanted nothing but to remain in power, seeking their own interests and motivated by hatred and jealousy."[20] One might put it a bit more kindly by saying that the agency heads understood the "interests of Egypt" differently from Sadat. Their posts gave them particular perspectives on what was good for Egypt.

Within a year after assuming the presidency, Sadat attacked what he termed the "power centers" that threatened his rule, forcing out simultaneously six cabinet ministers and three party chiefs. Perhaps even more interesting for understanding the dynamics of the "big shuffle" is what happened to those who stood by Sadat in the political crisis of May 1971, when so many top agency officials fell. John Waterbury recounts their fates in a footnote:

Ashraf Marwan, married to Nasser's daughter, gave Sadat tapes that incriminated Sabri. He became Sadat's advisor on Arab affairs until 1978 and then was dropped. Muhammed Sadiq was arrested in late 1972. Mumduh Salim went on to be prime minister but then was given an honorific post advisor after 1978. Hassanein Heikal was fired from the editorship of al-Ahram in 1974. 'Aziz Sidqi had had no public role since 1978. Hafiz Badawi, who became speaker of parliament, was dropped in favor of Sayyid Mar'ai. Dakruri, Darwish, 'Abd al-Akhir, and Mahmud were all put on the Discipline Committee of the ASU; two went on to governorships and two to cabinet positions. All had disappeared by the late 1970s. 'Abd al-Salam al-Zayyat survived as an M.P., but was briefly arrested in 1980 and again in 1981. Hussain Shafa'i of the RCC was made a vice-president and then replaced by Husni Mubarak in 1975. Those who fared best were Mahmud Fawzi, who retired with honor, and Sayyid Mar'ai, who remained an influential but somewhat marginal figure in the early 1980s.[21]

The "big shuffle" is not a one-time event nor is it reserved for enemies. It is a mechanism for deliberately weakening arms of the state and allied organizations – a kind of deinstitutionalization – in order to assure the tenure of the top state leadership.

[20] Anwar el-Sadat, *In Search of Identity: An Autobiography* (New York: Harper & Row, 1977), p. 207.
[21] Waterbury, *Egypt of Nasser and Sadat*, p. 352 n.

Nonmerit Appointments

The power of appointments that lies in the hands of state leaders involves more than merely dismissing people from positions. Appointments are a source of patronage that can be doled out selectively to prevent the development of centers of power within the state itself. The result is that some third-world states take on an almost familial character (for a few, one could just as well drop the "almost"), displaying many of the characteristics of much less bureaucratized and complex patrimonial systems.[22]

Probably the most popular method here is to appoint top agency officials who have deep personal loyalties to the state leaders. In India, Syria, Egypt, and elsewhere, one finds in recruitment to critical state posts patterns of kinship ties; of common regional origins (at times, limited to a single town or several villages); of shared ethnic, tribal, or sectarian backgrounds; of school connections; and of other sorts of personalities. In Iraq, for example, many top officials are from one family group, the Begat section of the Albu Nasir tribe, and primarily from the small town of Takri in the northwest.

In those countries where strongmen have retained tight grips and continue to make the effective rules, appointment to the state bureaucracy, state-owned enterprises, and government parties on the basis of personal loyalty is a means of mitigating powerful centrifugal forces. In postrevolutionary Mexico, for example, the top elite has nurtured a series of reinforcing personal, political, and business ties. At the foundation of all these linkages is membership in what Roger D. Hansen calls the Revolutionary Family.[23] In Sierra Leone, as far back as colonial times, tribal chiefs moved to monopolize positions in missionary and state schools. It was "the sons, brothers, relatives, and wards of chiefs . . . who had benefited from such educational opportunities."[24] Their attempt, which later proved to contain considerable merit, was to ensure that those with the backgrounds to assume leadership from the British colonialists would have strong personal ties to them. Where the dilemma of state leaders is acute and the sustained

---

[22] On neopatrimonialism, see S. N. Eisenstadt, *Traditional Patrimonialism and Modern Neopatrimonialism*, vol. 1 of *Sage Research Papers in the Social Sciences, Studies in Comparative Modernization Series* (Beverly Hills, CA: Sage 1973): 129.

[23] Roger D. Hansen, *The Politics of Mexican Development* (Baltimore: John Hopkins University Press, 1973), p. 129.

[24] Gershon Collier, *Sierre Leone: Experiment in Democracy in an African Nation* (New York: New York University Press, 1970), p. 85.

support coming from political mobilization eludes them, vulnerability can be contained by reinforcing organizational functional ties with close personal relationships. In addition, such relationships may be a hedge if one does fall from power.

Egyptians have formalized ties of personal loyalty much more than people in most societies. There one finds the institution of *shilla*, an intimate grouping of about a half-dozen people. Membership in each *shilla* is unambiguous; there is no question of who is part of the group and who is not. Each forms on the basis of friendships made in school, the university, the army, and the like. Egyptians often talk about the *shilla* as a kind of family.[25] In prerevolutionary Egypt, the military academy served as the setting for an important *shilla* whose members included Nasser, Sadat, Amir, and others who later helped overthrow the monarchy. Political life in Egypt continues to be rife with appointments based on *shilla* membership. The *dawrah* in Iran, a similar sort of informal group, created a hidden overlay to Tehran's formal political dealings during the rule of the Shah.[26]

Another basis for appointment to state positions is co-optation of those who might otherwise develop threatening power centers outside the state organization. Hansen has commented on co-optation at the apex of Mexican politics. He notes that the personal gains are both illegal (such as unauthorized landholdings) and legal (such as special trucking contracts). In either case, "the co-opters and the co-opted who reach the top of the Mexican political ladder generally reap financial rewards that cushion their later years."[27]

Waterbury makes a similar point for Egypt and notes additionally that the corruption tolerated by state leaders on the part of those they have co-opted can be a further source of political control:

For leaders like Nasser and Sadat, whose popular mandates to rule were always of dubious validity and whose trust in their peers was always minimal, corruption could be used to wed potential rivals to the regime. The elite would be allowed to play its crass material games, records would be kept of their activities, and were they ever to become politically threatening, legal action could be taken against them.[28]

---

[25] Robert Springborg, *Family, Power, and Politics in Egypt: Sayed Bey Marei – His Clan, Clients and Cohorts* (Philadelphia: University of Pennsylvania Press, 1982), p. 98 ff.

[26] James Alban Bill, *The Politics of Iran: Groups, Classes and Modernization* (Columbus, OH: Charles E. Merrill, 1972), pp. 44–9.

[27] Hansen, *Politics of Mexican Development*, p. 126.

[28] Waterbury, *Egypt of Nasser and Sadat*, p. 349.

Besides appointments motivated by personal loyalty and co-optation, a third basis for recruitment into the public sector is "ethnic bargaining." This standard involves a special sort of co-optation, based on group identity. Cynthia H. Enloe notes that appointments based on ethnicity have been used to divide potentially threatening concentrations of power and to bind critical elements of the population to the state "by bonds stronger than simply fear or legalistic compliance."[29] Perhaps the most formal ethnic bargain was the one that gave shape to Lebanese politics after 1943. The allotment of posts from the presidency to seats in parliament to positions in the bureaucracy was accomplished on a confessional (religious) basis in this nonmeritocracy.

Kenneth Kaunda, president of Zambia, juggled tribal, ethnic, and sectional divisions masterfully. While carefully selecting his cabinet on an ethnic basis, he repeatedly chided state officials and politicians about their calls to the public based on ethnic identification. Raising such issues, he exhorted, could only foment conflict. But in a footnote to an article, Robert Molteno points out how Kaunda constructed a government:

1969 and 1970 saw the step-by-step reduction of Bemba predominance. In January 1969 the President's new Cabinet included two additional Easterners and one additional member from North-western. In August the central committee was dissolved. The interim replacement committee included major Eastern and North-western leaders again. In September Vice President Kapwepwe was stripped of his major portfolios, and three additions to the Cabinet were made from the relatively under-represented Central, Luapula, and North-western Provinces. And in November 1970 the President chose a new, Tonga speaking Vice-president, Mr. Mainza Chonza.[30]

Where loyalties to other groups run high and where the state's rules confront heavy opposition, state leaders take great care in making appointments. Their goal is not simply to construct a "representative" bureaucracy or military, in which the proportion of various ethnic groups in the state agency reflects the proportion in society at large. Nor is their aim to expand state authority by following formal organizational principles in extending the reach of the state. Rather, allocations of posts reflect the loyalty of particular groups, the threat of other groups, and the

---

[29] Cynthia H. Enloe, *Police, Military and Ethnicity: Foundations of State Power* (New Brunswick, NJ: Transaction Books, 1980), p. 7.
[30] Robert Molteno, "Cleavage and Conflict in Zambian Politics: A Study in Sectionalism," in William Tordoff (ed.), *Politics in Zambia* (Manchester, UK: Manchester University Press, 1974), 95n.

importance of specific state agencies. The most loyal elements, often the tribe or ethnic group of state leaders themselves, are assigned to the agencies that are potentially most threatening to state leaders and that would exercise the most control in society, such as the military. (A good rule of thumb for quickly ascertaining the group most loyal to state leaders is to note the background of the minister of the interior and the commander of the palace guard.) Likewise, those from the least trustworthy groups may be co-opted into more marginal, low-budget agencies.

Shaul Mishal recounts that King Abdullah of Jordan assigned Palestinian elites to senior positions in the ministries of agriculture, economics, education, development, and foreign affairs. These appointments came after Jordan's annexation of the West Bank and its Palestinian population in 1949. The Palestinians, as a group, were much less trustworthy in Abdullah's eyes than the Bedouin tribal groups of the East Bank. Even among the Palestinians, the king rewarded those who had facilitated annexation and "also tended to use the appointments policy to placate or co-opt his enemies."[31] The real centers of power, however, were not the agencies under Palestinian direction but the offices of the prime minister, the ministry of the interior, and the army (the Arab Legion). There, those from Bedouin tribal groups constituted the most important appointees. "While trying to give the army a national character by recruiting Palestinians," Mishal writes, "the central authorities encouraged the concentration of loyal [East Bank] elements in key positions and in elite combat units."[32]

Appointments based on personal loyalty, co-optation, and ethnic bargaining can further limit the ability of states to make the binding rules in a society. Waterbury made this point regarding the Egyptian *shilla*: "By its very nature the *shilla* vitiates ideological and programmatic politics and maximizes the wielding of group influence for personal gain."[33] Mishal echoes the point for Jordan: "The absence of uniform procedures in the public service in terms of broad discretion in hiring and firing also led to weakness in the staff units of the Jordanian administrative system."[34] The state's prerogatives come to be bounded in much the same ways that

---

[31] Shaul Mishal, "Conflictual Pressures and Cooperative Interests: Observations on West Bank – Amman Political Relations, 1949–1967," in Joel S. Migdal (ed.), *Palestinian Society and Politics* (Princeton, NJ: Princeton University Press, 1980), p. 176.

[32] Ibid., p. 177.

[33] Waterbury, *Egypt of Nasser and Sadat*, p. 346.

[34] Mishal, "Conflictual Pressures and Cooperative Interests," p. 178.

historical patrimonial regimes were limited. Now, however, these limitations come in the context of a remarkable growth in the size and complexity of state organizations.

Overlapping Bureaucratic Functions: Building a Praetorian Giant

In states with limited abilities to apply rules and mobilize support, proliferation of government agencies serves another purpose besides expanding the number of appointments and avenues for using patronage. Building bureaus with overlapping functions acts to limit the prerogatives of any single arm of the state. Although this may not be the most "rational" form of administration in terms of efficiency in implementing policies, it does fit into conception of the policies of survival quite well. The state has become a labyrinth of public agencies absorbing large populations of workers, but the coordination of agencies has been limited in some instances by the political survival goals of state leaders. Ability to implement social policy has suffered badly. Eugene Bardach has noted that to get something done – to devise and implement a policy of any sort – states must assemble machines.[35] Without coordination, states have merely the unassembled parts of that machine.

Nowhere is the balancing of powerful state institutions more obvious than in the armed forces. Syria is representative of countries in which state leaders have essentially built two or more autonomous sets of military forces. Besides its regular armed forces, the Syrian regime under the leadership of President Hafez al-Assad created Defense Units, with a total of between 12,000 and 25,000 troops, and Struggle Companies, with another 5,000 men. Both acted as the regime's praetorian guard.[36] The regular armed forces were not deployed in the capital city, Damascus; rather, the Defense Units ringed the capital. Loyalty to the president is critical in a praetorian guard, so it is not surprising that in Syria the Defense Units were under the leadership of Rifaat al-Assad, President Assad's brother. The Struggle Companies were led by Adnan al-Assad, a cousin of the president. In addition, a special segment of the Defense Units protected the Alawis, the ethnic group to which the al-Assad family belongs. Jamil

[35] Eugene Bardach, *The Implementation Game: What Happens After a Bill Becomes a Law* (Cambridge: MIT Press, 1977), p. 36.
[36] Hanna Batatu, "Some Observations on the Social Roots of Syria's Ruling, Military Group and the Causes for Its Dominance," *Middle East Journal* 35(Summer 1981): 331–44.

al-Assad, another brother, led this unit. Even in a state confronting as difficult a security situation as that faced by Syria – four major wars in the fifteen years from 1967 to 1982 – the goal in building military forces was not simply to create as coherent and coordinated a fighting machine as possible. Isolation of units from one another, appointments and deployments on the basis of loyalty, and the creation of overlapping functions – all became central elements in the politics of survival in Syria.

Fear of joint action against state leaders leads in some countries to uncoordinated branches of the military. In others, elements of the armed forces, particularly the praetorian guards, are deployed against other military units of the state. In still other cases, the praetorian guard's overlapping functions are tolerated because such an arrangement offers greater opportunities for direct control by state leaders. In India, paramilitary police forces in the Border Security Forces, the Central Reserve Police, and the Home Guards numbered about half a million in the mid-1970s. As Myron Weiner stated,

A critical feature of these agencies is that they are not part of the military, and hence not under the control of the Defense Ministry. Nor are they under the control of the state governments, as are the state police. The paramilitary forces are directly under the control of the Home Ministry. This means that the prime minister has control of a quasi-military force for dealing with domestic crises.[37]

Dirty Tricks

With the Carter Administration's emphasis on human rights and the awarding of the Nobel Prize to Amnesty International, probably no aspect of the politics of survival has received as much recent notoriety as "dirty tricks." These actions by top-ranking state personnel include imprisonment and deportation, strange disappearances, torture, and the use of death squads. Although such actions have been directed occasionally at rival leaders within the state itself, these means have often been used against those in non-state organizations who are considered threatening by state officials. Removal of key figures is used to preempt the emergence of competing centers of power and to weaken or destroy groups already powerful enough to threaten the prerogatives of top state rulers.

[37] Myron Weiner, "Motilal, Jawaharlal, Indira, and Sanjay in India's Political Transformation," in Richard J. Samuels (ed.), *Political Generations and Political Development* (Lexington, MA: Lexington Books, 1977), p. 74.

One example of undermining rival power centers came in the ministate of Brunei in Southeast Asia. In August 1962, the Brunei People's party won all the seats in the elected Legislative Council. A rebellion by the party broke out after the sultan, who considered the People's party threatening to his hold on power, refused to convene the council. With the aid of British troops, the rebellion was quashed, and approximately 2,500 members of the party and its military wing were imprisoned. Twenty years later, nine of the original prisoners were still being held without trial.[38]

Dirty tricks can be used even in relatively benign ways (compared with torture, lengthy imprisonments, and death squads). In Sierra Leone, state leaders moved against the Sierra Leone Labour Congress when it called two brief national strikes in 1981. President Siaka Stevens retaliated by invoking emergency powers (a favorite mechanism to open the door to various dirty tricks) and arresting 179 labor leaders and journalists. They were held without charge for periods of up to a month.[39]

Building Coalitions and a Domestic Balance of Power

Despite attempts by state rulers with narrow power bases and limited mobilizational capabilities to weaken state agencies and other social organizations, there are important boundaries to such actions. State agencies, after all, collect taxes and police the streets. Large businesses produce goods that earn badly needed revenues in the world economy. Other social organizations and state agencies may provide important communications systems, maintain social stability, or produce other important social goods. The demands by international and transnational actors alone for debt repayment and for critical products of the country make it impossible for state leaders to weaken all centers of power in the state or society heedlessly.

Production of wealth and revenue collection are two fundamental concerns of state leaders that demand the development of complex, large organizations. Leaders of states in whose societies wealth is produced through the relatively easy process of extraction (e.g., mining, oil drilling) and that

---

[38] *Amnesty International Report 1983* (London: Amnesty International Publications, 1983), p. 189.
[39] U.S. Department of State, *Country Reports on Human Rights Practices for 1981* (Washington, D.C., 1981), p. 221.

81

can raise a large portion of their revenues through rent (e.g., petroleum sales or royalties) may be less compelled to create powerful agencies or allow complex social organizations to gain footholds. In nonrentier states, however, state leaders must either bring the necessary agencies under central control in order to assure adequate production and revenue collection or find some way to cope with large, complex agencies and organizations that retain threatening bases of power.

The simplest method of coping with these threatening power bases is to follow the old dictum that the squeaky wheel gets grease. Those agencies and organizations whose services and products are of direct benefit to a regime that cannot bring them under central control may be bought off with state resources, prerogatives, discriminatory tax policies, and the like. Here again one is struck by the patrimonial characteristics of such regimes.[40] A method demanding somewhat more political skill is to enter into loose, often shifting coalitions with the strongest agencies and non-state organizations. In these coalitions, rulers seek to play off agencies against one another, as well as to create an alliance directed at other threatening groups, such as laborers or peasants.

Although industry still takes a decided back seat to agriculture and other raw-material producers in the great majority of third-world countries, the concentration of capital in industry poses problems for political rulers. The power stemming from both foreign and local capital contrasts with the lack of a firm base for the state's rulers, despite the great expansion of the state organization itself. Local capital in particular, frequently reinforced by nonmarket solidarity derived from kinship and friendship ties, is in a position to make effective claims for state resources and favors. State-owned enterprises are in a similarly strong position to make demands upon vulnerable state leadership. As Peter Evans has noted for Brazil, "The most important resources the local partners may possess is political power, and the local partners with the most direct political leverage are state-owned firms."[41]

State leaders may carve out for themselves some area for maneuver in balancing state-owned enterprises, local capital, multinational firms, and other important state agencies (including the military) against one another.

---

[40] See Gerald A. Heeger, *The Politics of Underdevelopment* (New York: St. Martin Press, 1974), especially p. 53.
[41] Peter B. Evans, *Dependent Development: The Alliance of Multinational, State, and Local Capital in Brazil* (Princeton, NJ: Princeton University Press, 1979), p. 212.

Effective use of budgets and other prerogatives, along with other measures of the politics of survival, such as shuffling heads of state-owned enterprises, may prolong the life of a regime. It would be mistaken, however, to confuse such maneuvering with effective state autonomy. Without sufficient coherence and coordination of state agencies to effect mass political mobilization, state leaders are reduced to ruses and stratagems – building and rebuilding coalitions and balances of power while using state resources to reinforce the existing distribution of power and wealth in the society. Such mechanisms may turn out to foster economic growth, but they do not create a more capable, autonomous state.

When successfully practiced, the politics of survival can lead to stability and longevity of regimes even when their leaders have not dislodged others who apply different rules and strategies of survival. In fact, as we have seen, keeping state leaders afloat may paradoxically involve the systematic weakening of the state's agencies. Since the era of decolonization, leaders may have experienced a learning curve with respect to how to survive in the churning waters of politics where states have relatively little social control over broad segments of their societies. Leaders and future leaders of states may have taken note of the risks involved in rushing headlong into ambitious programs of social change. They may have witnessed the dangers inherent in pursuing full social agendas through their agencies to carry out far-reaching policies of change. Their own tenure is brought into question by these Frankensteins – the bureaus they have created – as long as widespread political mobilization remains beyond their grasp. Learning can come from watching the precarious grip of those who preceded them; the brief three-year rule of Algeria's independence hero, Ahmed Ben Bella, may have been very instructive to the man who deposed him, Houari Boumedienne. Also, mechanisms to deal with the threats and risks of rival centers of power can be learned by state leaders. Use of death squads, for instance, spread from South America to Central America to countries as distant as Indonesia.

The conclusion is not that leaders of third-world states that have successfully displaced strongmen and achieved predominance are pure, while all those in states that have not achieved these goals rise to power as cynical connivers and manipulators of personnel. Engaging in the politics of survival does not mean that a leader has never had the slightest interest in using the state as a vehicle for progressive social change. Indeed, such a leader frequently ascends to power with a full social agenda. It is the structure of the dilemma that such a leader faces in power – the danger of fostering the growth of powerful state agencies in the absence of adequate political mobilization – that causes a critical shift in priorities. No agenda is worth anything if its sponsor has not lasted through the hazards of politics. Political survival becomes the prerequisite for achieving any significant long-term social change. It becomes the central issue occupying the attention of state leaders. Programs for social change may still be the basis for public rhetoric and even for policy statements and legislation, but at the apex of the state, the politics of survival denudes state agencies of their capabilities to see those programs through.

The Politics of Administration

The politics of survival at the top has an important effect on those at a much lower level of the state hierarchy, bureaucrats entrusted with implementing policy. Implementors are usually far from the sight of state leaders – often even from the sight of the top personnel in their agencies – and they pose little danger of creating power centers that could threaten the position of state leaders. Nonetheless, they are crucial in determining whose authority or rules – the state's or the strongmen's – will take hold in region after region. Scholarly literature on political and social change, unfortunately, has paid civil servants little heed. "Many observers," write Douglas S. Van Meter and Carl E. Van Horn in their discussion of state policy failures, wrongly point "to insufficient planning or the inadequacy of the program itself."[42] These bureaucrats are, in fact, crucial players in the political process. The indirect impact of the politics of survival upon these implementors, their centrality to the implementation of politics, and the calculus of social and political pressures they face place them in a critical role to influence whether states can actually accomplish what their leaders purport. Who are these implementors? Grindle describes them as

a corps of middle-level officials who have responsibility for implementing programs in a specific, relatively constricted area – a state, a district, a province, or an urban zone – and who are held responsible for program results by their superiors. This corps of individuals – the first and second ranks of the field administration – maintains frequent contact with national or regional superiors, but also has occasion to interact with the clients of government agencies and with opponents of the pro-

---

[42] Donald S. Van Meter and Carl E. Van Horn, "The Policy Implementation Process: A Conceptual Framework," *Administration and Society* 6 (February 1975): 449.

grams at local levels. These middle-level officials may have considerable discretion in pursuing their tasks and, even when it is not defined as part of their formal duties, they may have a decided impact on individual allocation decisions.[43]

In short, implementors are the state personnel who take the programs, legislation, and policy statements of leaders and are responsible for acting on those guidelines, making them the rules of daily behavior. They must make policy work at the ground level.

Who affects the behavior of implementors? The most obvious people they need to look to are their supervisors. After all, these are the officials at the regional and national levels who are supposed to produce results and who are in charge of overseeing those below them in the bureaucratic hierarchy. Next are the clients of the program – those intended to benefit from, or be regulated by, the rule changes involved in the policy. In addition, there are regional actors from other state agencies and from the government-sponsored party, who take a keen interest in the allocation of resources and the changing of rules within their jurisdictions. Finally, there are non-state local leaders, such as landlords or moneylenders, those referred to earlier as strongmen. These are the people who have fashioned for the local population the existing strategies of survival – the rules of behavior – and whose social control is jeopardized by the state rules and strategies conveyed by a new policy.

In negotiating through the maze of pressures and cross-pressures generated by all these groups, implementors are motivated by careerism, a set of standards with which they can weigh pressures and evaluate the possible impact on their professional standing. The degree to which the implementor weighs pressures from one quarter or another to ascertain their effect on his career varies from state to state, even region to region. Where the accountability and control within the agency are high, and especially where supervisors are willing to protect their officials from other groups' pressures, then agencies tend to have high morale and to follow the purposes laid down in law and policy statements. Morton H. Halperin has described highly motivated personnel as believing "that what they are doing makes a difference and promotes the national interest"[44] (at least as

---

[43] Merilee S. Grindle, "The Implementor: Political Constraints on Rural Development in Mexico," in Merilee S. Grindle (ed.), *Politics and Policy Implementation in the Third World* (Princeton, NJ: Princeton University Press, 1980), p. 197.

[44] Morton H. Halperin, *Bureaucratic Politics and Foreign Policy* (Washington, D.C.: Brookings Institutions, 1974), p. 54.

they understand it). Even here, however, careerism stands out. "Above all," Halperin continued, "the career official must believe that there is room for advancement in the organization and that the organization is seeking to protect his opportunities for advancement."[45] One could add the flip side of the coin: the career official must believe that the organization can protect him from ouster or demotion due to attacks by those opposing policy goals.

The politics of survival at the apex of the state can diminish accountability and control below tremendously. First, appointment of agency leaders on the basis of their loyalty to the ruler or their ethnic affiliation cuts into the efficient operations of a bureau and its ability to supervise efficiently. Such appointments also undermine the unity of purpose of the agency's personnel and the motivation that comes from the belief that toeing the line furthers the national interest.

Second and probably more important, the frequent shuttling in and out of new agency heads can have a devastating impact on policy implementation. New agency chiefs come in with their own policy agendas. By the very nature of policy and its assault upon existing rules, it cuts into the interests of strongmen who receive disproportionate benefits from their own existing rules. It is the implementor who must do battle with these strongmen, all the while risking an assault by them on the policy itself and on the career of the implementor. If the agency chief is to be shuttled out of the agency in a matter of months – and along with him his agenda of programs – the implementor becomes very reluctant to confront the intense pressures local leaders can exert in order to push forward a policy that will disappear with its originator. With the new chiefs, no doubt, will come new burning priorities and innovative policies.

In Mexico, where the whole implementation process is subject to the shadow of the *sexenio*, policy implementation takes on a special rhythm. The first two years of a presidential administration are taken up with the tremendous task of shuffling people among agencies. Agency chiefs must familiarize themselves with new surroundings and set priorities. By the last third of the *sexenio*, implementors become extremely cautious, fearing too public an identification with any policy that might be out of favor in the next administration. Top-level personnel are already distracted by the politicking for new positions. Only in the middle two years of the period is there a major push toward reform, hardly enough to ensure the staying

[45] Ibid.

power needed. Implicit through all this is, as Grindle notes, "the need to promote one's own career or that of one's superior."[46]

The bureaucrat has too much at stake, especially his own career, to become closely identified with any one policy. Anthony Downs has commented on the inevitable "leakage of authority" as a policy moves through an agency.[47] Where accountability and control are crippled and where the "big shuffle" is under way, that leakage can turn into a massive hemorrhage. Careerism in these cases leads to resistance by implementors to the policies handed down from above. Resistance most often takes the form of what Bardach calls "tokenism," which "involves an attempt to appear to be contributing a program element publicly while privately conceding only a small ('token') contribution."[48]

Bureaucrats in the Third World have been singled out by scholars and foreign aid officials alike for their slothfulness, their lack of will, and their lack of commitment to reform. Very little attention has been paid by these scholars to the calculus of pressures these bureaucrats face that makes them so "lazy" or "uncommitted." Success for public policies does not lie around the corner in a "new breed" of implementor. It certainly will not be found in an exclusive focus on new management techniques.

The consuming obsession for careerist implementors is to prevent the upward flow of information to their supervisors and agency chiefs that would indicate the implementers are not "handling" the situation. As Bardach notes in the American context, "A great deal of energy goes into maneuvering to avoid responsibility, scrutiny, and blame."[49] This generalization is even stronger for those third-world cases where frequent shuffles at the top make officials in the upper reaches of the bureaus even less patient with implementors who cannot keep local situations local. The implementor must hunker down while somehow assessing who may pass undesirable information upward and what can be done to stop it.

It is usually not the intended beneficiaries of social programs who pose serious threats to the implementor. They often lack the contacts and means to publicize failures in implementation or reach and influence national political leaders with damaging information about the poor implementation of policy. Their voices are often muted, as well, because of their

---

[46] Grindle, *Bureaucrats, Politicians, and Peasants in Mexico*, p. 169; see also p. 160 ff.
[47] Anthony Downs, *Inside Bureaucracy* (Boston: Little Brown, 1967), p. 134.
[48] Bardach, *Implementation Game*, p. 98.
[49] Ibid., p. 37.

dependence on local strongmen who are staunchly opposed to state policy initiatives. They are dependent on those whose rules and strategies are threatened by the state's social policy. This policy, then, is not targeted at a free-floating clientele but at people susceptible to the sanctions of the local threatened leaders. Potential "beneficiaries" of a policy may at the same time face the resulting loss of benefits they reap from the status quo – the failure to secure a tenancy, the denial of credit, or the loss of a job. Their current working strategies of survival make it dangerous to demand rightful benefits from state policies and to finger the implementor as the villain in the implementation process.

The potentially damaging groups for the implementor are the regional officials from other state agencies or the government-sponsored party and the local strongmen themselves, whose rules are threatened by the new policy. What the implementor often confronts is a set of complex accommodations between these two groups. Local leaders, through the social control they exercise, perform critical functions for state and party personnel. They turn out the vote (where there are elections), they maintain stability, they provide access to constituencies. In turn, the state officials and party personnel return favors. When implementors threaten the existing power structures, it is these personnel who can convey to higher state or party officials the information that could damage the career prospects of the implementors. Implementors in Mexico, for example, found that any reformist strategy on their part "was often met at the local level by the resistance of state or local party chiefs whose personal interests would be harmed if the peasants were encouraged to escape from the bonds of the dependency and exploitation."[50] Where the politics of survival is working at the apex of the state, those in the middle levels of administration learn that the calculus of pressures changes for them, as well. The implementors must learn how to stem the upward flow of negative information by accommodating those who make the rules below.

Politics at the Local Level: Accommodation and the Capture of the State

For those interested in discerning how third-world societies are ruled and the influence of politics on social change, the local level often holds the richest and most instructive hints. It is here that implementors become

---

[50] Grindle, *Bureaucrats, Politicians, and Peasants in Mexico*, p. 180.

involved in triangular relationships with strongmen, on the one hand, and with other state and party officials, on the other. A web of unexpected state-society relations results – unexpected, at least, for those who have observed only the politics of the capital city. The impact of state policies may be quite different from that anticipated by a scholar looking only at the scope of public policies undertaken and the vast apparatus the state organization has available to effect those policies. It has all too often been assumed by observers that "once a policy has been 'made' by a government, the policy will be implemented and the desired results of the policy will be near those expected by the policymakers."[51]

Grindle summarized the web of local politics in Mexico as a "system of accommodation and payoff." In this system, "the governors, the caciques, and other political actors have far more to gain from the present system than they would if they championed the political rights of their followers."[52] A community study in Mexico reported similar conclusions: "It is possible to understand why the PRI [the dominant party] has guarded zealously the outcome of the gubernatorial and state deputy elections. Any inroads of the opposition into these offices would upset the economic and political system of the spoils."[53]

Myron Weiner painted a similar picture in discussing India's politics leading up to Indira Gandhi's declaration of an emergency in 1975. "The system," he wrote, "gave a great deal of power to individuals at the local level who were often able to impede the carrying out of national policies."[54] Frankel drew the same sorts of conclusions in analyzing India's policy on rural cooperatives. Despite the tremendous powers for the Department of Cooperation written into legislation, the policy was a striking failure. Frankel hinted at the entanglement of implementors with local strongmen:

The Department of Cooperation, functioning in local environments of entrenched hierarchies, and generally unsympathetic to the egalitarian goals of national policy, preferred to operate in ways more congenial to the interests of the existing power structure. . . . Contrary to the basic intention of the government's policy in using the cooperatives to mobilize local resources for investment, schemes for

---

[51] Thomas B. Smith, "The Policy Implementation Process," *Policy Sciences* 4 (June 1973): 198.

[52] Grindle, *Bureaucrats, Politicians, and Peasants in Mexico*, p. 179.

[53] Antonio Ugalde, *Power and Conflict in a Mexican Community: A Study of Political Integration* (Alberquerque: University of New Mexico Press, 1970), p. 122.

[54] Weiner, "Motilal, Jawaharlal, Indira, and Sanjay," p. 72.

cooperative credit were being transformed into public subsidies on the cost of private investment (and in come cases, consumption and moneylending activities) for the more affluent landowning classes."[55]

Accommodation at the local level means that no single group – not the implementors, not the local politicos, and not the strongmen – monopolizes power. Local politics reflects the bargaining strength of each of the actors. Implementors, as noted, must guard against any damaging flow of information and must avoid scrutiny from above. Nevertheless, since they allocate so many of the resources that come through the state pipeline, they are often in a strong bargaining position at the local level. In cases where accountability and control still have some meaning in their agencies, they use their bargaining power to protect their careers by narrowing the perimeters of what can be done with the resources they allocate. Where, on the other hand, effective supervision has all but disappeared, implementors can use their leverage for personal gain with little regard for the overall purpose of any given policy. In either case, bureaucrats at the regional and local level remain key actors in determining who gets what and what they can do with it. The state bureaucracy, then, cannot avoid but being a major factor in the local allocation of resources. The limitation on state power, of course, is that the allocation may deviate tremendously from the prescriptions set out in law and policy statements in the capital city.

District leaders, state governors, local party chiefs – the local and regional politicos – face constraints and opportunities similar to those of the implementors. The closer the scrutiny from above, the more they must narrow the perimeters of acceptable behavior. Where supervision is lax, they can use their budgetary discretion, their contacts with top-level state leaders, and the force at their disposal for personal gain. Like the implementors, however, they are vulnerable to damaging publicity and are dependent on those who exercise social control – the strongmen – for any sort of popular mobilization they need to carry out.

Perhaps the most interesting figures of all in the web of political bargaining are the strongmen. As time goes on, they become reliant on state resources – from contracts to handouts – in order to maintain the dependency of their segment of the population. While the social control they exercise enables these strongmen to make demands upon the state, the fragmentation of their petty baronies – of their rules and organization –

[55] Frankel, *India's Political Economy*, 196–7.

hurts them as well. Frequently, their inability to develop a significant organizational basis among themselves means that the actual volume of resources filtering through state agencies to them is relatively small. Because effective maintenance of strongmen's social control, which is obviously in their own interests, willy-nilly creates the stability enjoyed by a regime, state leaders have little incentive to invest a large proportion of state funds in areas of strongmen's control. Thus while the state resources that strongmen garner may seem bountiful in the context of poor rural areas or urban slums, these resources are a disproportionately small share of total state revenues. The larger sums are reserved for the bigger centers of power, such as the armed forces, private industry, and state-owned enterprises, which can threaten top state leaders directly.

In proffering their strategies of survival, the strongmen use a share of the state resources at their disposal to bind the population to them. The latitude they have in how they use the resources depends in great part on the bargaining power of the implementors. In short, the strongmen are wedded to state resources and personnel in order to maintain their local control. Yet their most basic purposes are antithetical to those of the state. State leaders view the state as a mechanism to create a single jurisdiction – a rule of law in which the rules are the same from border to border. This is a desideratum of the modern state. These strongmen, whether they are village chiefs, urban caciques, or rich peasants, work for precisely the opposite effect. They seek to maintain their own rules, their own criteria for who gets what, within much more limited bounds. While in some respects they would like to enhance the state, or at least the resources it can make available to them, they must also thwart the state from achieving its leaders' most fundamental purposes and from achieving a position from which to offer viable strategies of survival to the population directly.

Such contradictory impulses, and the delicacy of the equilibrium strongmen seek in simultaneously embracing and foiling the state, lead them to try to maximize control over as much of their environment as possible. Also, they find the parameters set by implementors in the accommodation process irksome. In practice, many strongmen have captured parts of states. They have succeeded in having themselves or their family members placed in official state positions to ensure the allocation of resources according to their rules, rather than the rules propounded in the rhetoric and policy statements generated in the capital city or those put forth by a strong implementor.

The state has become, then, the grand arena of accommodation. Such accommodation takes place on at least two levels. First, local and regional strongmen, politicians, and implementors accommodate one another in a web of political, economic, and social exchanges. Their bargaining determines the final allocation of state resources that have made their way to the region. Second, accommodation also exists on a much grander scale. The local stability that strongmen can guarantee – as long as they provide workable strategies of survival to the population – is critical to the overall stability of the regime. State leaders accept this stability, which they garner even without building a complex, institutionalized apparatus, in exchange for their implicit consent not to contest actively the strongmen's control in local areas or even their capture of the state's tentacles. The strongmen end up with an enhanced bargaining position or with posts in the state itself that influence important decisions about the allocation of resources and the application of policy rules.

Conclusion

Tokenism on the part of bureaucrats, frequent reshuffling of cabinets, and human rights abuses by state officials are not random or idiosyncratic happenings in the Third World. Nor are they simply explained as the products of depraved, mendacious, or inept regimes and leaders. Society's structure, I have argued in this essay, affects politics at the highest levels of the state and the actions of the implementors of state policy at much lower levels. If one wants to understand the capabilities and characters of state leaders – their ability to make the rules for their population and the degree to which the politics of survival predominate over other agenda items – one must start with social structure. Where social structure has not been marked by strongly entrenched strongmen or where such strongmen have been weakened, state leaders have greater opportunities to apply a single set of rules – the state's rules – and to build channels for widespread, sustained political support. In such instances, leaders are in a position to pursue broad social and political agendas. The struggle for survival need not become so consuming as to weaken the state's abilities to carry out any other public policies.

The emphasis in this essay has been on other circumstances – societies in which social control is vested in numerous local level social organizations. Here, rules of behavior have been dictated by critically placed strongmen – landlords, caciques, bosses, moneylenders, and others. Their ability to pose themselves between segments of the population and critical resources such as land, credit, and jobs, has enabled them to devise viable strategies of survival for their clients. This structure of society, with its fragmentation of social control, has denied the state the ability to mobilize these clients politically. The altered priorities of state leaders (survival over social change), the style of state politics ("big shuffles," "dirty tricks," etc.), the structure of the state organization (redundant agencies), the difficulties in implementing policy, the calculus of pressures on the implementor, the capture of the tentacles of the state – all these have derived from the fragmented structure of society.

The entanglement of implementors of policy with the leaders of local social organizations has put state resources at the disposal of these strongmen. The argument thus comes full circle. We start with the fragmented social control exercised by these local leaders and the impact of this social structure on the state. We now see the impact of the state – its resources, policies, and personnel – on the structure of society. And what we find in numerous third-world cases is the strengthening of the fragmented social control of the local leaders and their particular rules. Added to their land, credit, and jobs – the elements upon which they have based the strategies of survival that they offer their clients – are the bountiful resources of the state. The local leaders have become the brokers for the contracts, jobs, goods, services, force, and authority that filter through the bureaucratic tentacles of the state. In short, a society fragmented in social control affects the character of the state, which, in turn, reinforces the fragmentation of the society.

For the near future, at least, the prospects for building cohesive states, which can apply their rules and policies effectively, are not bright in societies with fragmented social control. The strong bargaining position and the capture of the tentacles of the state by urban and rural caciques or any other such strongmen make the outlook for widespread political mobilization by state leaders in these societies even more remote. The dilemma of state leaders has intensified in many countries. Without mobilization, state leaders' ability to pursue innovative programs or to coordinate state agencies that can exercise significant autonomy in the face of other power centers remains limited. Scholars who have focused on these limitations of states, particularly those who have studied what happens after a policy is adopted, have put forth the image of the weak state.

Even while limited by the fragmentation of social control, states have grown almost everywhere and have expanded their resources steadily. State agencies and resources have become a major presence in their societies, although at times they have had rather unexpected impacts. Images presented by researchers of strong corporate or bureaucratic authoritarian states reflect the impingement of state agencies on nearly every aspect of social life. Resources and prerogatives of the state affect the way society is organized, and they help maintain a particular sort of social and political stability. It would be misleading, however, to infer from the expansion of the state organization, from its coalitions with capital, and from the importance of its resources in rural areas and urban slums that the state is necessarily autonomous. Reshaping society, whether through an independent position in alliance with foreign and domestic capital or through reformist social policy, is way beyond the capabilities of many third-world states. Policies intended to bring about radical redistributions in wealth or political and social power in the end frequently have the opposite effect and actually strengthen the existing distributions. States in fragmented societies are more likely to remain arenas for accommodation than to become sources for major changes in peoples' social behavior.

PART III

A Process-Oriented Approach

CONSTITUTING STATES AND
SOCIETIES

4

An Anthropology of the State

STRUGGLES FOR DOMINATION

From the writing of Thomas Hobbes's *Leviathan* in the seventeenth century, more than a century before the full blooming of capitalism and industrialization, thinkers have grappled with the increasingly powerful state and its role in society. After the industrial revolution, classical social thinkers, such as Marx, Weber, and Durkheim, devoted themselves to issues surrounding what Karl Polanyi later called the Great Transformation.[1] Their interest, too, was drawn to the state and its relationship to the momentous social and political changes overtaking European societies.

Some writers, such as the Hegelians, put the state – and the idea of the state – at the center of the sweeping social and political changes overtaking Europe. Others, including Marx, rejected the primacy of the state and saw the source of historical change in other forces in society, notably the organization of production. But even Marx and others who saw the motor of change outside the formal political realm felt called upon to address the notion of the transformative state.

The underlying questions in this volume resonate with the themes of the classical debates in social theory about major societal transformations and the relationship of the state to them. When and how have states been able to establish comprehensive political authority? When have they succeeded in defining the prevailing moral order or in determining the parameters of daily social relations, whether in preserving existing patterns or forging new ones? When and how have states been able to establish the economic agenda for their societies – to appropriate resources and to shape patterns of investment, production, distribution, and consumption? And

---

[1] Karl Polanyi, *The Great Transformation: The Political and Economic Origins of Our Time* (Boston: Beacon Press, 1944).

when have other social forces, whether entire social classes or tiny cliques, thwarted or co-opted the state and had their own way in devising effective symbolic systems, molding daily social behavior, and shaping the patterns of economic life?

As in the classical debates of the last two centuries, the decades since World War II have seen the fashions of scholarship swing between society-centered and state-centered theories in explaining social transformation. In the last decade or so, theorists confronting the major social and political transformations of the last half milleniumin have leaned toward state-centered approaches. They have explicitly acknowledged the central institutional role of the state in determining patterns of domination in society.[2]

But, in both the periods of state-centered explanations and those of society-centered ones, while many empirical researchers wrote nuanced accounts of association and authority, many middle-range and grand theorists have unfortunately tended to treat states and societies in all-too-undifferentiated terms. In presenting states or civil societies as holistic, some scholars have given the misleading impression that at key junctures in their histories states or societies have pulled in single directions. State-centered theorists (when that sort of explanation has been fashionable) have taken this tendency so far so as to reify and anthropomorphize the state. By treating the state as an organic entity and giving it an ontological status, they have obscured the dynamics and patterns of the struggle for domination in societies.

In this chapter, I argue how we can go beyond establishing a balance in scholarship between state and society, nudging the needle away from the extreme state-centered side of the guage. The need is to break down the undifferentiated concepts of state and society in order to understand how

---

[2] By domination, I refer to the ability to gain obedience through the power of command. Weber used such a designation for domination in *Wirtschaft und Gesellschaft*. See Max Rheinstcin, ed., *Weber on Law in Economy and Society* (Cambridge, MA: Harvard University Press, 1954), pp. 322–37. The motivation to obedience can be coercion or voluntary compliance that comes when one sees the rulemaker as the legitimate authority. (Weber speaks of the sources of domination in slightly different terms, seeing domination as a virtue of one's interests, the monopoly position of the dominator, or by virtue of authority, the power to command and the duty to obey [p. 324].) Domination, as used here, is thus more inclusive a term than just coercion or just legitimate authority. Domination can be localized or it can be exercised broadly over society. The term hegemony, on the other hand, while also including elements of coercion and legitimate authority, includes only domination exercised broadly over society.

each pulls in multiple directions leading to unanticipated patterns of domination and transformation.

By presenting a means to disaggregate state and society, I do lose some of the elegance of nomothetic theories of power, such as statist approaches from the rational choice perspective. Such nomothetic theories see the process by which states or specific social groups come to dominate, even in widely different circumstances and time periods, as occurring through a single logic, such as the single-minded drive of the state to garner larger revenues.[3] As inviting as such logic is, an all-encompassing theory of this sort presupposes a more general theory of human social, psychological, and political systems that simply does not exist now, nor is it likely to in the foreseeable future.

This essay points to the need for a more historically specific treatment of power. The need beyond the approach outlined here is for what the anthropologist Manning Nash has called "closely viewed crucial instances" – case studies reflecting the rootedness of the scholar in the society – in order to make persuasive comparative generalizations.[4] But such a treatment of power and social control does leave room to indicate (I hope elegantly) how to discern the key building blocks of states and societies, and their interactions, even if the varying combinations do lead to different results in different circumstances.[5] In this chapter, I will suggest an anthropology of the state, a means of disaggregating it through a focus on the different pressures that officials on four different levels of the state encounter. Pressures occur within what I call society's multiple arenas of domination and opposition. These arenas also help us break down the other critical components of societies besides the state organization. For the other parts of society, I first will propose that we need to move away from theories that rob social forces besides the state of their volition and agency, as well as from theories positing an integrated framework for societies, such as a ruling class, that accounts for the dominant patterns of behavior and belief. Later, in looking at the junctures of state and society, I will suggest the need to differentiate between society as a whole and civil society in order to analyze society's interaction with the state.

---

[3] For a good recent example, see Margaret Levi, *Of Rule and Revenue* (Berkeley: University of California Press, 1988).

[4] Manning Nash, *The Cauldron of Ethnicity in the Modern World* (Chicago: University of Chicago Press, 1989), p. viii.

[5] Nash wrote, "Which building blocks ... are invoked to construct a category and what boundary forged to set the category off from others is historically specific." Ibid., 5.

My central argument is that struggles for domination in society are not simply over the question of who controls the top leadership positions of the state (as is so often the assumption in journalistic and academic writing). Nor are such battles always among large-scale social forces (entire states, social classes, civil society, and the like) operating on some grand level. Struggles for domination take place in multiple arenas in which the parts of the state are related not only to one another but each is a single social force in a field of interacting, at times conflicting, social forces. The individual parts of the state may respond as much (or more) to the social field in which they operate – the other social forces in the arena – as they do to the rest of the state organization. A state official implementing birth control policies in Orissa, India, for example, may have to take local landlords, religious leaders, and businesspeople into account as much as distant supervisors and parliaments, and his or her consideration of these figures may lead to a distinctly different disposition of program resources from what was conceived in Delhi. I argue that in order to glean the patterns of domination, one must focus on the cumulation of struggles and accommodations in society's multiple arenas. Such a focus is possible only by conceptually breaking down states and societies and the junctures between them. In some cases, the results of the numerous struggles may move a society toward integrated domination, in which the state or other social forces establish their power broadly. In other instances, the conflicts and complicities in the multiple arenas may lead to dispersed domination, where neither the state nor any other social force manages to achieve countrywide domination and where parts of the state may be pulled in very different directions.

Some arena struggles may be limited to a depressed urban slum or a far-off, neglected village; others may be countrywide and extend to the seat of state power itself. In the various settings are born the recursive relationship between state and society, the mutually transforming interactions between components of the state and other social forces. Conflicts flare up over specific thrusts and parries: attempts by the state to increase tax collection, efforts by local figures to gain control over particular state offices and resources, initiatives by state agencies to regulate certain behavior, attempts by local strongmen to extend the area of their own dominance, and more. Such struggles end up reshaping both the state and the other social forces.

Often, the initiatives of states or others in society have been provoked by some of the fundamental changes associated with the Great Transformation – the growth of cities, the increased use of inanimate sources of power, the decline of agriculture in terms of total domestic production, and so on. These changes have swept beyond Europe to every nook and cranny of the globe. Capitalism and the model of the strong European state have reverberated through every continent, precipitating massive dislocation and mixtures of appropriation of new ideas and methods, reactions against them, and adaptations of them to local circumstances. These processes have constituted an onslaught on existing distributions of critical resources – land, other sources of wealth, personal connections, representation of meaningful symbols, and so on – setting off new and renewed battles and accommodations throughout societies. At times these struggles have resulted in integrated domination as the state has played a leading role, but in other instances such centralization has proved elusive, ending in dispersed domination.

The continuing encroachment of the European-centered market into Anatolia in the early decades of the nineteenth century is a case in point of the latter sort of societal transformation. Reşat Kasaba has shown how Greek merchants, well placed in the western provinces, took advantage of the new opportunities in trade with Europe to increase their own wealth tremendously.[6] These merchants, located in the port cities of the Mediterranean, had long enjoyed relative autonomy in their commercial dealings, without close supervision by the state. And, in the mid-nineteenth century, when trade was booming, they faced few constraints, as well, from the European states with which they traded. Bureaucrats of the Ottoman Empire understood that the state would have to inject itself into this flourishing trade if it were going to survive. To some degree, they succeeded in devising a centralization of administration that would curb the growing power of the merchants. But the new circumstances that the linkage between the European market and the merchants had forged meant that the beleagured Ottoman state could no longer enjoy control over prices of grains and other raw materials, as it had in the past. It found itself accommodating to the new power of the merchants (e.g., appointing some to important government positions or giving them a forum for participating in the actual administration of their localities) and, in so doing, radically transformed itself in the course of the nineteenth century. Rather

---

[6] Reşat Kasaba, "A time and place for the nonstate: social change in the Ottoman Empire during the 'long nineteenth century,'" in Joel S. Migdal, Atual Kohli, and Vivienne Shue (eds.), *State Power and Social Forces* (New York: Cambridge University Press, 1994).

than moving headlong toward centralization and increased state domination, the Ottoman state ended up adopting a series of contradictory measures that promoted the Greek merchants and their goals as much as the state's aim for control over these scattered commercial processes.

Whether the impetus lies in the spread of world capitalism or in other factors, it is the struggles and accommodations that these new circumstances have precipitated that are key. I am interested in developing an approach that can shed light on the nature of domination in society, where one might fruitfully look in studying persistence and change in patterns of domination exercised by states and other social forces. I also will propose a number of core propositions, educated guesses, as to when and where we might expect to find certain patterns of domination prevailing.

Third-world settings have thrown the struggles for domination in societies into stark relief.[7] In the countries of Africa, Asia, and Latin America, established social relations and institutions have come under severe pressure during the last century and more as most areas outside Europe changed into what Eric R. Wolf called "dependent zones of support" in a single capitalist world.[8] New state structures, led by those who harbored ambitious aims for far-reaching governance of daily life, have only intensified that pressure, especially in the period since World War II.

In the fading embers of feudalism in England and France, the Wars of the Roses and the Fronde, among other struggles, illuminated the intense, ground-level disputes associated with the attempts to impose states upon those societies and the backlash of social forces against the aggrandizing states. Max Beloff put it well: "In the sixteenth and seventeenth centuries, the modern idea of political sovereignty, the notion that over every man and every foot of ground, there must exist some single supreme authority was still something to be argued and fought over rather than the underlying presumption of all political action."[9]

Third-world societies, with their blend of expanding state organizations, entrenched local power relations, and market-induced economic and

---

[7] The term Third World is not used with any special precision or analytical rigor here. A good case for the limitations in the term and its utility, nonetheless, is found in Christopher Clapham, *Third World Politics: An Introduction* (Madison: University of Wisconsin Press, 1985), chap. 1.

[8] Eric R. Wolf, *Europe and the People Without History* (Berkeley: University of California Press, 1982), p. 296.

[9] Max Beloff, *The Age of Absolutism, 1660–1815* (New York: Harper and Row, 1962), p. 20.

social flux, can offer similar insights for the twentieth century. Here, norms and rules, regulations and laws, symbols and values, have been objects of intense, if sometimes hidden, discord. State autonomy and class formation – so glibly, perhaps even teleologically, assumed and expected by recent state-centered theories – have not at all been assured outcomes. The need in social science is for an approach that pinpoints the struggles for domination that lie at the heart of twentieth-century social and political change. The approach here portraying the state in society not only will have relevance for the Third World but will depict useful ways for understanding state and society in Europe, including the former Communist states, and North America, as well.

My starting purview is those spaces in society – the arenas of domination and opposition – where all sorts of social forces, including the institutions of the state, engage one another. I suggest boring in on the clashes and coalitions between state organizations and other social organizations (and their unexpected results) as these various social forces attempt to impose their own stamp on ordinary life, everyday social relations, and the ways people understand the world around them. The guide here highlights the relations between states and other social forces by simultaneously scanning and breaking down three phenomena, a task akin to watching the three rings of a circus. They are the society; the state itself; and the actual junctures, the engagements and disengagements, of state and society. In the remainder of this essay, I will look at each of these rings in turn.

Society

Because society is so complex and amorphous, so difficult to grasp, one common method for using the concept in social theory has been to impute to some general integrated framework the ability to establish patterns for all (or most) of society's disparate parts. Social scientists drawing on Marxism have portrayed the ruling class or the hegemony generated by a combination of the ruling class and the state as dominating across society. Where society is seen as pulling in different directions, the struggles are understood to be between this class and other broadly constructed social classes. Like the Marxists, liberal social scientists have often accepted axiomatically that the existence of society presupposes the exercising of some sort of hegemony, or society-wide domination. For them, the integrated framework is the consensus of norms, partially expressed within the authoritative structure of a somewhat constrained state, about how individual and group competition proceeds over the question of who gets what.[10] Social struggle comes through a set of plural interests competing for influence over public policies, all under the umbrella of well-established rules of the game. Recent state-centric theories have also accepted the notion of society-wide domination or hegemony, only they have been more prone than either the Marxists or liberals to focus explicitly on the frameworks and authority created by the society's state organization.[11]

The approach to society offered here questions the presumption of a unifying framework (whether a ruling class, a consensus of norms about competition, or the state) to explain patterns of domination and distribution in all cases. I ask an empirically prior question: Have the outcomes of struggles in multiple arenas aggregated to create, in fact, broad classes with cohesive projects that can shape a society or a widely agreed upon normative framework or a state organization capable of containing competition? And, if one indeed finds such classes or frameworks or states, must one assume that they will hold together indefinitely?

In the case of the Marxists, unified social classes and wide-ranging social struggles for dominance – class struggles – have often been easier to find in imaginative theorizing than in real societies. Class, noted E. P. Thompson, has become a broad heuristic device when, in fact, it is the particular result of historical conditions only in certain places and only at certain times: "Class, as it eventuated within nineteenth-century industrial capitalist societies, and as it then left its imprint upon the heuristic category of class, has in fact no claim to universality."[12] Referring to the

---

[10] Vincent notes that the consensus that is assumed by liberal theorists is a collective good. But, he complains, "the pluralists seem at times to conjure this collective good out of thin air." Not all groups may accept the basic framework; he explains, "Groups can be as oppressive, mean-minded and destructive of liberty as any state." Andrew Vincent, *Theories of the State* (Oxford: Basil Blackwell, 1987), p. 216.

[11] See Peter B. Evans, Dietrich Reuschmeyer, and Theda Skocpol, eds., *Bringing the State Back In* (New York: Cambridge University Press, 1985). Vincent notes of the liberal pluralists that "they were trying to theorize an idea of the state incorporating maximal diversity of group life and some kind of central authority." He noted that some have argued "that the State was smuggled in through the backdoor." Vincent, *Theories of the State*, p. 210.

[12] E. P. Thompson, "Eighteenth-Century English Society: Class Struggle without Class?" *Social History* 3 (May 1978): 150. Stedman Jones ends up taking a different position from Thompson but is even more adamant about the tenuous relationship between heuristic devices and what was found in history. "One should not proceed upon the assumption that 'class' as an elementary counter of official social description, 'class' as an effect of theo-

agrarian-capitalist mix in nineteenth-century England, Thompson wrote, "It arose, like *every* real historical situation, from a particular equilibrium of forces; it was only one of the seemingly infinite number of social mutations (in which each, nevertheless, maintains a generic affinity to others arising from a comparable conjunction) which actual history provides in such profusion."[13] In other countries of Europe and in other parts of the world, cohesive classes, which can lead society or around which the primary struggles in society revolve, may or may not exist at all or, when they do, may or may not succeed in achieving some sort of broad class project.

The Egyptian business class of the 1930s, as Robert Vitalis demonstrates, could in limited instances engage in broad forms of collective action. But in some of the critical issues revolving around state-fostered markets, the business class, despite all its privileges, did not develop unified class domination. Instead, rival coalitions of businessmen aligned with different elements of the state, each coalition seeking to secure access to the state's investment resources. The result was not only deep conflicts among the business class itself but also the undermining of the state and its policies, as well. Isma'il Sidqi, the strong-armed leader who took over the government in 1930, needed the businessmen as much as they needed him. In the end, however, neither could achieve their goals: Sidqi was forced to resign by 1933 and businessmen continued to pursue their conflicting interests in dispersed arenas, with no semblance of a unified influence on society. The idea of a highly integrated social class working toward some large class project that can reshape society may be an elegant metaphorical device, Vitalis points out, but these metaphors "can obscure as much as they reveal about the nature of the institutions, strategies and power of capitalists."[14]

Similarly for liberal theorists, battles over the distribution of authority have not always produced hegemony for specific rules of competition. The

retical discourse about distribution or production relations, 'class' as the summary of a cluster of culturally signifying practices or 'class' as a species of political or ideological self-definition, all share a single reference point in an anterior social reality." Gareth Stedman Jones, *Languages of Class: Studies in English working class history, 1832–1982* (New York: Cambridge University Press, 1983), pp. 7–8.

[13] E. P. Thompson, *The Poverty of Theory and Other Essays* (New York: Monthly Review Press, 1978), p. 255 (author's emphasis).

[14] Robert Vitalis, "Business conflict, collaboration, and privilege in interwar Europe," in Migdal, Kohli, and Shue (eds.), *State Power and Social Forces*, p. 198.

struggles in societies have often been over who establishes the procedures, rather than competition over the course of public policy within an overarching legitimate framework for all of society. The establishment of legitimate authority over a large territory in which plural competition can occur has, like unified class rule, been exceptional in twentieth-century history and the result of distinctive historical conditions.[15] Even in as established a democracy as India, Atul Kohli argues, integrating frameworks of authority are difficult to find today.[16] In fact, the opportunities provided by democracy for mobilization have opened the way for new groups, especially the lower and lower-middle strata, to expand their participation in politics substantially. The result has been an increasingly fragmented politics, with few institutional or normative frameworks that could contain increasingly vitriolic competition.

State-centered theories encounter similar difficulties when they assume the state organization is powerful and cohesive enough to drive society. That assumption, too, is open to empirical verification. In addition, it has frequently led to the tendency to strip the other components of society of their volition or agency, portraying them as malleable putty in the hands of the most powerful element of society, the state.[17] Such a perspective leaves us at a loss to explain such instances as Catherine Boone's Senegalese case.[18] Rather than finding an increasingly capable state in the postcolonial years, Boone observed that political practices seemed to undermine the administrative capacities and resource bases of the

[15] In Gramsci's language, these historical contingencies are "conjunctural." Antonio Gramsci, *Selections from the Prison Notebooks*, ed. Quitin Hoarc and Geoffrey N. Smith (New York: International Publishers, 1971). There has been a tendency among liberal theorists to deny the existence of a real society in cases where an integrative framework, with clear rules of the game, does not exist. Shils, for example, has spoken of such cases as proto-societies. But that simply accepts the reality of the bounded nature of society and the linking of associative behavior and common memories while denying the status of society where conflict still exists over the framework for action. See Edward Shils, *The Constitution of Society* (Chicago, University of Chicago Press, 1972).

[16] Atul Kohli, "Centralization and powerlessness: India's democracy in a comparative perspective," in Migdal, Kohli, and Shue (eds.), *State Power and Social Forces*.

[17] "The inhabitants of countries also possess social attributes like language, a cultural heritage, and a common history.... Unlike the country's political structure, the common attributes of *society* do not possess any representative agency that speaks for the whole." Reinhard Bendix, John Bendix, and Norman Furniss, "Reflections on Modern Western States and Civil Societies," *Research in Political Sociology* 3 (1987): 2 (authors' emphasis).

[18] Catherine Boone, "State and ruling classes in postcolonial Africa: the enduring contradictions of power," in Migdal, Kohli, and Shue (eds.), *State Power and Social Forces*.

Senegalese state. The state itself came to be based on a system of patronage in which chiefs and other local-level authorities exercised a tremendous degree of discretion in local arenas. These local patterns of domination came to be rooted in the state organization, crippling it and making it unable to deal with the pressing problem of eroding national production that left the state with a drastically declining tax base. Authoritative and autonomous forces in society shaped the state as much or more than they were shaped by it.

Social forces in society represent powerful mechanisms for associative behavior. These forces encompass informal organizations (such as Senegal's patron-client networks, or friendship groups and "old-boy" networks in other societies) as well as formal organizations (such as businesses and churches). They can also be social movements, including those held together by common, strongly motivating sets of ideas (even where obvious organizational ties are absent).[19] Such movements may range from those dedicated to squatters' rights to ones focusing on questions of ecology. Capabilities of social forces to exercise power starts internally. The efficiency of their hierarchies, their ability to use to advantage resources at hand, their adroitness in exploiting or generating symbols to which people develop strong attachments, all affect their ability to influence or control behavior and beliefs.

But there is another dimension, as well. Social forces do not operate in a vacuum. Their leaders attempt to mobilize followers and exercise power in environments in which other social forces are doing the same. And there is rarely a neat division of the population or of issues that keep social forces out of one another's way. In my approach, the focus is on these environments – these arenas of domination and opposition – where various social forces engage one another over material and symbolic issues, vying for supremacy through struggles and accommodations, clashes and

---

[19] The existence of a social organization, formal or informal, necessarily implies domination. Note Weber: "A circle of people who are accustomed to obedience to the orders of leaders and who also have a personal interest in the continuance of the domination by virtue of their own participation in, and the benefits derived for them from, the domination, have divided among themselves the exercise of those functions which will serve the continuation of the domination and are holding themselves continuously ready for their exercise. This entire structure will be called organization." Max Rheinstein, ed., *Max Weber on Law in Economy and Society* (Cambridge, MA: Harvard University Press, 1954), p. 335. I use the broader term, social forces, to signify such relations of domination in organizations but also to signify where there is obedience in movements where no clear organization is present.

coalitions.[20] These are not simply policy arenas in which various groups attempt to shape public policy. In addition to contestation over governmental policy, struggles and accommodations take place over the basic moral order and the very structure within which the rights and wrongs of everyday social behavior should be determined: Who has the right to interpret the scriptures? Who is to be respected over others? What system of property rights will prevail? How will water and land be distributed within the context of the prevailing system of property rights?[21]

Various social forces endeavor to impose themselves in an arena, to dictate to others their goals and their answers to these and related questions. Their aims may vary and may be asymmetrical. Some people use social forces for extracting as much surplus or revenue as possible; others look for deference and respect or doing God's will or simply power to rule other people's behavior as an end in itself. Whatever the motivation and aims, attempts at domination are invariably met with opposition from others also seeking to dominate or from those trying to avoid domination. Rarely can any social force achieve its goals without finding allies, creating coalitions, and accepting accommodations. Landlord and priest, entrepreneur and sheikh, have forged such social coalitions with power enough to dictate wideranging patterns of belief and practice. Frances Hagopian demonstrates how in Brazil, the authoritarian military regime found it had to reinstate accommodations with local traditional oligarchic elites after it had instituted a political system of domination that it believed had rid Brazilian politics of these old forces: "The military was no more successful at cleansing the political system of patronage politics than it was at purging the state of the traditional political elite."[22] The old patrons' ability to manipulate resources in order to achieve

---

[20] An arena is not necessarily spatially limited but rather is a conceptual locus where significant struggles and accommodations occur among social forces.

[21] Arenas of domination and opposition thus differ in some fundamental respects from Lowi's arenas of power. Such arenas of power, he writes, include "events, issues, and leadership [which should] be studied within defined areas of governmental activity. These areas are, in effect, the functions of government defined more broadly than a single agency, more narrowly than government with a single political process." Theodore J. Lowi, *At the Pleasure of the Mayor: Patronage and Power in New York City, 1898–1958* (New York: The Free Press, 1964), p. 139. In contrast, arenas of domination and opposition are not functions of government (although they may include government actors) nor are they limited to governmental activity.

[22] Frances Hagopian, "Traditional politics against state transformation in Brazil," in Migdal, Kohli, and Shue (eds.), *State Power and Social Forces*, p. 44.

domination in local arenas forced the state's leaders to seek an implicit coalition with them.

Coalitions and accommodations may not only enhance a social force's ability to attain its goals, it may also transform those very goals. As a social force's constituency changes, it may incorporate a new material basis as well as new ideas and values into its constitution. To state this point in slightly different terms, in addition to a social force's capabilities, its social and ideological basis (whom it serves and with what goals or agenda) also may change radically as a result of its interactions in an arena. It makes little sense, then, to try and understand outcomes by deriving actions from a fixed set of goals, as too much social science does today. Those ends themselves may very well be in flux. In China, both the Nationalist regime in the 1930s and the Communist one from the late 1940s on were themselves transformed as they recruited different segments of the Shanghai working class as pivotal constituencies. Elizabeth J. Perry notes how deeply affected the Kuomintang was as it used organized crime to help it incorporate semiskilled workers from North China and how the Communist state absorbed the goals of the labor elite as it attracted the more skilled artisans from the South.[23]

Power or social control can expand along three dimensions in order to extend a social force's domination. First, within an arena, a social force can dominate in an increasing number of issue areas, from dictating what crops to grow to providing credit to defining the nature of salvation. Second, arenas themselves can grow to incorporate a larger share of the population and a larger territory. The alignment of forces over which language people should use, for example, may begin in a particular city and spread to incorporate large portions of a country and its population. And, third, a social force can use the resources it garners in any one arena to dominate in other arenas composed of different sets of social forces. Chiefs in some countries of postcolonial Africa, for instance, used their command in tribal territories to catapult themselves into national questions such as issues of family planning.

Social forces attempt to appropriate the resources and symbols at hand to further their goals, and they often have wildly different abilities to do that. The mix of key elements in an arena – its physical geography,

---

[23] Elizabeth J. Perry, "Labor divided: sources of state formation in modern China," in Migdal, Kohli, and Shue (eds.), *State Power and Social Forces.*

material resources, human resources, forms of social organization, and trove of beliefs – are the raw materials with which the patterns of relationships among social groupings are determined. Patterns of domination come as social forces, with their already unequal abilities and access to resources, seek to utilize and manipulate these key elements of the arena's environment. The introduction of new factors into an arena – such as additional capital, compelling ideas, or innovative forms of social organization – or the depletion of old elements also benefits and harms social forces in very different ways. These shifting factors set off new and renewed struggles in arenas. Sometimes those struggles proceed slowly and quietly; at other times, they can be fraught with violence and recurring upheaval.

The struggles and accommodations of social forces in any local or regional arena of domination and opposition have not been hermetically sealed affairs. Resources have been reallocated from one arena to another in order to influence the outcome of struggles. Social forces have enhanced their position by sporting resources garnered from outside, by reassigning trusted personnel, or by riding on the backs of pervasive and powerful symbols. Factors such as the overall structure of production in society, existing institutional arrangements, and the saliency of certain symbols all influence who is in a position to reallocate resources and symbols from arena to arena.

Creating the conditions for domination in society and maintaining dominance – the reproduction of power within society – are the products of the many ongoing struggles and accommodations in multiple arenas. Our approach to society analyzes whether particular social forces can create an integrated domination. That is, can they prevail within given arenas to produce resources and support – a material base and a normative framework – that can be used to dominate locally and then be carried into other domains to create society-wide domination? Or do the struggles in the arenas result in a pattern of dispersed domination by limiting the creation of authoritative, legitimate forces that can dominate broadly across society?

The State

Any number of scholars have offered formal definitions of the state, most of which draw heavily on the notions of Max Weber.[24] These definitions

---

[24] Max Weber, *Economy and Society* (New York: Bedmister Press, 1968), vol. 1, p. 64; and Rheinstein, ed., *Max Weber on Law in Economy and Society*, p. 342.

have not differed tremendously from one another. They have tended to emphasize its institutional character (the state as an organization or set of organizations), its functions (especially regarding the making of rules), and its recourse to coercion ("monopoly of the legitimate use of physical force"[25]). At the core of these definitions lies the question of domination or authority in the state's claimed territory and the degree to which the state's institutions can expect voluntary compliance with their rules (legitimacy) or need to resort to coercion.

One work, for example, considers "the state to be a set of organizations invested with the authority to make binding decisions for people and organizations juridically located in a particular territory and to implement these decisions using, if necessary, force."[26] Another looks at the state as a power organization that engages in "centralized, institutionalized, territorialized regulation of many aspects of social relations."[27] By the "power" of the modern state, authors usually mean what Michael Mann has called infrastructural power, "the capacity of the state actually to penetrate civil society, and to implement logistically political decisions throughout the realm."[28]

Scholars understand the state to be the culmination of a process transcending the old localized organizations in societies, which had previously made the rules. It is "a more impersonal and public system of rule over territorially circumscribed societies, exercised through a complex set of institutional arrangements and offices, which is distinguished from the largely localised and particularistic forms of power which preceded it."[29] Since the sixteenth century, the theories maintain, the emergence of this new sort of public power with its large standing armies, formidable bureaucracies, and codified law has made the old forms of rule antiquated. The

---

[25] Max Weber, "Politics as a Vocation" in H. H. Gerth and C. Wright Mills (trans. and eds.), *From Max Weber: Essays in Sociology* (New York: Oxford University Press, 1946), p. 78.

[26] Dietrich Reuschemeyer and Peter B. Evans, "The State and Economic Transformation: Toward an Analysis of the Conditions Underlying Effective Intervention" in Evans, et al., *Bringing the State Back In*, pp. 46–7.

[27] Michael Mann, *The Sources of Social Power*, vol. 1, "A History of Power from the Beginning to A.D. 1760" (New York: Cambridge University Press, 1986), p. 26.

[28] Michael Mann, "The Autonomous Power of the State: Its Origins, Mechanisms and Results," in John A. Hall (ed.), *States in History* (Oxford: Basil Blackwell, 1986), p. 113. Also see John A. Hall and G. John Ikenberry, *The State* (Minneapolis: University of Minnesota Press, 1989), pp. 1–14.

[29] Roger King, *The State in Modern Society: New Directions in Political Sociology* (Chatham, NJ: Chatham House, 1986), p. 30.

state has forged close-knit nations out of societies that had been but loose associations of local groups. It is simply assumed that there is no longer any dispute that the state is the framework for the authoritative making of rules: "In the modern world only one form of political unit is recognized and permitted. This is the form we call the 'nation-state.'"[30]

Although there is much to recommend these definitions, they also pose certain problems. For one, they tend to feature one dimension of the state, its bureaucratic character. The accent on this side of the state highlights its capabilities, its proficiency in achieving a fixed set of goals and in implementing formal policies. A whole other aspect to the state exists that many of these definitions do not capture well, the formulation and transformation of its goals. As the state organization comes into contact with various other social forces, it clashes with and accommodates to different moral orders. These engagements, which occur at numerous junctures, change the social bases and the aims of the state. The state is not a fixed ideological entity. Rather, it embodies an ongoing dynamic, a changing set of aims, as it engages other social forces. This sort of engagement can come through direct contact with formal representatives, often legislators, or, more commonly, through political parties closely allied with the state.

Resistance offered by other social forces to the designs of the state, as well as the incorporation of groups into the organization of the state, change its social and ideological underpinnings. The formulation of state policy is as much a product of this dynamic as it is a simple outcome of the goals of top state leaders or a straightforward legislative process. The results of the engagement with (and disengagement from) other social forces may modify the state agenda substantially; indeed, they may alter the very nature of the state.[31] Even as self-consciously an ideological state as that in postrevolutionary China – a state, as Vivienne Shue puts it, that set out to do nothing less than reinvent society – found itself transformed by its engagement with other social forces.[32] Mao's China, to be sure,

---

[30] Anthony D. Smith, "State-Making and Nation-Building," in Hall (ed.), *States in History* (New York: B. Blackwell, 1986), p. 228.

[31] Alfred Stepan's use of the term "political society," which he adapted from Gramsci, opens the way to consideration of the changing basis of the state's symbolic system and its behavior. Political contestation, Stepan argues, is within the framework of "political society" and is about "control over public power and the state apparatus." Alfred Stepan, *Rethinking Military Politics: Brazil and the Southern Cone* (Princeton, NJ: Princeton University Press, 1988), p. 4.

[32] Vivienne Shue, "State power and social organization in China," in Migdal, Kohli, and Shue (eds.), *State Power and Social Forces*.

112

framed state policies in the language of class struggle, defending social-ism, and raising revolutionary consciousness. But the state's goals and actions were colored by the social networks that, in Shue's terms, insinu-ated themselves into all aspects of economic, social, and political relations, affecting the character of the state at both local and national levels.

Problems with existing conceptions of the state go beyond their disin-terest in the changing foundation upon which state goals are built; they exist even on the issue of capabilities, which is the heart and soul of these definitions. Authors have a troubling tendency to take too seriously actual states' abilities to make their decisions for people binding. The penchant to exaggerate states' capabilities has stemmed from the near ubiquity of states in the struggles in society's multiple arenas, as well as from the pre-sumptions of state officials themselves.

In the twentieth century, there have been very few places on earth, whether in the most remote corners of a country or in the heart of a capital city, where the state organization has not been one of the key social forces engaged in arenas of domination and opposition. Sometimes its initiatives have triggered intensified social battles; in other instances, it has simply reacted to the forays of other social forces. At times, it has championed economic development and redistribution. At other times, its agenda has been to preserve existing patterns of economic domination. But in only rare instances (a number of which have been in Africa[33]) during the last several generations has the state been largely absent during conflicts over who exercises power in any segment of society.

Along with technological change and industrialization, the idea of the transformative state has been, to be sure, one of the defining characteris-tics of the modern world. Indeed, what has distinguished the modern state from most other large-scale political organizations in history, such as empires, has been its imposition into the "mattering maps" of its subjects. Mattering maps place people in relation to others in their ordinary lives.

But it is not only who matters in people's lives; for, as Rebecca Goldstein noted in her novel *The Mind-Body Problem*, "Who matters is a function of what matters." She continued, "The map in fact is a projec-tion of its inhabitants' perceptions. A person's location on it is determined by what matters to him, matters overwhelmingly, the kind of mattering

---

[33] Victor Azarya and Naomi Chazan, "Disengagement from the State in Africa: Reflections on the Experience of Ghana and Guinea," *Comparative Studies in Society and History* 29 (January 1987).

that produces his perceptions of people, of himself and others: of who are the nobodies and who the somebodies, who the deprived and who the gifted, who the better-never-to-have-been-born and who the heroes."[34] Transformative states set about trying to influence how people place themselves in mattering maps, the content and ordering of the symbols and codes determining what matters most to them. Concern with mattering maps implied that transformative states simply could not let any struggle over domination within its official boundaries go uncontested;[35] state leaders want the state to matter most, enough to die for.

With only isolated exceptions, leading state officials have adopted the goal of heading a transformative state. They have seen the state as an organization that can (or, at least, should) dominate in every corner of society. It should mold how people see themselves on mattering maps – define the moral order and set the parameters of daily behavior, or, minimally, authorize and defend other social organizations to undertake some of those tasks. Even in recent cases of privatization and liberalization of markets, for example, a frequent underlying assumption is that the state should not entirely abdicate economic questions to markets. It should seek to carve out limits to the autonomy of those markets and, at the same time, to authorize, regulate, and defend their operation.[36]

In short, throughout the territory they claim to govern, most state leaders have maintained that the state should have primacy. In some instances, that has meant efforts to stake out autonomy for powerful social forces with which state leaders are allied, such as markets, churches, or families. But, commonly, the quest is for the state to exercise that autonomy directly – to impose centrally its own systems of meaning and boundaries for acceptable behavior on people's mattering maps, in everything from sexual unions to labor-management relations.

State leaders attempt to create an aura of invincibility about the state. The more the state seems all-powerful, the more likely are subjects to accept it in their ordinary lives and, in the process, reduce the burden of

---

[34] Rebecca Goldstein, *The Mind-Body Problem: A Novel* (New York: Random House, 1983), p. 22.

[35] By transformative, we do not necessarily mean progressive. Even a state seeking to preserve an existing order must be transformative if it is to have its way in the context of international changes sweeping over its boundaries.

[36] "The state is as central to the economics of development as to its politics." Peter Evans and John D. Stephens, "Studying Development since the Sixties: The Emergence of a New Comparative Political Economy," *Theory and Society* 17 (1988): 723.

enforcing all its dictates. In fact, those social scientists who wittingly or unwittingly exaggerate the capabilities of the state become part of the state's project to present itself as invincible. State sovereignty, the actual imposition of supreme state authority over its claimed territory, has simply too often been taken for granted.[37]

Despite their best efforts and to their never-ending frustration, state leaders have not had a clear way of imposing their domination – their systems of meaning, their rules for social behavior, and their economic plans – upon society. All states have not succeeded in reshaping mattering maps, as their leaders have envisaged. Like any other organizations, states have real limits to their power: what they can do and what they cannot do, when they can collect taxes and when not, which rules they can make binding and which not. Ambitious goals for states – aims of actually penetrating throughout the society, regulating the nitty-gritty of social relations, extracting revenues, appropriating resources that determine the nature of economic life, and controlling the most dearly held symbols – have seldom been approximated, certainly not in the case of most new or renewed state organizations in the Third World.

One of the reasons that much recent literature on states has consistently overestimated their power and autonomy is the homogeneous way that works present them. The focus all too frequently has been on the very top leadership, the elites in the upper echelon of the state organization, as if they alone are the state, as if their wills are re-created faithfully throughout the labyrinth of state branches and bureaus. Note in Mann's statement how the interest in states and their top leadership go hand in hand: "My principal interest lies in those centralized institutions generally called 'states,' and in the powers of the personnel who staff them, at the higher levels generally termed the 'state elite.'"[38]

---

[37] King writes that "the constitutional state is characterised by a unitary sovereignty which becomes manifest in a single currency, a unified legal system, and an expanding state educational system employing a single 'national' language. A literary tradition in this 'national' language erodes cultural particularism, and a system of national military conscription, which replaced the local recruitment of ancient military units, also tends to overcome 'peripheral' or localist identities." Roger King, *The State in Modern Society: New Directions in Political Sociology* (Chatham, NJ: Chatham House, 1986), p. 51.

[38] Mann, "Autonomous Power of the State," p. 112. The identification of the state with its top elites or leadership, with its own distinct interests and perspectives that are independent of specific other socioeconomic interests, does not mean that authors do not recognize what King (*The State in Modern Society*, p. 53) calls the "plurality of foci" of the state. But these foci are seen largely as differentiated institutional expressions of a fairly singular will.

But the state is far from the re-creation of the aims and wills of the state elite. Like the ideological basis of the state and its formulation of policy, the implementation of policies also reflects the dynamic of the state's engagement with other social forces. To understand what happens to the state and its policies as state leaders attempt to shape and regulate society, one must look at the multiple levels of the state. Social scientists must develop a new anthropology of the state. They need a method that looks carefully at its different parts (just as anthropology often focuses on small portions of society); they require an approach that analyzes how its various components, often impelled by conflicting interests and pulling in different directions, relate to one another. Such an anthropology would reject the assumptions implicit in many studies concerning the smooth interlocking of relations within and between organs of the state organization or of a state that simply reflects the will of its top leaders.

Personnel in the various components of the state organization operate in markedly different structural environments. Various units of the state have diverse histories of their own, leading to differing sorts of esprit de corps, senses of purposefulness, and insularity by their staffers or politicians. The first step in understanding the different directions in which components of the state pull is to identify the forces that constitute the various environments in which state officials operate. Only then can a researcher begin to inquire about the weights of these forces for different parts of the state in particular circumstances.

Five types of social forces and groups stand out as immediate factors that impinge directly on state officials: (1) supervisors (at least for state personnel not elected nor at the very top of the hierarchy); (2) underlings, state employees that one directly or indirectly supervises; (3) peers, staff in other agencies or politicians at roughly similar levels; (4) domestic social forces, those not part of the state organization but from within the society (including clients of state policies, blocs of voters, contractors, and others); and, perhaps, (5) foreign social forces from the international system.

The state, then, does not generate a single, homogeneous response to an issue or problem, or even necessarily a varied but coordinated set of responses. Rather, its outcomes – the formulation and implementation of its policies – are a series of different actions based on the particular calculus of pressures that each engaged component of the state faces in its particular environment of action. Those environments of action, the loci of conflicts and coalitions, of pressure and support, involving parts of the state and other social forces, are what we have termed the arenas of domination and opposition.

There is certainly little guarantee that the sum of actions of the various components of the state, each facing distinctive struggles within the particular arenas in which it engages other social forces, will represent some harmonious mesh. The outcome can just as likely be a sum of ill-fitting responses that stem from the different components of the state as they respond to their various arenas of domination and opposition. As Shue writes of Maoist China, "Frontline officials, despite their status as agents of the state, frequently found it advisable, or easier, or more natural, or just in accord with their own convictions, to throw in their lot with local people and departmental associates, against the impersonal requirements of the state bureaucracy above them."[39]

At different points in the state organization, the calculus of pressures on state officials differs markedly depending on the particular array of forces in their arenas and their relative weight. To speak of the overall autonomy of states, as much recent theory does, might not at all be the best initial point of inquiry for those studying the state. Researchers must first ask about the autonomy of the various components of the state, for which the calculus of pressures differs so markedly. What sorts of social forces predominate at different points in the state hierarchy and why? Does the calculus of pressures allow for discretionary room for state officials and representatives? Do supervisors influence decisions of state personnel, or are they outweighed by other social forces?

It would be impossible, of course, for any researcher to study the calculus of pressure for each state official. In order to simplify the task, we can identify four levels of the state organization, from bottom to top, as the trenches, the dispersed field offices, the agency's central offices, and the commanding heights. On the first three levels, those involved in an anthropology of the state must carefully choose instances that can illuminate processes and trends beyond the specific cases – the sort of choice that social or cultural anthropologists have had to make in selecting the "right" village for study.

The Trenches. At the bottom of the state hierarchy, in the political trenches, stand the officials who must do daily battle with other social

---

[39] Vivienne Shue, "State power and social organization in China," in Migdal, Kohli, and Shue (eds.), *State Power and Social Forces*, p. 71.

forces. They must execute state directives in the face of possibly strong societal resistance. They are the tax collectors, police officers, teachers, foot soldiers, and other bureaucrats mandated to apply state rules and regulations directly. Their contacts are with the intended clients, targets, and beneficiaries of official state policies. For state personnel in the trenches, pressures come not only from supervisors but also directly from intended clients and from lower-level figures in other large social organizations or heads of small-scale organizations who stand to lose or gain by the state's policy success. They must confront the local businessman or farmer or the local representative of a national labor union. These other social forces that weigh in on the actions of lower-level state officials may reinforce the pressure of supervisors or may act in an entirely different direction.

The Dispersed Field Offices. A notch higher in the state hierarchy are the regional and local bodies that rework and organize state policies and directives for local consumption, or even formulate and implement wholly local policies. The dispersed field offices include the bureaus, legislative bodies, courts, and military and police units that work exclusively within a circumscribed territory within the larger territory claimed by the state as a whole. These organs make key decisions about local appropriation of resources funnelled through national ministries or garnered locally. Where will state schools be built? How will local postal distribution be organized? Which villages will benefit from the digging of new tube-wells or irrigation canals? Who will be hired in the trenches?

Among those at the level of the field command stand provincial governors and legislators, district police chiefs, members of local school boards, and the officials who Merilee S. Grindle has called the implementors. These implementors are middle-level bureaucrats, the first and second ranks of the field administration, who have the task of organizing the execution of policy in a given region.[40] Like their underlings in the trenches, implementors face supervisors in their agencies but ones who usually are physically far removed. Implementors are responsible for the course of a policy once it (and the resources attached to it) are passed from the capital city to the regions where it will be installed. Their supervisors are cen-

---

[40] Merilee S. Grindle, "The Implementor: Political Constraints on Rural Development in Mexico," in Grindle (ed.), *Politics and Policy Implementation in the Third World* (Princeton, NJ: Princeton University Press, 1980), p. 197.

trally located, looking after implementors throughout the country, as well as their own interests in the midst of capital city intrigues. In fact, if one could pinpoint a place in the state hierarchy where supervision is likely to be most lax, it might be here, due both to distance of supervisors from the scene and their lack of familiarity with local conditions.

At times, to be sure, the calculus of pressures for state personnel in the provinces can include strong elements from the capital city, but it encompasses, too, powerful doses of pressure that are only dimly understood by top party chiefs, national ministers, and central government parliamentarians. National politicians usually face directly only those social forces incorporated into the state's central political process. The different goals and social origins of these additional, local forces may inject local politicians and implementors into a process that substantially changes state goals at this level from those dictated in the capital city.

If state personnel in the dispersed field offices can avoid the magnifying glass of supervisors and national politicians, they still may face intense pressures from peers in other local or regional components of the state organization. The positions of implementors and regional politicians often afford them wide discretion; the profound differences from region to region necessitate their broad adaptation of central state directives to local circumstances. What is more, in third-world states a large proportion of local capital may come through the hands of those in the state's dispersed field offices. That combination of discretion and resources makes them the objects of intense competitive pressures. It is of little surprise that those with substantial resources to distribute face scrutiny from other local politicians and implementors. All have an enormous stake in the discretionary and nondiscretionary resources in the hands of any other implementors or politicians, as well as in how those implementors apply directives received from above or how they craft purely local laws and rules.

Politicians and implementors in the dispersed field offices are in a nexus that also draws the considerable weight of domestic and foreign social forces – those that are well represented and powerful – from the provincial or local level. Regional representatives of countrywide organizations, such as political parties, religious groups, and large multinational and domestic corporations, take a keen interest in the activities of those in the dispersed field offices. So, too, do the overall leaders of powerful regional organizations, including heads of regional businesses, large agriculturalists, and others.

The Agency's Central Offices.   In the capital city are the nerve centers that constitute the various agencies' central offices, the places where national policies are formulated and enacted and where resources for implementation are centrally marshalled. These offices are staffed by national parliamentarians and heads of ministries or agencies of the state. It is these various central offices that have overall responsibility for the state's attempts to penetrate and regulate society in particular realms of social life. They may be responsible for housing, welfare, education, revenue collection, conscription, security, or other broadly defined, but still limited, social areas. Or they may be the center for generating overall legislation but with no executive responsibilities.

Those heading central offices are most often directly accountable to the top leadership of the state, the president's office or some equivalent, but pressures come from a number of other directions, as well. For one, they are engaged in an endless process of bargaining with each other. In their negotiations, both in their competition and cooperation, they face the tough pressure that their peers can bring to bear on them. They compete, after all, for tight resources, and they build countless temporary coalitions with other agency chiefs and legislators to forward their own agency's perspective on an issue.

The solidarity of the agency's central staffers helps shape its distinctive perspective. Part of that solidarity grows out of self-serving aims – the protection of individual careers and common turf – which are reinforced by the patronage (largely appointments) controlled by heads of the agency's central offices. In fact, where other pressures – from the state's top leadership, other central agency commands, and non-state social forces – are muted, the large bureaus of the state may end up as little more than extended patronage networks. But pressures from within an agency itself can have other effects besides fostering an arena of patronage. The special perspective of the agency puts pressure on its chiefs. They face a rocky road within their own bureaus or parliamentary groups if they fail to represent those perspectives faithfully.

Finally, those in the central offices often must deal with the most powerful forces in society from outside the state organization. Of these, large capital enterprises, both domestic and foreign, are the most prominent. Others may include political parties, large labor unions, major media organs, and religious organizations. Although powerful social forces may operate on different levels of the state, well-organized social classes, communal groups, and other key social organizations weigh in heavily on state policy making at the level of an agency's central offices. Each brings its own special advantages – large membership, performance of essential social functions, capital, perhaps even a shared background with key state officials – to bear on the process. Many have wide-ranging interests and, as a result, inject themselves not only into the workings of a single central agency but also into the bargaining among a number of state agencies.

In some cases, a particular social force, or combination of them, has been so powerful that central agencies have been little more than an expression of that social force's perspectives and interests. More commonly in recent decades in the Third World, there has been a discernible differentiation between the interests of a single social force and those of the sum of the agency's central offices. Powerful social forces, to be sure, still have exerted exceedingly strong pressures but now as parts (often the dominating parts in a given arena) of the various calculus of pressures weighing on top-level bureaucrats and politicians.

The effects of underlings in the dispersed field offices and, below them, in the trenches can often be muted in the agency's central offices. Again, the lack of proximity of the dispersed field offices creates an important chasm between them and the agency's central offices. Similarly, depending on the sort of policy the agency is projecting, it may face only limited pressure from the actual targets or clients of those policies. Where the implementation of policy is to a diffused, nonorganized clientele (e.g., requirements for vaccinations as opposed to, say, regulation of foreign-owned corporations), the pressure applied directly to the central agency command may be relatively light. The most intense pressures may come from within the capital city itself, both from inside the state organization and from other centrally organized social forces.

The Commanding Heights.   At the pinnacle of the state are the commanding heights, housing the top executive leadership. Social scientists have devoted much ink to studies of state leaders. Presidents, prime ministers, even juntas, certainly do not work in obscurity as do those in the trenches, the dispersed field offices, and even, at times, an agency's central offices. But the attention of social scientists has not frequently focused on the structural strains between them and other layers of the state.[41]

---

[41] For a good exception seen John Waterbury, *The Egypt of Nasser and Sadat: The Political Economy of Two Regimes* (Princeton, NJ: Princeton University Press, 1983).

Research has not often systematically analyzed the limitations placed on the commanding heights (a phrase used here with some hint of irony) by the larger organization of the state itself. Little work can be found beyond writers making the usual nod to bureaucracies and noting how recalcitrant top state leaders find them.

The leadership of the state obviously shares essential purposes with those in the levels below them. After all, leaders' own triumphs build on the success of the other components of the state. The revenues they garner depend on the lowliest tax-collectors; their security rests on the performance of foot soldiers and police on the beat; their legislative agenda lies in the hands of parliamentarians and bureaucrats. The ultimate power bases of top leaders and their ability to transform agendas into actual accomplishments demand functioning legislatures, efficient courts, and complex, well-organized bureaus to formulate and adjudicate rules, as well as to push these rules to, and mobilize resources from, the society. Their success depends, too, on numerous components of the state, including schools and others, working together to present a coherent system of meaning.

These same state leaders, however, also find themselves beset with differences with respect to other officials of the state. Those in other components of the state maintain perspectives that reflect their circumscribed arenas and the distinctive calculus of pressures associated with those arenas. State personnel in the trenches and in the dispersed field offices are limited territorially; their regional bases often lead them to respond to the arenas in the locales that they serve. Even where states regularly shift them from region to region, they still must deal day-in and day-out with the pressures of their immediate environment, which reflect the distinctiveness of their locale. While supervision may not change substantially when they are shifted, the rest of the calculus of pressures – from underlings, peers at their own level in the state, and domestic and foreign social forces – does shift and induces corresponding adjustments by them. For these state officials, the goal of state domination is caught in a web of local rivalries and coalitions with local social forces.

Those in the central offices of agencies do not develop such territorial perspectives, of course, but they, too face distinctive arenas and specific sorts of issues with which they deal. Their perspective stems from the purview of their ministries and bureaus. Parliamentarians, similarly, are limited by the regional constituencies they serve or their particular specialty in the legislature. For leaders at the state's commanding heights, then, the array of perspectives in the rest of the state organization generates unexpected conflict. When top state leaders speak with the minister of defense, they hear that security and defense are by far the most important elements of the national interest. The minister of education asks what could be more important for the nation's future than a literate, skilled citizenry and workforce. Individual health adds up to national health, insists the minister of health.

State leaders at the commanding heights face pressures from all of them but may not identify fully with any of them. In other words, an agency's central offices, whose actions are themselves the outcome of different arrays of pressures in varying arenas, become simply one pressure point in the top state leadership's own arena of domination and opposition. The forces pressuring the commanding heights come from a broader field than those affecting the lower levels of the state. The power of important international actors and the heads of the weightiest indigenous social forces, who can gain direct access to the top, only exacerbate the conundrum for the top leaders of the state.

To conclude this section, there has been an unfortunate tendency in social science to treat the state as an organic, undifferentiated actor. States have been assigned an ontological status that has lifted them apart from the rest of society. As a result, the dynamics of the struggles for domination in societies, in which components of the state have played differing roles in various arenas, have been obfuscated. Those struggles have not only been about who seizes the commanding political heights in society. They have involved alliances, coalitions, and conflicts among social forces in multiple arenas, including components of the state.

Varying perspectives (parochial or universal, regional or countrywide) within state components have derived from the distinct arenas of domination and opposition in which they operate. The sum of all the components' responses to the distinctive mix of pressures in the particular arenas in which they engage other social forces together have created the outcomes of the state. What is certainly true is that the cacophony of sounds stemming from the wildly different arenas in which components of the state interact often have resulted in state actions that bear little resemblance to the original schemes or policies conceived by leaders of the state or by particular state agencies.

But state policy outcomes have been more than just the sum of independent actions by different components of the state. One portion of the relevant arena for each part of the state has been yet other segments of the state organization. In fact, one can inquire into the roots of particular forms of the state, such as democratic checks and balances or tyranny, by tracing the evolving relationship of the state's components to one another in light of the other environmental forces that these various parts of the state encountered.

To trace such an evolution, we need develop an anthropology of the state – the study of the parts of the state in their environments and of the relationship of the parts to one another. The four levels of the state that I have delineated are simply one tentative scheme that allows us to see components of the state in various arenas of domination and opposition. Alternative ways of breaking down the state may illuminate other dimensions of state behavior as its components engage a variety of social forces.

Whatever the particular anthropology of the state that is selected, we can conclude the following: The more diverse and heterogeneous the arrays of pressures that various components of the state encounter on their different levels, especially when there are strong pressures applied by multifarious domestic and foreign social forces, the less likely is it that the state ends up with complementary behavior by its many parts and the less likely is it that it can successfully convey a coherent system of meaning. Despite its international stature and its sheer bulk in society, the state may be a crippled giant in the quest for domination. That bulk will surely mean that it cannot be ignored in conflicts over domination in society, but more meaningful initiatives and more coherent actions may come from other social forces.

The Junctures of States and Societies

The results of the engagement and disengagement of states and other social forces are tangible, even momentous, but outcomes rarely reflect the aims and wills embedded in either. The clash of social forces, including the state, is mediated through the struggles and accommodations in society's numerous arenas. For the social scientist, the challenge is to understand how those diffused struggles alter society's disposition of resources, the nature of its stratification, the character of its gender relations,[42] and the content of its collective identities. In the end, those local

---

[42] Of all elements concerning identity and the state, probably the least remarked upon has been gender. One good exception is a recent book by Parpart and Staudt. They write, "For us, gender is at the heart of state origins, access to the state, and state resource

interactions cumulatively reshape the state or the other social organizations, or, most commonly, both; these interactions are the foundation of the recursive relationship between the state and other social forces.

The cumulative result of engagements and disengagements in multiple arenas has been that societies have assumed "all manner of shapes," as Anthony Smith put it.[43] Smith's observation seems, at first glance, rather unremarkable; of course societies have ended up with all manner of shapes. But Smith's comment, as he notes, flies in the face of much prevailing social theory. In contemporary social science writing, where states and societies have been portrayed with broad brush strokes, different states and societies have had an uncannily uniform look. So much contemporary scholarship blurs the rich diversity produced in various societies' multiple arenas. The meeting grounds of states and other social forces have been ones in which conflict and complicity, opposition and coalition, corruption and co-optation have resolved the shape of countrywide social and political changes. They have determined whether domination is integrated or dispersed, as well as the varying contours of integrated or dispersed domination.

Some arenas of domination and opposition have achieved periods of stable relations among their social forces in different times and places, but these may have been more the exception than the rule. A Nicaraguan earthquake, a Bengali tidal wave, the absorption of fundamentalist Islam in southern Lebanon, changing birth rates in Mexico, the penetration of the world economy throughout the Third World – all have created winners and losers and thus changed the balance of forces in various arenas. Through its distinctive ideology and organization, the modern state was at the core of destabilization of existing arenas in the nineteenth and twentieth centuries. The common core of ideology among the leaders of transformative states has been to create a hegemonic presence – a single authoritative rule – in multiple arenas, even in the far corners

allocation. States are shaped by gender struggle; they carry distinctive gender ideologies through time which guide resource-allocation decisions in ways that mold material realities. Through their ideological, legal, and material efforts, states foster the mobilization of certain groups and issues. This mobilization usually benefits men rather than women. While over the long haul, state action may submerge and obscure gender conflict, over the short term, the obviousness with which male privileges are fostered may actually aggravate that conflict." Jane L. Parpart and Kathleen A. Staudt, "Women and the State in Africa," in Parpart and Staudt (eds.), *Women and the State in Africa* (Boulder: Lynne Rienner, 1989), p. 6. Also, see chapters 2, 3, and 10.

[43] Smith, "State-Making and Nation-Building," pp. 229–30.

of society. The goal has been to penetrate society deeply enough to shape how individuals throughout the society place themselves on mattering maps. The organization of the state has been to effect such far-reaching domination. It has included vertically connected agencies, designed to reach to all pockets within the territory, and specialized components to promote the state's system of meaning and legitimacy (e.g., schools), to make universal rules (legislative bodies), to execute those rules (bureaucracies), to adjudicate (courts), and to coerce (armies and police). Major policy initiatives by the state have led to a massive inundation of new elements (from fresh ideas to personnel and hard cash) as well as to the depletion of others through taxation, conscription, relocation, mass murder, or other means. Even the most benign states have made extraordinary demands upon those they have claimed as their subjects: to sequester their children in state institutions for thirty hours per week, to dispose of their bodily wastes in only prescribed ways, to treat their sick exclusively with state-licensed healers, to prove a proprietary relationship to land solely through state-issued deeds, and so on. Whatever their specific programs, states have shaken up existing relationships of social forces in society's arenas, renewing active struggles for domination.

In the multiple meeting grounds of states and other social components, some social forces have tied their own fortunes to that of the state or accepted it as the appropriate organization to establish the proper practices for all of society. But, in other instances, some forces have sought to appropriate resources, positions, personnel, even whole bureaus of the state for their own purposes. Still others in society, such as peasants or slum-dwellers, who were already dominated by other social forces, have also, at times, actively or quietly resisted the attempts of officials to impose new state domination. These struggles and accommodations in the junctures between components of the state and other social forces have produced a range of outcomes. We can capture these in three ideal types of results. First is total transformation. Here, the state's penetration leads to the destruction or subjugation of local social forces and to the state's domination. In such cases, the components of the state successfully transform how the people of an arena place themselves on the mattering map. Forced migration, replacement of the locals by a settler population, widespread use of violence, and other draconian means may nullify or destroy local dominating social forces and the contours of mattering maps. Where there is no severe social dislocation, it is unlikely that total transformation will occur within a single generation.

Second is state incorporation of existing social forces. In this type, the state's injection of new social organization, resources, symbols, and force into an arena enables it to appropriate existing social forces and symbols in order to establish a new pattern of domination. But it also forces changes and accommodations on the part of the state's components as they adapt to the specific patterns and forces in the arena. These changes in local components of the state may then affect the state's overall coherence – its ability to reallocate resources, establish legitimacy, and achieve integrated domination.

Third is existing social forces' incorporation of the state. In this type, the presence of the state's components spurs adaptation by dominating social forces, but does not produce radical changes in the pattern of domination. Or, in some cases, the new state presence does generate new patterns of domination, but ones in which new non-state social forces rise to the top. In either case, the contours of the mattering maps that result among the population are not the ones envisioned by state leaders. The organization and symbols of the state's components are appropriated by the local dominating social forces. In this scenario, the transformation of the local components of the state is so extensive as to harm significantly the state's overall chances of achieving integrated domination in society. Michael Bratton, for example, points to how the establishment of marketing boards and cooperatives for peasants in African states has precipitated arrangements not at all intended, or even imagined, by political leaders. Peasants reacted to the state initiatives by setting up their own informal trading networks. Bratton dismisses the notion that the interpenetration of parts of the state apparatus with this second economy implies some sort of state domination: "When public officials accept bribes to turn a blind eye to an illegal activity, they are not extending the state's authority but reducing it. And when officials engage in private accumulation and trade – even if only through relatives, intermediaries, and employees – they are acknowledging that their behavior is not governed by legal commands. The participation of state officials in the second economy amounts to a deconstruction of formal architecture of the state in the face of a more compelling set of social imperatives."[44]

Finally, the state may fail altogether in its attempt at penetration. Disengagement or lack of engagement of the state in the local arena will result

---

[44] Michael Bratton, "Peasant-state relations in postcolonial Africa: patterns of engagement and disengagement," in Migdal, Kohli, and Shue (eds.), *State Power and Social Forces*.

in little transformative effect upon the society – and limited effects of the society upon the state. Failures to engage in arena struggles in even the most remote parts of the country can affect the state in the capital city by denying state components their resources and support from the larger society.

Only rarely have real cases approached the two extreme ideal-types, total transformation or disengagement. Most have offered some variant of the middle two types, where state components and other social forces have been involved in a recursive relationship, that is, mutually transforming struggles. In fact, not only may states and other social forces alter one another, they may also affect the very integrity of the other through encroachment. In the midst of such struggles and accommodations, the boundary between the state and other parts of society may continually shift, as powerful social forces in particular arenas appropriate parts of the state or as the components of the state co-opt influential social figures. While state leaders may seek to represent themselves as distinct from society and standing above it, the state is, in fact, yet another organization in society. And, as one organization among many, it is subject to the pushes and pulls in society's arenas that can change the line between it and other social forces.

In parts of colonial Africa, for example, the British attempted to extend the scope of the colonial state by incorporating tribal chiefs as paid officials. Many chiefs, for their part, gladly accepted the salary and any other perquisites that they could garner but often ignored the directives from their superiors in the state hierarchy. The demarcation between the state and other parts of society in such instances was difficult to locate and was in constant flux. Chiefs were state officials but sometimes – indeed, many times – simply used their state office and its resources to strengthen their previous roles as chiefs.

To talk of the relations between state and society as if both always have had firm boundaries, as much recent social theory does, is to miss some of the most important dynamics of transforming struggles.[45] Chiefs, like other state employees and officials, play multiple roles. State organizations

---

[45] I am indebted to Timothy Mitchell for illuminating the point about the shifting boundary between states and societies. See Timothy Mitchell, "The Effect of the State," working paper presented at the workshop on state creation and transformation of the Social Science Research Council's Committee on the Near and Middle East, Istanbul, September 1–3, 1989.

may succeed in having them suppress roles with different norms (as members, for example, of kinship or tribal groups) while performing their state duty. The desire to mold special state norms and suppress the norms of other roles is one reason that states attempt to create their own space for officials, such as separate state office buildings or new capital cities. In state-designated space, the assumption goes, officials would be less likely to succumb to the logic of the struggle being played out in specific arenas. But states may fail to "capture" chiefs or other state workers, resulting in the domination of the norms of other social forces.

In arena after arena, then, social forces have reorganized to deal with the new reality of ambitious states. Where those forces have created or found the spaces and methods to sustain, sometimes even augment, their own social and economic power outside the framework of the state's moral order and its rules, the society comes to be characterized by dispersed domination. Here, neither the state nor any other social force has established an overarching hegemony; domination by any one social force takes place within an arena or even across a limited number of arenas but does not encompass the society as a whole. Social life is then marked by struggles or standoffs among social forces over questions ranging from personal and collective identity and the saliency of symbols to property rights and the right to use force. People's mattering maps remain remarkably diverse in such a society.

Even in those twentieth-century cases closer to the ideal type of dispersed domination, the state has rarely been a negligible actor. The junctures of the state with other social forces have taken place in the multiple arenas of society, and in most cases the state's agencies have created a formidable presence, precipitating realignments of local forces. But the components of the state have not achieved total transformation or even successful state incorporation of local powerful social forces in all or most of these settings. This pattern contrasts with integrated domination, which is inclusive, or society-wide. In cases of integrated domination, the state, whether as an authoritative legal system or a coercive mechanism of the ruling class, is at the center of the process of creating and maintaining social control. Its various components are integrated and coordinated enough to play the central role at all levels in the existing hegemonic domination. That domination includes those areas of life regulated directly by the state, as well as the organizations and activities of society that are authorized by the state within given limits.

In analyzing the junctures of state and society, many theorists have simply assumed the existence of integrated domination. The concept of civil society has been widely used by a number of liberals, Marxists, and statists to capture the relation between state and other parts of society, reinforcing the presumption of integrated domination in society.[46] The notion of civil society, to be sure, has had different shades of meaning in various theoretical contexts – in the works, for example, of Hegel and Gramsci.[47] But despite their differences, for many theorists, civil society has been a convenient term with some surprising commonalities. Various writers have used the concept to acknowledge the existence of sundry interests in society while still being able to treat them as if, on some level, the entire society (even the state, in many writings) pulls together in a single direction.[48] Note how Stepan, in his book on military politics, speaks

---

[46] Hegel put forth the notion of civil society as one that emerges from the interdependence of individuals, their conflicts, and their needs for cooperation. Those needs give rise to the state; and it is the law, the principle of rightness, that links civil society to the state. *Hegel's Philosophy of Right* (Oxford: The Clarendon Press, 1942), pp. 122–3, 134–5. Marx reacted to Hegel's conception, arguing that the state is merely the mechanism to defend privileged propertied interests in civil society. He understood civil society in a material sense, the expression of particular property rights: "'Bureaucracy' is the 'state formalism' of civil society." David McLellan, ed., *Karl Marx: Early Texts* (Oxford: Basil Blackwell, 1979), p. 68. Gramsci noted that besides the educative agencies of the state helping maintain hegemony, there are, "in reality, a multitude of other so-called private initiatives and activities [that] tend to the same end – initiatives and activities which form the apparatus of the political and cultural hegemony of the ruling classes." This, for Gramsci, is civil society. Gramsci, *Selections from the Prison Notebooks*, p. 258.

[47] One difference among them has been the direction of causality: does the state create civil society or does civil society bring about the state? Whereas Hegel believed that society created the demand for the state, others, including Stepan, have argued that the state can create civil society. Otto Hintze alluded to this mutuality of the state and civil society and the role of the state in creating its own civil society, using the term "nationalities" instead of civil society: "The European peoples have only gradually developed their nationalities; they are not a simple product of nature but are themselves a product of the creation of states." Otto Hintze, "The Formation of States and Constitutional Development: A Study in History and Politics," in Felix Gilbert (ed.), *The Historical Essays of Otto Hintze* (New York: Oxford University Press, 1975), p. 161.

[48] Bendix et al. do note that "civil society comprises only a segment of the population." Those not in civil society tend to be marginal sorts – those abandoned by their parents, homeless people who do not participate in the market, illegal immigrants, etc., "Reflections on Modern Western States and Civil Societies," p. 23. John Keane sees even larger elements of European societies that have been excluded from civil society (most of those who are not white, heterosexual male citizens). *Democracy and Civil Society: On the Predicaments of European Socialism, the Prospects for Democracy, and the Problem of Controlling Social and Political Power* (New York: Verso, 1988), p. 14.

130

of civil society in an anthropomorphic way: "Civil society must consider how it can make a contribution to the democratic control of military and intelligence systems."[49]

Civil society assumes the existence of a normative consensus or hegemony of fundamental ideas among social forces, even among contending groups; this consensus represents a prevailing moral or social order. For many writers, civil society expresses the ties that bind all, or nearly all, of society together, whether those are property rights or mutually felt needs or any other factors. Until the last decade or so, most theories posited a hand-in-glove relationship between state and civil society.[50] This interpretation does not mean that there are never tensions between the state and civil society or questions about the boundary between the two. The concept of *pouvoirs intermédiaires*, intermediary institutions, has been used to signify a civil society in which organizations guard a degree of autonomy from the state. Such autonomy leaves open the possibility of some differences between the state and non-state associations.

But the critical point is that in most social science writing state and civil society are mutually reinforcing, even when differences prevail between them. It is the existence of widely held norms, property relations, or modes of social behavior in the myriad organizations across the totality of society – that is, the existence of civil society – which reinforces the dominance of the state and allows it to rule without constant recourse to coercion or without an outlay of resources that would cripple it. Conflicts may persist on particular issues, but implicit agreement prevails over the rules for interaction and competition. For the most part, it is the legal framework of the state that establishes the limits of autonomy for the associations and activities that make up civil society.

Only recently in Latin America, Eastern Europe, and even Western Europe has there developed a discourse that takes more seriously the possibility of civil society versus the state.[51] Even among those holding this

---

[49] Stepan, *Rethinking Military Politics*, p. 128.

[50] Bendix, et al., note that "the independence of private associations is a synonym for civil society" and that for civil society to exist, a "consensus" is required between state and society. "Reflections on Modern Western States and Civil Societies," pp. 14–15.

[51] In the 1980s, the term "civil society" came to be used by analysts of Eastern Europe. They were looking for a way to break the theoretical umbilical cord between state and civil society. For them, the term civil society implied a spunky society, which develops autonomy through organizations in opposition to the state. See, for example, Andrew Arato, "Empire vs. Civil Society: Poland 1981–2," *Telos* (1981–2): 19–48. For a critique, see

position, the strain between civil society and the state is seen in overarching terms between these two integrative entities. Civil society is still an aggregate of diverse interests, which on one level pull in a single direction. Together, they attempt to oppose the state's moral order and impose one of their own.

There are several problems with analyzing the junctures of state and society through such a view of civil society. For one, as I have discussed elsewhere, even within civil society, various social forces are not always aggregative and inclusive, leading to a hegemony of fundamental ideas.[52] We need to develop a much more careful understanding of the constitutive elements in civil society and not assume it is made up only of interest groups and private voluntary organizations, which tend to create a harmonious consensus in society. Also, an integrative view of civil society misses entirely cases of dispersed domination. Society and civil society are not synonomous; the heterogeneous struggles in society's multiple arenas of domination and opposition, in which social forces pull in different directions, also affect the state profoundly. The way the concept of civil society is most commonly used leaves no room for these dispersed struggles over society's moral order. As Naomi Chazan points out, "Civil society encompasses only one portion of what has become a complex and diverse associational scene. What distinguishes those groups incorporated in civil society from other associations is their partial nature: they are separate from but address the state."[53] Society as a whole may include other organized components (not just marginal individuals), which strive to make their own rules and institute their own moral orders, without addressing the state directly.

Many contemporary societies have included significant elements that have struggled against all or many of the claims of the state to be the organization in society with supreme authority. Some social forces have not lent their support to the state's universal pretensions or, for that matter, the pretensions even of a civil society pitted against the state. Their rela-

Zbigniew Rau, "Some Thoughts on Civil Society in Eastern Europe and the Lockean Contractarian Approach," *Political Studies* 35 (1987): 573–92. On Western Europe, see Keane, *Democracy and Civil Society* (see, for example, 31–2).

[52] Joel S. Migdal, "Civil Society in Israel," in Ellis Goldberg, Reşat Kasaba, and Joel S. Migdal (eds.), *Rules and Rights in the Middle East* (Seattle: University of Washington Press, 1993).

[53] Naomi Chazan, "Engaging the state: associational life in sub-Saharan Africa," in Migdal, Kohli, and Shue (eds.), *State Power and Social Forces*, p. 278.

tion to the state has been one of resistance (overt or covert) or one in which they have sought to transform or appropriate part of the state for their own purposes. Similarly, their orientation to the other forces that make up civil society has often ranged from disinterest to outright hostility.

The multiple arenas of society and the interactions among them have been the cauldrons within which the contingent, particular historical outcomes have been brewed for each society and its state. The ultimate form of the state (democracy or some other type of government), its goals, its capabilities, its scope, its domination by particular social forces or its autonomy, as well as the form, systems of meaning, capabilities, and autonomy of other social forces, all these have been determined through these critical struggles and accommodations in the multiple arenas of society and the relationships among arenas. States do not succeed in establishing their own domination by default. In fact, they may end up as much the transformed as the transformative states.

In brief, scholars need ask if and how the struggles in various arenas carry over to other arenas and, possibly, to domination in the society as a whole. Have resources and support generated in struggles and accommodations in one arena then been carried into other domains in society, possibly to create an integrated domination? Integrated domination, whether by states, social classes, civil society, or any other groupings, results from successful reallocation of resources and support garnered from activities in one arena into other arenas.[54] What Sidney Tarrow has called the "vast issues, roiling conflicts, and deep-seated social and economic cleavages" in societies cannot be understood divorced from the more limited arena conflicts. It is in the latter that people "organize their relations with the state, reconcile or fight out conflicts of interest, and attempt to adapt politically to wider social pressures."[55] The ability of any social force, including the state, to develop the cohesion and garner the material and symbolic resources to project a meaningful presence at the society-wide level depends upon its performance in more circumscribed arenas. In those

---

[54] In the United States, social theorists have been particularly reticent about admitting that the state is, in fact, exercising supreme authority. More often the emphasis has been on social organizations that regulate themselves, with little attention as to how the state creates the authoritative legal framework within which markets and other social organizations function. See Gary C. Hamilton and John R. Sutton, "The Problem of Control in the Weak State," *Theory and Society* 18 (January 1989): 15–16.

[55] Sidney Tarrow, "Introduction," in *Territorial Politics in Industrial Nations* (New York: Praeger, 1978), p. 1.

arenas, it must dominate successfully enough (close to total transformation or, at least, incorporation of existing social forces) so as to be able to generate resources for application in other arena struggles and, ultimately, the society as a whole. Whether any social force, from social classes to the state, will succeed to be the basis for integrated domination is far from a foregone conclusion.

5

Why Do So Many States Stay Intact?

On the face of it, it is puzzling that more states do not simply fall apart. Why do their components not fly off in a thousand different directions? It has happened to some in recent years: Lebanon, Yugoslavia, Somalia, Liberia, Zaire, even the vaunted Soviet Union. Why not to others? What can account for the staying power of so many state organizations, most with tens of thousands of workers toiling in hundreds of different agencies with countless sets of varying procedures, goals, interests, pressures, and incentives? All these are scattered across variegated territories with diverse populations. The potential for interagency turmoil, mad grabs for scarce resources, forces pulling in different directions, contestation of internalized global forces, and conflicting priorities seems endless – and all that in an organization harboring the feasibility for inflicting tremendous violence.

Surveying European expansion across five centuries, David Strang found remarkable ability of non-European polities – at least those that were recognized as sovereign – to survive.[1] He found only eleven that went from sovereign to dependent status between 1415 and 1987, and fifteen non-European polities that merged or underwent dissolution. What was striking about the last half of the twentieth century was how many states were created – unprecedented numbers in the annals of world history – and how few disappeared, dissolved, or imploded.

In fact, during the years of the Cold War, one is hard pressed to point to more than a handful of cases in which states vanish or fall apart – perhaps Pakistan and Nigeria for a spell, certainly Lebanon, and then some

---

[1] David Strang, "Anomaly and Commonplace in European Political Expansion: Realist and Institutional Accounts," *International Organization* 45 (Spring 1991): 143–62.

odd instances such as Egypt, Syria, and the United Arab Republic. At the same time, social scientists wrote volumes on how frail so many states have been. They used terms such as quasi-state or soft state or weak state to indicate the vulnerability of many political entities, both to outside forces and to organized domestic groups.[2] Does not state weakness also indicate a fragility that would lead many to shatter irrevocably?

The disintegration of vast empires after World War I and World War II coupled with the powerful idea of self-determination led to a proliferation of new states, many extremely weak in terms of internal coherence and their ability to effect public policy that could change people's behavior in intended ways. In the two decades following World War II alone, the number of states more than tripled. Indeed, the middle of the twentieth century became the heyday for states as practically the universal political form.

Now, at the dawn of the twenty-first century, we live in the age of the state as survivor. New political forms, led by the European Union and powerful nongovernmental organizations, loom on the horizon. Book after book has appeared describing how the state's sails have been trimmed.[3] Others have predicted its imminent demise with such chilling phrases as "the Lebanization of the world."[4] The state is increasingly portrayed as

---

[2] See for example: Robert H. Jackson, *Quasi-States: Sovereignty, International Relations, and the Third World* (New York: Cambridge University Press, 1990); Joel S. Migdal, "Studying the State," in Mark I. Lichbach and Alan S. Zuckerman (eds.), *Comparative Politics: Rationality, Culture, and Structure* (New York: Cambridge University Press, 1997).

[3] See for example: Joseph A. Camilleri and Jim Falk, *The End of Sovereignty? The Politics of a Shrinking and Fragmenting World* (Brookfield, VT: E. Elgar, 1992); Ivo D. Duchacek, Daniel Latouche, and Garth Stevenson, *Perforated Sovereignties and International Relations: Trans-Sovereign Contacts of Subnational Governments* (New York: Greenwood Press, 1988); John Dunn, *Contemporary Crisis of the Nation State?* (Cambridge, MA: Blackwell, 1995); Julie A. Erfani, *The Paradox of the Mexican State: Rereading Sovereignty from Independence to NAFTA* (Boulder, CO: Lynne Rienner, 1995); Gidon Gottlieb, *Nation Against State: A New Approach to Ethnic Conflicts and the Decline of Sovereignty* (New York: Council on Foreign Relations Press, 1993); Christine Ingebritsen, *The Nordic States and European Unity* (Ithaca: NY: Cornell University Press, 1998); Peter Katzenstein, *Tamed Power* (Ithaca, NY: Cornell University Press, 1997); Edmond J. Keller and Donald Rothchild, *Africa in the New International Order: Rethinking State Sovereignty and Regional Security* (Boulder: Lynne Rienner, 1996); Gene M. Lyons and Michael Mastanduno (eds.), *Beyond Westphalia?: State Sovereignty and International Intervention* (Baltimore, MD: Johns Hopkins University Press, 1995); Claus Offe, *Modernity and the State: East, West* (Cambridge, MA: MIT Press, 1996); Michael J. Shapiro and Hayward R. Alker, *Challenging Boundaries: Global Flows, Territorial Identities* (Minneapolis: University of Minnesota Press, 1996).

[4] Jean-Marie Guehenno, *The End of the Nation-State* (Minneapolis: University of Minnesota Press, 1995), p. 35.

the crippled Leviathan, whose life-support system might give way at any time. But reports of its near-death seem decidedly premature – state weakness has not meant state collapse.

In the next two sections, I review several reasons offered by scholars to explain why states stay intact. The first involves the role of forces from the international environment, which become internalized domestically in both states and societies. The second draws from organization theory and its emphasis on the trade between states and their subjects: loyalty and support in exchange for selective access to public goods. A third reason focuses on a variant of exchange, where the state serves as an umbrella and money tree for diverse patron-client ties.

While these factors help us in understanding some of the elements that fend off disintegrative forces, they do not tell us enough. The main argument of the paper in the final section is that certain areas of state-society interaction can create meaning for people in society, and that meaning, in turn, can naturalize the state. Naturalization means that people consider the state to be as natural as the landscape around them; they cannot imagine their lives without it. If that belief is widespread, it provides a powerful antidote to disintegrative forces, even in the face of continued weakness in delivering goods, effecting policy, and gaining efficiency.

We will explore three overlapping areas where meaning and practice are created – the generation of law in society, the use of public ritual in a context in which politics is seen as theater, and the constitution and continuing reconstitution of public space. We are not yet at the point where we can specify under what conditions meaning is created in these three areas leading to a bolstered state, and where the opposite happens. But it is important at this point to explore these areas of state-society relations in order to understand their underlying relationship to state cohesion and disintegration.

A Global Environment Empowering States

What can we draw from those writing on states as to why more of them do not fall to the countless centrifugal forces within them and within their populations? For most writers, the question did not arise at all or was brushed aside.[5] As James N. Rosenau aptly put it, the literature gives the

---

[5] Jackson, Rosberg, Rosenau, and Strang are clear exceptions. See: Robert H. Jackson and Carl G. Rosberg, "Why Africa's Weak States Persist: The Empirical and the Juridical in

impression that "the state is to politics what the hidden hand is (à la Adam Smith) to economics."[6] Many ignored the question of state stability, instead naturalizing the concept of the state in their writings. By the early nineteenth century, they argued, states had become "the sole constitutive elements of the international system at the exclusion of others."[7] As the normative and juridical way to organize governance – in fact, as nearly the only successful way the twentieth century saw to establish rule – the state came to seem as much a part of the landscape as mountains and rivers. Little reason existed to question its presence or its future.

International law and the international society of states consecrated its form and worked to preserve, not only the society of states as a whole, but frequently individual states as well. Indeed, Jackson and Rosberg maintain, that if we were to take another criterion besides the juridical existence of states, such as whether states effectively control all of their territory, we could count many more of them as having failed to remain intact. They write that "one cannot explain the persistence of some 'states' by using a concept of the state that does not give sufficient attention to the [international] juridical properties of statehood."[8] Jackson referred to the international conditions that sustained states as "negative sovereignty."

While a few scholars investigated how international conditions propped up states, most simply took the state's continued existence for granted. In addition, the bedrock assumptions of International Relations theory reinforced the idea of the inviolability of the state. Models emphasized its rationality, thereby assuming its integrity and coherence.[9] International Relations thinkers dealt with states almost exclusively as independent variables, rather than dependent ones.[10] While these writers were reacting against pluralist approaches, systems theory, and Marxist notions, they too – like those they reacted against – simplified the state, treating its complex internal workings as unproblematic.

Statehood," *World Politics* 35 (October 1982): 1–24; James N. Rosenau, "The State in an Era of Cascading Politics: Wavering Concept, Widening Competence, Withering Colossus, or Weathering Change?" *Comparative Political Studies* 21 (April 1988): 13–44; Strang, "Anomaly and Commonplace in European Political Expansion."

[6] Rosenau, "The State in an Era of Cascading Politics," p. 14.

[7] Hendrik Spruyt, *The Sovereign State and its Competitors: An Analysis of Systems Change* (Princeton, NJ: Princeton University Press, 1994).

[8] Jackson and Rosberg, "Why Africa's Weak States Persist," p. 4.

[9] Lars-Erik Cederman, *Emergent Actors in World Politics: How States and Nations Develop and Dissolve* (Princeton, NJ: Princeton University Press, 1997), p. 29.

[10] Ibid., p. 213.

Realist theorists tended to ignore the internal dynamics of states that might tear them apart and looked, instead, to the configuration of states to explain state stability. The rationality of states, realists argued, frequently leads stronger ones to support weaker ones in an effort to prevent another stronger state from achieving world domination.[11] But Strang has demonstrated that realist theories cannot account for the state stability that he found across five centuries. At the same time that realist and neorealist theories gripped International Relations theorists, comparativists in political science and sociology made many similar assumptions in their efforts "to bring the state back in."[12]

Starting with the collapse of the Berlin Wall, however, it became increasingly difficult to think of states as inviolable. Words like "dissolution," "anarchy," and "collapse" crept into titles of works on states.[13] Constructivists and those using norms-based approaches began to question the old assumptions of International Relations theory,[14] and "state-in-society" displaced the notion of a totally autonomous, sovereign-ruling authority.[15] In the post–Cold War era when state weakness more often has led to state disintegration, and in a period in which scholars have given prominence to the internal complexity of the state, the question of why some states fall apart and others stay together has become both more urgent and more accessible.

During the Cold War, the argument goes, the very structure of world politics propped up teetering states. Superpower competition resulted in bountiful resources for states even in remote parts of the globe, high

[11] Kenneth Waltz, *Theory of International Politics* (Reading, MA: Addison-Wesley, 1979).

[12] Peter B. Evans, Dietrich Reuschemeyer, and Theda Skocpol, eds., *Bringing the State Back In* (New York: Cambridge University Press, 1985).

[13] See Cederman; Robert Kaplan, *The Ends of the Earth: From Togo to Turkmenistan, from Iran to Cambodia, A Journey to the Frontiers of Anarchy* (New York: Knopf, 1997); Klaus Schlichte, "Why States Decay: A Preliminary Assessment" (Mimeograph, 1997).

[14] See for example: Alexander Wendt, "Constructing International Politics," *International Security* 20 (1995): 71–81; Michael N. Barnett, *Dialogues in Arab Politics: Negotiations in Regional Order* (New York: Columbia University Press, 1998); Peter Katzenstein, *Culture of National Security: Norms and Identity in World Politics* (New York: Columbia University Press, 1996); Audie Klotz, *Norms in International Relations: The Struggle against Apartheid* (Ithaca, NY: Cornell University Press, 1995); Martha Finnemore, *National Interests in International Society* (Ithaca, NY: Cornell University Press, 1996).

[15] Joels S. Migdal, Atul Kohli, and Vivienne Shue, eds., *State Power and Social Forces: Domination and Transformation in the Third World* (New York: Cambridge University Press, 1994); Peter Evans, *Embedded Autonomy: States and Industrial Transformation* (Princeton, NJ: Princeton University Press, 1995).

incentives for their parts to hang together, and relief for them from much of their traditional role in defending borders against outside attack. Now, with the end of the Cold War and the increased intensity of economic globalization, the buzz is that the state is at the end of its rope. State weakness, in the absence of the old international props, might now translate directly into state collapse.

The termination of the Cold War, indeed, has brought an increase in the collapse of some states – enough to spur thinking about why they dissolve.[16] But the vast majority, even ones that seemed to be little more than propped-up artifacts of East-West competition, have remained intact and, for the moment, seem in no threat of disintegration even when public funds have been squandered and public policies, largely ignored.

Part of the reason for the relative stability of the state is that the international factors supporting and sustaining states did not all disappear with the end of the Cold War. Embassies and ambassadors, the United Nations and the World Bank, foreign aid and international agencies – all implicitly or explicitly have designated the state as the proper representation of the people in a given space. As strong as economic and environmental factors have been in making the state's boundaries quite porous, we have had a countervailing set of international regimes that have encouraged, sustained, and legitimated states as the proper form of rule.[17] As Strang argues, the stability of states can be explained, in large part, "by the cultural constitution of the Western state system as a community of mutual recognition."[18]

It is very rare indeed that international organizations and procedures have not promoted the state as the interlocutor of populations. One recent exception to the rule has been the restrictions placed by the United Nations on the Iraqi state with respect to its Kurdish population following the Gulf War. But that is a true rarity. More common is a case such as that portrayed in Peter Dauvergne's article on the Solomon Islands.[19] There, a state whose

---

[16] Kaplan, *The Ends of the Earth*; Schlichte, "Why States Decay"; Cederman, *Emergent Actors in World Politics.*

[17] Finnermore, *National Interests in International Society*, pp. 2–3; Klotz, *Norms in International Relations*, p. 24.

[18] Strang, "Anomaly and Commonplace in European Political Expansion: Realist and Institutional Accounts," p. 162.

[19] In Peter Dauvergne, "Weak states and the environment in Indonesia and the Soloman Islands," Working Paper presented at Australian National University (Canberra: Department of International Relations, 1997).

administrative capacity is as low as one could imagine gains succor from a host of international organizations and nearby foreign governments.

International institutions, such as the UN, not only have consecrated the state as the normatively appropriate way to organize rule over people, they also have empowered it by helping shape what it does and how it is constituted. International agencies have made all sorts of assumptions about how the state should occupy itself. It is expected not only to protect its population but to improve people's material lives, ensure their dignity, organize many of their activities, rectify the condition of women and children and indigenous peoples, and much more.

In other words, fairly rigid normative expectations envelope the state. And while these norms bind it, at the same time they empower it. It must undertake tasks that even a century ago were the marks of only a few regimes or none at all – educate youth in public schools, protect the environment, regulate the labor market, and so on. Even where states have failed miserably to put children in classrooms or affect workers' everyday conditions, they still have built huge state agencies assigned to education and labor. All states, whether they regularly succeed in implementing international norms or not, have constructed a sprawling state bureaucracy devoted to social issues, a fearsome security apparatus, and an extensive court system. These are now imperatives for all states, even if just to *appear* to tackle these sorts of issues. Even weak states have gained international legitimacy, not to speak of an extensive bureaucracy, as they have gone through the motions of putting international norms into practice domestically.

Numerous state bureaus, from agricultural extension to child welfare, have plugged into international agencies. Those international connections have made related state agencies in different countries look remarkably similar, even if their effectiveness differs substantially from state to state. Membership in an international organization, such as the World Health Organization, has shaped states' data collection (in fact, it has demanded data collection as a central activity), procedures, base of knowledge, and approaches to their subject of concern. The effect, at least on the surface, has been a worldwide homogenization of practices, norms, and technical expertise. Little states, big states – they all look remarkably alike, even if some are much more effective than others in putting these international norms to work in the domestic environment.

And their leaders have made the same sorts of claims of territoriality, sovereignty, autonomy, and independence. They issue similar calls for the obedience of their populations and for governing the minutiae of personal life – demanding taxes, regulating sexual relations, putting limits on parents' authority. And they consist of bureaus and agencies that look notably alike from one side of the globe to the other. In short, globalization has deepened and strengthened practices that enhance the state's role as much as it has generated practices that bypass the state.

But no matter how developed international norms have been about the proper form and practices for governance or how blustery leaders have been about the inviolability of their states, international support and claims for sovereignty cannot alone explain how and why states stay intact. A focus on global factors should not obscure the overriding importance of the make-up of the state and its relation to those it claims to rule. It also should not make us less aware of those global forces that weaken the state nor hide how superficial the integration of international norms and practices may be. Internalized international institutions may mean very different things in different domestic environments.

Even the direct propping up of states by neighbors or world powers and by international agencies through foreign aid, technical assistance, and military support goes only part of the way toward explaining the remarkable resiliency of so many states. So many states are shot through with corruption, inefficiency, and incapacity to put international intentions into practice with their own populations that we cannot rely only on the elaboration of international norms and the proffering of international support to explain how states stave off their own collapse.

The Organizational Imperatives of the State

Organizational theorists have given some sense of why any organizations, including states, remain intact. But their approaches are only partially satisfying. To some extent, that is because so much of what they have written assumes the integrity of organizations and does not question their cohesion. A kind of functionalist undertone seeps in to many of the discussions: Human beings have goals, wishes, and hopes; organizations exist as ways in which people connect to one another to realize those ends. In other words, organizations exist simply because people have a need for them. Göran Ahrne writes, "In the beginning there is organization. The basic human experience is belonging and dependence."[20] Different pressures

---

[20] Göran Ahrne, *Social Organizations: Interaction Inside, Outside and Between Organizations* (Thousand Oaks, CA: Sage Publications, 1994), p. 5. Ahrne notes the belief that func-

and opportunities that units of the organization encounter may have divisive effects, but its leaders at the top of the hierarchy of authority and control formulate strategic responses and adjust organizational structure to meet the challenges.[21] This process is what organizational theorists have called adaptation.

Because state organizations deal with fundamental needs, such as personal security, there is a temptation to say that they are there because people need them to be. But this formulation tells us very little about why state organizations are the dominant mode to fill these needs – why not some other type of organization? – or why some of these organizations may fail and others not.

To be fair, sociologists have recognized the possibility (perhaps even probability) that organizations will fail. Arthur L. Stinchcombe got the ball rolling by proposing that young organizations are more likely to die than old ones.[22] In the case of states, however, Stinchcombe's analysis runs into difficulties; young states have fared remarkably well over the last four decades. Michael T. Hannan and John Freeman, arguing that organizations' inertia diminishes the chances for successful adaptation, maintain that different environments "select" organizations that fit the specific local conditions well and cause ones that are ill-suited to the environment to fail.[23] Their thinking leads to the notion that organizations necessarily look quite different from one environment to another, but, again in the case of states, one is at pains to say why states the world over look so similar.[24]

More recently, Ahrne has simply pointed to what organizations have to do to avoid failure. "Positions have to be fitted together into a working

tionalist thinking dominates organizational theory: "According to Alexander the anti-functionalist movement has won a total victory. But the presumed functionalist organization theory is still alive. The fact that much of the organization theory Burrell and Morgan regarded as functionalist has survived the downfall of functionalist social theory seems to indicate that organization theory has a life of its own." Ahrne, *Social Organizations: Interaction Inside, Outside and Between Organizations* (Thousand Oaks: Sage Publications, 1994), p. 30. Ahrne goes on to argue that organization theory "has liberated itself from paradigmatic dependencies [like functionalism]" (p. 31). I have my doubts.

[21] Michael T. Hannan and John Freeman, "The Population Ecology of Organizations," *American Journal of Sociology* 82 (1994): 161–2.

[22] Arthur L. Stinchcombe, "Organizations and Social Structures," in James G. March (ed.), *Handbook of Organizations* (Chicago: Rand-McNally, 1965).

[23] Hannan and Freeman, "The Population Ecology of Organizations," p. 161.

[24] Jitendra V. Singh, David J. Tucker, and Robert J. House, "Organizational Legitimacy and the Liability of Newness," in W. Richard Scott (ed.), *Organizational Sociology* (Brookfield, VT: Dartmouth, 1994).

unit in order to counteract centrifugal forces. Even if the fit between positions is rarely perfect, centripetal forces are developed to balance the influences from the surrounding social landscape."[25] In other words, organizational dissolution is always a real possibility; only those that develop countervailing means to offset pressures toward collapse will survive and succeed. But this fashioning of the issue is somewhat unsettling in its use of the passive voice ("centripetal forces *are* developed"). Who is developing them and how? Why do they succeed and others not?

Too often, these questions have been glossed over in organizational theories, many of which now use an agency-structure approach in reference to public or collective goods. This approach maintains that organizations' centripetal forces derive from their ownership or control of such goods. By making individuals' access to these goods or resources dependent on membership in or affiliation with the organization – or, what is even more important, on the performance of obligations to the organization by fulfilling prescribed roles – centrifugal forces leading to dissolution or disaffection are kept at bay.

In other words, a simple trade takes place: individuals submit to the control of their personal behavior by paying dues, undertaking tasks, and taking orders (all of which act to keep the organization together) in exchange for access to resources, such as personal security, admission to the health club, and wages. To be sure, this approach still leaves holes in our understanding of who organizes, why organizations take the form they do, and why only some organizations overcome the problems of inertia that threaten the delivery of goods to individuals. But it goes a long way toward helping to understand organizational integrity, including the cohesion of states. As Ahrne writes, "Incentives and persuasion are centripetal forces in any organization contributing to the upkeep of authority."[26]

While states are subject to the same logic as other organizations in terms of maintaining themselves by being the gateway to collective goods, they also form a special kind of organization in this regard. Note Krasner's understanding:

With regard to both breadth and depth, sovereign states have become increasingly formidable institutions. They influence the self-image of those individuals within their territory through the concept of citizenship, as well as by exercising control, to one degree or another, over powerful instruments of socialization.

[25] Ahrne, *Social Organizations*, p. 104.   [26] Ibid., p. 111.

144

Why Do So Many States Stay Intact?

With regard to breadth, states are the most densely linked institutions in the contemporary world. Change the nature of states and virtually everything else in human society would also have to be changed. Hence, even though environmental incentives have dramatically changed since the establishment of the state system in the seventeenth century, there is little reason to believe that it will be easy to replace sovereign states with some alternative structure for organizing human political life.[27]

States are, indeed, complex organizations that often reach deeply and widely into everyday life. As organizations, they include individuals who actually are part of the organization (officials) and those outside the organization subject to its control. And the latter are divided between those with a distinctive affiliation – citizenship – and those, such as tourists or resident aliens, without that status. The multiple levels of bargains that any state has with all these different sorts of individuals, while in some ways diffusing its risks, also demand unusual complexity in providing different, sometimes contradictory, products to different groups. States that fail in their side of the basic bargain with those inside the organization (e.g., by not paying soldiers or bureaucrats), or with citizens in very different sorts of arrangements (e.g., by closing channels through which to influence officials or by leaving the door open to immigration that might affect citizens adversely) or with other residents (e.g., by not providing adequate security or by closing the door to immigration that might allow family reunions) are likely to face very serious centrifugal pressures.

States, more than many other sorts of organizations, may be subject to coming apart at the seams simply because there are so many seams. Their sheer complexity, Offe indicates, eats away at their organizational integrity. He quotes Dieter Grimm's phrase on the "decomposition of state power by increase of functions" and notes:

The state's claim to rational decision-making suffers from the fact that multiplication of the responsibilities is accompanied by a corresponding increase in instances, authorities, and administrative agents. This results in an internal pluralization and fragmentation of departmental perspectives within the administration, an escalation of the respective rivalries, and, on the whole, an increasing unpredictability of the resulting long-term and "synergetic" effects of individual policies which are nearly impossible to coordinate.[28]

[27] Stephen D. Krasner, "Sovereignty: An Institutionalist Perspective," *Comparative Political Studies* 21 (April 1988): 76.
[28] Offe, *Modernity and the State*, p. 63.

In sum, organizational theorists have given some sound reasons for why organizations remain intact, particularly how the provision of selective access to collective goods creates strong centripetal forces. But their approaches still leave us wondering why organizations look as they do, why they do not take different forms, and why other basic bargains might not lead to the replacement of existing structures. While the motivation of individuals has been clearly portrayed – they are rational bargain hunters looking to make the best choices they can to fulfill their wishes – the structure itself, its form and function, has stayed somewhat murky. These questions are amplified when we turn to states, where the multiple-level bargains in which they engage pose additional challenges of maintaining loyalty and where their utter complexity adds to already strong centrifugal tendencies. In short, many states have demonstrated abiding weakness – gross inefficiencies in maintaining bargains with a large and complex population. If it is organizational coherence that keeps states intact, why do the many states that demonstrate incoherence continue to exist?

Historical institutionalists have tried to grapple with some of these questions. Their arguments have gone beyond the rationality that underlies the organizational bargain – individuals' access to collective goods in exchange for fulfilling obligations. Centripetal forces stem too, they have emphasized, from routine. In other words, scholars using this approach have favored looking at habit in any given situation more than at utility maximization. Thomas A. Koelble notes:

When making decisions, individuals do not ask the question "how do I maximize my interests in this situation?" but instead "what is the appropriate response to this situation given my position and responsibilities?" In the majority of situations, rules and procedures (that is, institutions) are clearly established, and individuals follow routines. They follow well-worn paths and do what they think is expected of them.[29]

Historical institutionalists, then, have acknowledged the calculation of individuals, but they have emphasized that this sort of individual reckoning cannot be understood in a disembodied way. It takes place within a context, within the confines of rules and procedures of the organization. Moreover, after a while, individuals do not bother with the demanding course of rationally processing every possible choice that they encounter. Instead, their behavior becomes routinized within the possibilities that

---

[29] Thomas A. Koelble, "The New Institutionalism in Political Science and Sociology," *Comparative Politics* 27 (January 1995): 233.

existing organizations afford. Individuals do not need to be presented with the best possible choice by organizations in each instance for them to fulfill their obligations, because they are not always maximizing their utility. In most cases, they opt simply to "satisfice," in James G. March and Johan P. Olsen's terms.[30]

To be sure, this approach takes the pressure off organizations. States (and other organizations) remain intact even when they cannot put together the best choices for individuals, even when coordination and synergy among policies are low. In these instances, one can imagine even weak and inefficient state organizations continuing to exist. The habit of obeying and fulfilling other obligations adds important centripetal energy to combat disintegrative tendencies. Individuals are reluctant to abandon whimsically their states.

But the focus continues to be on the individual navigating his or her way through a labyrinth that remains quite mysterious. Little attention is paid to the content of the labyrinth, the organization itself. And the individual is a strangely passive being. He or she has become a creature of habit, and there are all too few signs of any affective tie to the organizations that fill needs or fulfill wishes.

We are left in the end with individuals who are either relentlessly rational or maddeningly passive. Little heed has been taken of Murray Edelman's caution of a generation ago: "To explain political behavior as a response to fairly stable individual wants, reasoning, attitudes, and empirically based perceptions is ... simplistic and misleading. Adequate explanation must focus on the complex element that intervenes between the environment and the behavior of human beings: creation and change in common meanings through symbolic apprehension in groups of people of interests, pressures, threats, and possibilities."[31]

Inefficient States Keep on Going

Organizational and international factors tell us about the nuts and bolts that hold parts of the state together as well as the global props that help sustain it. But they only skim the surface of how its population affects

---

[30] James G. March and Johan P. Olsen, *Rediscovering Institutions: The Organizational Basis of Politics* (New York: Free Press, 1989).

[31] Murray Edelman, *Politics as Symbolic Action: Mass Arousal and Quienscence* (Chicago: Markham, 1971), p. 2.

the state's cohesion. That factor is dealt with mainly by theorizing about material distributive issues. A key tenet of organizational theory is that organizations (here, states) maintain themselves by eliciting maximally efficient conduct from members, which they do by most effectively distributing public goods selectively. The conclusion would be that the most efficient organizations in this regard would have the best chances of survival.

But, as Marshall W. Meyer and Lynne G. Zucker have shown, "maximally efficient conduct is often not attained" and organizations nevertheless continue to exist.[32] States are prime examples of often inefficient, sometimes highly inefficient, organizations that keep on going. Benedict Kerkvliet portrays a Philippine state repeatedly failing to fulfill its promises with respect to agrarian reform.[33] But it still remains very much intact, and, indeed, is held in high esteem even by those patiently waiting for reform. The remarkable survival of what at first blush seem like pitifully weak states demands explanations that explore issues beyond efficiency and material distribution and, as Kerkvliet suggests, more nuanced understandings of what "weak" and "strong" entail.

One possibility suggested in some of the Asia Pacific cases is that states may survive as a result of odd bargains in which elements of the state participate. These bargains are between patrons and their clients. At times the patrons inhabit state offices and, at times, not. In either case, elements of the state provide cover for these exchanges. In addition, its administrative apparatus does not interfere too much with existing bargains between patrons and clients. It is in these bargains that meaningful exchanges of material goods and compliance are actually made. There is little Weberian rationality in the provision of services here, nor is there organization theory's maximal efficiency. Instead, the state's stability rests in good part on its integration into a web of strongman-follower ties.

While grossly inefficient in their own ability as coherent actors to provide security and material benefits to the population, states may provide a secure framework for numerous, disjointed patron-client bargains to flourish. The state, despite its weakness in providing the kinds of services

---

[32] Marshall W. Meyer and Lynne G. Zucker, *Permanently Failing Organizations* (Newbury Park: Sage, 1989), p. 47.

[33] Benedict Tria Kerkvliet, "Land Regimes and State Strengths and Weaknesses in the Philippines and Vietnam," in Peter Dauvergne (ed.), *Weak and Strong States in Asia-Pacific Societies* (Australia: Allen & Unwin, 1998).

demanded by international norms – security from crime, defense of human rights, development, protection of the environment – may continue to exist by being propped up by other powerful organizations or figures. It is often in the interest of the patrons to sustain the state because of the flow of international resources through the state (which they can appropriate) and because of the fig leaf international legitimacy can provide for their activities.

For the clients of, say, the Solomon Islands, the state seems to carry very little meaning in their everyday lives. Inefficiencies abound. As Dauvergne points out, while the capital city is in a state of disintegration, state officials sit idly in their offices.[34] It is patrons, for better or for worse, to whom the population must look for any sort of help. Remarkably, the author points out, the state remains unchallenged. Part of the reason may be the low saliency that the state has in people's minds and how little it affects their daily lives. It may not be worth rebelling against. Certainly, too, international props and quick state responses to pressure points have served the Solomon Islands political leaders well.

Still, one must wonder about long-term stability. International agents pour in sums that are not insubstantial in local terms to the state, making such funding a highly valued prize. As long as there is effective collusion among the patrons, inside and outside the state, regarding the distribution of those sums, the state remains intact. But that collusion of patrons seems quite fragile in its own right, as Somalia, Lebanon, Rwanda, and other cases have demonstrated.

If the Solomon Islands are an example of a fairly stable state – at least to date – that is extremely weak, some Southeast Asian states show much more robustness. Part of the ability of states, such as Indonesia, to remain intact stems from their well-developed and effective coercive arms using violence to lower the risk of opposition to them. For some of these states, patron-client ties are important, as well, and the relationship of the state to these ties can be a stabilizing factor. But coercion alone cannot keep a state intact (e.g., Iran under the Shah, or the USSR) and some states' weakness does not derive from their relationships to powerful patrons. For example, the enduring weaknesses of the Indonesian state, as Harold Crouch demonstrates, derive more from its own internal structure than from giving way to strong patrons, and its ability to survive, even prosper,

---

[34] Peter Dauvergne, "Weak States and the Environment in Indonesia and the Solomon Islands," in Dauvergne (ed.), *Weak and Strong States in Asia-Pacific Societies*.

has not been seriously questioned.[35] How, then can we explain states' survival, even in the face of enduring weakness and even when ties to extra-state distributional methods (i.e., patrons) are not determining?

Constituting the State

A crucial but hard-to-get-at factor in the ability of the state, even a relatively weak state, to stay intact is its place in the meaning people generate about the world around them and their place in it. When states become naturalized – where their dissolution or disappearance becomes unimaginable to their subjects because of their longevity, provision of crucial goods and services, and other factors – they have a much greater chance of counteracting their own inefficiency and ineffectiveness. By no means is a hegemonic idea, such as the state's indispensability, a guarantee of the state's indefinite predominance – hegemonic ideas do falter in the course of history. But where such ideas reign, the state holds a hedge against some failures. In these instances, inefficiency in distributional questions and other aspects of policy implementation need not necessarily lead weak states down the plank to collapse.

Many states, including many relatively weak ones, have a deep impact on the structure of society and people's sense of meaning about themselves. At the same time, the structure of society and the meaning people generate in it affect the state and its chances for survival. State and society are in a mutually constitutive relationship. The state's centrality in people's lives, its relationship to ongoing conflicts in society, people's expressive relationship to it, all depend on its cohesion. And, simultaneously, these elements of state-society relations shape the form, content, and ultimately the viability of the state.

To understand why states do not fall apart means somehow getting at this doubly transformative process – at how society acts upon the cohesion and form of the state at the same time that the state acts upon the thoughts and actions of people, as well as where they find meaning. We can analyze a number of different areas to get at the mutually transformative state-society relations. In the following pages, I look at three of these, which can be fruitful in understanding the resiliency of many states. The three are law, public rituals, and informal behavior in the public sphere.

---

[35] Harold Crouch, "Indonesia's 'Strong' State," in Dauvergne (ed.), *Weak and Strong States in Asia-Pacific Societies.*

1. Law

While its meaning seems quite straightforward at first glance, as Robert Cover notes, "the word 'law' itself is always a primary object of contention,"[36] but it is in the interest of the state to present the law as if no such contention existed. In its raw form, law involves compelling people to behave in certain ways, but the institution of law implies a sense of justice and rightness that legitimates and obscures the process of forcing others to submit to a particular will. State leaders, especially, have had a very strong interest in presenting their idea of law as if no other meanings of it existed or mattered. They have wanted people to believe that there is no law other than state law and that people's sense of what is just and right finds expression in that law. The legitimacy of the state and its ability to gain people's obedience have depended upon it. Again, as Cover states:

There is not automatic legitimation of an institution by calling it or what it produces "law," but the label is a move, the staking out of a position in the complex social game of legitimation. The jurisprudential inquiry into the question "what is law" is an engagement at one remove in the struggle over what is legitimate.[37]

How do states successfully stake out a position in which their law becomes a strong legitimating factor in their rule, giving people a sense that the existence of justice and rightness depend upon the existence of the state and that their world would be topsy-turvy without it? To answer that question, I believe, one must move beyond some of the conventional understandings to a more pluralistic notion of law.

State law has traditionally been thought of in two ways. The first emphasizes social control. States have adopted laws as an efficient and predictable means to set the limits and parameters for behavior in the territory that they have claimed to rule, and they have backed up their prescriptions with the use and threat of tremendous violence. This sort of control has been directed both at those outside the organization (citizens, aliens, tourists) as well those staffing the state. In this view, then, law is a tool of the state to regulate and direct behavior, both

---

[36] Robert Cover, "The Folktales of Justice: Tales of Jurisdiction," in Martha Minow, Michael Ryan, and Austin Sarat (eds.), *Narrative, Violence and the Law: The Essays of Robert Cover* (Ann Arbor: University of Michigan Press, 1995), p. 174.
[37] Ibid., p. 175.

for controlling the population of a territory and for its own internal control.

The second meaning of law is one that involves self-limitation by states through the creation of, or at least respect for, individual and property rights. Here, it has been liberal states, in particular, that have advocated the notion of inalienable property and human rights, inviolable powers and privileges for individuals. Law here has involved states' creation of islands of action for individuals, especially in the context of a capitalist society, that cannot be constrained or regulated by the sorts of restrictive law found in the first category, law as social control.

Both of these notions of law stress the centrality of the state. It legislates and executes and adjudicates. It creates laws and implements them. The handful of states in the common law tradition do look outside the state organization itself for the basis of law, valorizing the origins of laws in practical everyday transactions and custom, but even in these cases it is state legislative bodies and judiciaries that formalize and validate codes of action. States stand at the center of self-limiting laws as well as ones geared toward social control; it is the state organization that determines, or at least codifies, what rights individuals have. The awesome force of the state – its police and judges and jails and executioners – stands behind its edicts.

To be sure, scholars and jurists have recognized that actual practice has not always conformed to state law. It has been contravened by outright criminality, of course, but also by customary law or social convention. Still, the essence of power in this state-centered view of law lies in the narrowness of the gap between state-imposed codes and social practice and in the acceptance by society of state law as the proper and just form of rule. This perspective on law, it seems to me, takes as unproblematic the question of why people should obey the law when there is little or no threat of state violence. In other words, what makes the law seem legitimate in their eyes beyond the big stick it wields?

Cover's comments about the conflicts over who gets to make law imply an alternative standpoint to the state-centered one, that of legal pluralism. It stresses the existence of multiple sets of laws in society, including those opposed to the state, others not controlled by the state but not necessarily in opposition to it, and still others complementary to state law. Some of these may be formal codes, such as Islamic law; others may be long-standing but much less formal, such as the law of the manor in feudal societies; and still others may be loose, recently generated sets of norms. This

152

last sort of law – "although 'law' may be too lofty or lowly a term to describe it,"[38] – consists of what various groups of people in society think is just and use as their guide to proper behavior.

In this alternative view, the notion of state law as singular is nothing more than a state-professed ideology seeking to enhance power and legitimacy. In fact, state law stews in a cauldron with numerous other sets of law – some friendly to it, some not.[39] This alternative perspective also notes that these other sets of laws and practices invariably have an effect on state law. Finkel characterized the differences between the state-centered and the legal-pluralist perspectives in this regard as "should the law [read, state law] follow the path laid by community sentiment [read, other sorts of law], or should the community follow the path the law has laid?"[40] In the legal pluralist view, state law often follows the path set by non-state forms of law.

The notion that state law has been or should be deeply affected by these other sets of law has not been universally accepted, by any means. The mainstream of legal theory has long held that governmental law, the official pronouncements of the state, constitutes the do's and don't's for society, and not the opposite. In this view, "people outside the institutions and offices of the 'legal system' receive rather than generate legal authority."[41] Through its rules and rights, law does shape and structure society – "law creates and maintains hierarchy and dominance in society."[42] But it is important to understand, too, how that society shapes and reshapes state law, as well.

If Cover is right that law is a powerful legitimating force – and I think that he is – then the ability of states to remain intact rests in part on their relationship to these other sets of law. The ability of other categories of law to subvert, strengthen, or transform state law has a deep impact on the chances for the state to hold together and be effective. Much of what law – state and others – does is to delineate a universe of meaning for people: what is acceptable and what not, what is right and what wrong. Law is not

---

[38] Norman J. Finkel, *Commonsense Justice: Jurors' Notions of the Law* (Cambridge, MA: Harvard University Press, 1995), p. 2.

[39] Mark Galanter, "Justice in Many Rooms: Courts, Private Ordering, and Indigenous Law," *Journal of Legal Pluralism (and Unofficial law)* 19 (1981): 56–72.

[40] Finkel, *Commonsense Justice*, p. 1.

[41] John Brigham, *The Constitution of Interests: Beyond the Politics of Rights* (New York: New York University Press, 1996), pp. 6–7.

[42] Susan Burgess quoted in Brigham, *Constitution of Interests*, p. ix.

just setting out what to do and what not to do, it is asserting what is right to do and what is wrong. When state law successfully creates a broadly shared meaning – what Durkheim would call social solidarity – it enhances the conditions for its own survival. Broad social solidarity reinforces the cohesion of the state. State law in such cases is taken by the population as a delineation of right from wrong. It becomes a critical process that "coalesce[s] groups with diverse concerns into a single political force and that infuse[s] individual participants with the intense affect that comes from defense of one's identity."[43] But where state law sits uneasily with other sets of law in the society, it undermines its own ability to give people that sense of meaning in their lives and to gain the legitimacy it desperately needs.

We still know very little about how different sets of laws interact. We also have little sense of how the transformation of state law through the interaction with other forms of law may help create a broadly shared sense of meaning for a population, including legitimacy that can enhance the state's cohesion. What we can suggest is that state law has been deeply affected by other sets of law, especially by what various groups of people in society have thought is just and have used as their guide to behavior. Lawrence M. Friedman demonstrated how remarkably U.S. law was transformed from the nineteenth to the twentieth century as a result of people's changing understanding of themselves and what proper behavior therefore should be.[44] Indeed, he goes so far as to say that the very meaning of the individual (or, better, individualism) changed, which has led to a very different legal system from that of a century ago.

In any society, significant social change brings with it a proliferation of sets of laws, of legal meanings. Those new legal meanings may turn into texts of resistance, as Cover calls them, threatening the cohesion of the state.[45] But where state law has been transformed by these other sets of law, where it has created the conditions for melding diverse sets of law generated in society, it has put states in a position to benefit from renewed, broadly shared meaning in society. In other words, social changes in elements of the public and the generation of new non-state forms of

---

[43] Edelman, *Politics as Symbolic Action*, p. 12.

[44] Lawrence M. Friedman, *The Republic of Choice: Law, Authority, and Culture* (Cambridge, MA: Harvard University Press, 1990).

[45] Robert Cover, "Nomos and Narrative," in Martha Minow, Michael Ryan, and Austin Sarat (eds.), *Narrative, Violence, and the Law: The Essays of Robert Cover* (Ann Arbor: University of Michigan Press, 1995), p. 150.

law among these publics can transform the make-up of the state (here, in legal terms), the very way the state is constituted. And the state, in turn, can transform society through its application of new law as well as by synthesizing different sets of societal law that may be at odds with one another. Where such a double transformation takes place, states come to be associated among those publics with what is right, gaining key legitimacy from that shared sense of meaning.

In the colonial context, where we might have expected the clashes of different sets of laws to be severe, we can find cases of transformation with unexpected results. The imperial powers' law interacted with previous ways of doing things in complex ways. Ornulf Gulbrandsen, for example, wrote about a people and an area, the Northern Tswana of the then Bechuanaland Protectorate, in which effective precolonial legislative and judicial bodies interacted with the newly imposed British law.[46] The result of the interaction, perhaps surprisingly, was the strengthening of the preexisting bodies, giving the society "considerable potentials to counteract the penetration of European categories and valuations."[47]

For the Tswana the maintenance of a system of law counteracting Britain's attempts to impose a singular, hegemonic law had interesting results. For one, their distinctive strong law "kept the British willing to retain the Protectorate in the face of the continuous pressure for annexation to the apartheid regime of South Africa."[48] It also prompted the British rulers increasingly to absorb Tswana leaders into the domain of state laws and institutions. Despite their inability to do what they had set out to do, that is, to create a British legal system, the colonial rulers found themselves gaining legitimacy from the changes society imposed upon them.

Martin Chanock uncovered a different African pattern. In his case, the attempt to impose British law had the unintended effect of actually creating de novo an African customary law, "for the perceptions of the traditional order arise from current concerns and are necessary to current conditions."[49] Chanock notes that the interaction of colonial state law with

---

[46] Ornulf Gulbrandsen, "Living Their Lives in Courts: The Counter-Hegemonic Force of the Tsawana *Kgotla* in a Colonial Context," in Olivia Harris (ed.), *Inside and Outside the Law* (New York: Routledge, 1996).

[47] Ibid., p. 127.

[48] Ibid., p. 152.

[49] Martin Chanock, *Law, Custom, and Social Order* (New York: Cambridge University Press, 1985), p. 8.

this new customary law (which the British pretended had prefigured colonialism) had, and continues to have, complementary effects:

For the colonization of Africa by western legal forms and institutions continues under the aegis of the growing legal profession, which in other circumstances, has been among the most verbally ardent of the opponents of colonialism. This process, however, is partly being legitimated by its presentation as a development of a customary law which is essentially African, a recapturing of a pre-colonial dynamic.[50]

Outside of colonial situations, too, states have had to rely on, respond to, and contend with other systems of law extant in society. In nineteenth-century Russia, the state had serious difficulties in providing some overall shared meaning for the society through law. Social changes that produced an active urban middle class pushed legal reformers at the end of the century to introduce "modern" codes derived from Western Europe, particularly France. Key principles of the new systems of law conflicted with the law of the manor for serfs and patriarchal law for women. The clash of varying sets of laws raised important questions. Were women and serfs (or former serfs) to be understood as rights-possessing individuals subject to state law or as subject to the authority of fathers and husbands? Could the Russian state afford to assert legal authority over aspects of life formerly ruled by males in families and lords of the manor and still maintain sufficient social stability?

As Laura Engelstein shows, the interaction of these varying sets of laws raised immediate and practical dilemmas.[51] How would the state treat "public women" (prostitutes), who were not subject to the authority of husbands or fathers? What would the role of the police be: guarding the morals implied by the other sets of law or treating women as rights-bearing individuals (which implied a whole different sense of what is right)? The state appeared confused, moving back and forth on the implementation of the new codes and unable to develop a coherent system of meaning across its vast territories. State law certainly was transformed but not in a direction that successfully incorporated and integrated the other sets of legal meanings in society. Increasingly, the Russian state found it difficult to generate a law that could produce

[50] Ibid., p. 238.
[51] Laura Englestein, "Gender and Juridical Subject: Prostitution and Rape in Nineteenth-Century Russian Criminal Codes," *Journal of Modern History* 60 (September 1988): 458–95.

broadly shared meaning in society, and its legitimacy and ultimate cohesion suffered as a result.

Scholars have only begun to scratch the surface of how different sets of law have affected one another. We cannot generalize about when state law has been successfully transformed in the interaction to reflect key changes in society and to generate a shared meaning for society. But if we are to get a handle on how and why states hold together (and why others do not), and on what kind of institutional adaptation that takes, we would be well advised to study the law as a key meeting point of state and society. The increasing autonomy of judicial institutions from other branches of the state in countries around the world may speak to the way in which law serves as a means for society to transform the state even where state bureaucratic, legislative, and executive institutions seem inflexible and impenetrable to popular influence.[52] The interaction of various forms of law, the transformation of state law, and the emerging role of the judiciary may help to explain both the adaptability of state organizations and the importance of the state in providing central meaning in people's lives.

2. Public Ritual

Sociologists have observed that organizations often persist despite regularly falling short of doing what they are supposed to do: "We are surrounded by organizations whose failure to achieve their proclaimed goals is neither temporary nor aberrant, but chronic and structurally determined."[53] States are among those that regularly fall short of passing efficiency tests, some failing abysmally. Their failures are hard to hide; they range from failure to supply security, as evidenced in crime, to the inability to deliver on their end of material bargains, such as not paying soldiers or bureaucrats. One way in which states have overcome their gross inefficiencies and grave difficulties in meeting central goals has been to gain loyalty and support other than through efficient allocation of public goods;

---

[52] Paula R. Newberg, *Judging the State: Courts and Constitutional Politics in Pakistan* (New York: Cambridge University Press, 1995); Mark J. Osiel "Dialogue with Dictators: Judicial Resistance in Argentina and Brazil," *Law and Social Inquiry* 20 (Spring 1995): 481–560; Martin Shapiro and Alec Stone, "The New Constitutional Politics of Europe," *Comparative Political Studies* 26 (January 1994): 397–420.

[53] Paul DiMaggio, "Foreword," in Marshall W. Meyer and Lynne G. Zucker (eds.), *Permanently Failing Organizations* (Newbury Park, Sage, 1989), p. 9.

they have garnered backing by blurring the line between state officials and citizens through the use of public ritual.

John W. Meyer and Brian Rowan argue that the survival prospects of organizations increase when they successfully adopt ceremonies that express institutional rules functioning as powerful myths. These ceremonies may conflict head on with the goals of efficiency; that is, organizations "dramatically reflect the myths of their institutional environments instead of the demands of their work activities."[54] In the case of states, this means that state organizations adopt ceremonies that appeal to the particularities of their population over procedures that maximize their efficiency. They "incorporate elements which are legitimated externally, rather than in terms of efficiency."[55] Expensive coronations, which can drain resources needed to achieve stated goals, for example, may affirm moral values by which many in society live and identify the state with those values in people's minds; they are acts of "national communion."[56]

Ritual and ceremony – it is impossible to conjure up states without thinking about them, from the grand entrance of judges into courtrooms to military parades.[57] State practice from the age of kings to the era of republics has been suffused with elaborate ritual. Ceremonies have had the effect of forging unity, whether of the king's physical body with the body politic or of scattered individuals into a unified carrier of sovereignty supporting a particular state organization.[58] "The central authority of an orderly society, whether it be secular or ecclesiastical," wrote Shils, "is acknowledged to be the avenue of communication with the realm of the sacred values."[59] Rituals and ceremonies connect the sacred to the notion of the nation and the mundane institutions of the state. States and societies both shape, and are shaped by, rituals and the beliefs that they support.

---

[54] John W. Meyer and Brian Rowan, "Institutionalized Organizations: Formal Structures as Myth and Ceremony," *American Journal of Sociology* 83 (1977): 341.

[55] Ibid., p. 348.

[56] Edward Shils, *Center and Periphery: Essays in Macrosociology* (Chicago: University of Chicago Press, 1975), p. 139.

[57] "Ritual is a stereotyped, symbolically concentrated expression of beliefs and sentiments regarding ultimate things." Shils, *Center and Periphery*, p. 154. Also, see his discussion of the term "ceremonial" on p. 155.

[58] See Emile Durkheim, *Elementary Forms of Religious Life* (London: Allen & Unwin, 1915): 427.

[59] Shils, *Center and Periphery*, p. 151.

Ritual and ceremony resonate with a theatrical ring. It is not surprising that theater and politics seem to have a twinned existence, mimicking each other and spilling over into each other's domains.[60] Marie-Hélène Huet opens her book on the French Revolution with the culmination of the trial of Louis XVI, that moment when the representatives of the people, one by one, stepped forward to pronounce on the question of "what penalty shall be inflicted?" Huet writes:

We are indeed within the register of the theater: the material organization, the public, the state, the loges, the ushers, the galleries. The distribution of elements: that noisy, frivolous, enthusiastic theater-going crowd of which Diderot was so fond, and the more sober representatives of the people, loudly declaiming a sentence the repetitiveness of which brought out its force. The text was in dialogue form, as in the theater; however, in this instance the dialogue went beyond the theatrical and bore within it, amid the tumult and the levity of the auditorium, a force that was truly revolutionary.[61]

This last sentence is almost a disclaimer of what was said earlier. Huet follows it by noting, "This theater was not theater, of course; under the exterior signs of a frivolous scene almost familiar in its frightening levity, History was unfolding."[62] But the temptation is strong to make what happens into theater or, as in the case of Lynn Avery Hunt's *The Family Romance of the French Revolution*, into a scripted story. In both works, the symbolic relationship of politics to a play or novel gives the gory events of the moment a shared and enduring meaning among the people. And, as the French Revolution vividly portrayed, the society can choreograph events as well as be choreographed by them. Hunt puts it this way, "I use the term *family romance(s)* in order to suggest that much of this imaginative effort [that is, the people's reconfiguring their relationship to political authority] went on below the surface, as it were, of conscious political discourse."[63]

The connection between politics and theater has been made repeatedly by observers, from Cicero to Hobbes to Burke. Edmund Burke, for example, saw close links between the two, approving the use of drama in

---

[60] James E. Combs, *Dimensions of Political Drama* (Santa Monica, CA: Goodyear Publishing, 1980).

[61] Marie-Hélène Huet, *Rehearsing the Revolution: The Staging of Marat's Death 1793–1797* (Berkeley: University of California Press, 1982), p. 3.

[62] Ibid., p. 4.

[63] Lynn Avery Hunt, *The Family Romance of the French Revolution* (Berkeley: University of California Press, 1992), p. xiv.

the case of the British monarchy and regarding it with horror in the case of France's revolutionaries.[64] One way commonly used to understand the relationship between theater and politics is to see how spectacles have been used by politicians to enhance their power. By creating spectacles, as does the theater, in which the public participates, state officials have sought to inscribe its laws within the spectator's mind, "not as foreign but as inherent, self-imposed, 'moral.'"[65]

Clifford Geertz also suggests an association between the state and theater, between ritual and power, one that may not always be instrumental.[66] His case came from the nineteenth-century Balinese state, Negara. Power in this instance was not foremost on the mind of political rulers. Indeed, they showed indifference to actual governing, hesitancy in regulating people's everyday actions, and lack of interest in territorial sovereignty. Their attention pointed "toward spectacle, toward ceremony, toward the public dramatization of the ruling obsessions of Balinese culture: social inequality and status pride. It was a theatre state in which the kings and princes were the impresarios, the priests the directors, and the peasants the supporting cast, stage crew, and audience.... Power served pomp, not pomp power."[67]

In this view the court-and-capital "is not just the nucleus, the engine, or the pivot of the state, it *is* the state.... It is a statement of a controlling political idea – namely, that by the mere act of providing a model, a paragon, a faultless image of civilized existence, the court shapes the world around it into at least a rough approximation of its own excellence."[68] In his study, Geertz deals with the threat of state dissolution directly. He sees a constant threat from the disintegrative forces of the "power system composed as it was of dozens of independent, semi-independent, and quarter-independent rulers."[69] But what underlies the staging of politics, the "controlling political idea" (or what we might label

---

[64] Edmund Burke in C. C. O'Brien (ed.), *Reflections on the Revolution in France* (London: Penguin, 1969); Stephen K. White, *Edmund Burke: Modernity, Politics, and Aesthetics* (Thousand Oaks, CA: Sage, 1994); Paul Hindson and Tim Gray, *Burke's Dramatic Theory of Politics* (Brookfield, VT: Avebury, 1988).

[65] Scott C. Bryson, *The Chastised Stage: Bourgeois Drama and the Exercise of Power* (Saratoga, CA: Anma Libri, 1991), p. 3; Murray Edelman, *Constructing the Political Spectacle* (Chicago: University of Chicago Press, 1988).

[66] Clifford Geertz, *Negara: The Theatre State in Nineteenth-Century Bali* (Princeton, NJ: Princeton University Press, 1980).

[67] Ibid., p. 13. [68] Ibid. [69] Ibid., p. 19.

the *master narrative*) is a strong counterforce to the disintegrative elements. Master narratives "operate as the unchallenged first principles of a political order, making any given hierarchy appear natural and just to rulers and ruled."[70]

Participation in the Balinese ritualized theater forged a sense of unity among those participating as well as an awareness that such unity was maintained, in great part, by the existence of the theater state. Have not politics and public ritual been related in similar ways in our time? Especially in an age where technology makes both the manipulation and dissemination of dramatic politics possible on a huge stage, theatrical images suffuse our current-day politics. The small box of television, in particular, transforms the complexity and ambiguity of politics into a moral tale with a readily understandable content and lesson. Edelman noted that "in the age of mass communications dramaturgy has become more central and the pattern it assumes more banal."[71] Staged dramas are constructions that "offer answers to troubling questions. They tell what conditions are healthy or threatening and who are responsible for success and misfortune."[72]

All the elaborate ceremonies that we associate with states – from inaugurations to press conferences – might not be, as we always thought, means to an end. They might, as in the Balinese case, be ends in themselves, an expression of a simultaneous unity among people (all are part of the production) and an order in which some command and others obey (different roles in the production). The state's officials play a leading role in people's minds in forging and maintaining that master narrative, the underlying dramatic unity, and in holding positions of authority.

Of course, such theater does not guarantee the state's survival. Particularly in conditions of rapid social and political change, when notions of the proper locus of political authority are in flux, old dramatic representations may lose their hold. Such a crumbling of the old drama has been commented on in the case of France's ancien regime.[73] But these authors,

---

[70] Sean Wilentz, *Rites of Power: Symbolism, Ritual, and Politics Since the Middle Ages* (Philadelphia: University of Pennsylvania Press, 1985), p. 4.
[71] Edelman, *Constructing the Political Spectacle*, p. 120.
[72] Ibid.
[73] Bryson, *The Chastised Stage*; Hunt, *The Family Romance of the French Revolution*; Huet, *Rehearsing the Revolution*.

too, note the importance in the midst of the French Revolution of scripting a new dramatic representation of unity and authority.

Still, both in the instances of the French Revolution and the Balinese state, those who use the theatrical metaphor present it as a tool used by states to mold and energize society. We can think of this line of thinking as the impresario theory of politics. This metaphor of theater implies an impresario or producer as one who puts together the production; in the case of politics, the producer is the supreme leadership of the state.[74] We can counterpose to that impresario model a collective one. Here the state is not totally free to cast people however it wants; elaborate staging alone will not save any state. The will of the actors, the reaction of the audience, even the attitudes of the stagehands – all count heavily in the eventual success or failure of the production, and all good producers take account of them in staging their spectacle. The state is not only responsive to the society, it is changed by the nature of the population and its beliefs.

Warding off the disintegrative forces pulling at the state involves creating a unity among some or all of the people, as the impresario model implies, and having the state shape itself to key beliefs in society, as the collective model suggests. It is a unity in which the ruled see their roles as tied in to those of friends and strangers around them, even to strangers they will never meet, including the officials of the state who demand their obedience. For state leaders, that means creating "a negotiated process relying on the skills of the theatre to achieve spontaneous cooperation between human actors."[75] Elaborate ritual has been key to forging a semblance of oneness among disparate peoples and groups. As in the theater, rituals have been used to arouse passions, to create affective ties between audience and spectators. Even the elaborate capital cities that every state has laid out and the costly public buildings they have erected are integral

---

[74] Runciman in *Pluralism and the Personality of the State* (New York: Cambridge University Press, 1997) contrasts this sort of model with a more pluralist model in the context of theatrical metaphors. He notes Hobbes's notion that all freedoms lie with the author of the drama, who is the sovereign (p. 237). He contrasts this view with that of Ernest Barker, the early twentieth-century British political theorist: "Initially, Barker is happy to describe all the state as a stage, just as he is to describe all the persons within it as actors treading across its boards. The literal image of the state, however, is rather too passive to convey that sense of agency on which Barker's idea of the state depends. So he extends his analogy to take in those agents – the dramatist and producer – with whom responsibility for the staging of any drama rests" (p. 251).

[75] Hindson and Gray, *Burke's Dramatic Theory of Politics*, p. 8.

parts of the theatrical production. Analyzing Edmund Burke, Paul Hindson and Tim Gray write:

The physical arena within which political drama was enacted, was another feature of great importance to Burke's dramatic metaphor. The arena should be imposing and majestic. It should overwhelm the imagination of the populace, and awe them into acquiescence. The arena should be the architectural summit of human achievement, vast, impressive, and sublime.[76]

E. P. Thompson, who certainly would not disparage the role of material forces in maintaining states' power and cohesion, noted that such forces go only so far in explaining why people obey: "A great part of politics and law is always theater; once a social system has become 'set,' it does not need to be endorsed daily by exhibitions of power . . . what matters more is a continuing theatrical style."[77] Theater molds "the images of power and authority, the popular mentalities of subordination."[78] And those images have remained important far past Geertz's and Thompson's nineteenth-century cases.[79] "Thrones may be out of fashion, and pageantry too," writes Geertz, "but political authority still requires a cultural frame in which to define itself and advance its claims, and so does opposition to it."[80] The ability of any state to remain intact rests on its ability to produce that cultural frame, linking itself to the sacred through a set of rituals, and to transform itself so as to fit into a cultural frame that has resonance among key elements of the population.

3. Informal Behavior in the Public Sphere

Whether one leans toward an impresario or collective model for the theatrical metaphor, the state's position is central. Its success comes in creating some harmonious whole out of disparate parts. Another dimension having a deep impact on the state's ability to remain intact lies outside its direct control. Yet this factor, too, is key in the fashioning of shared

---

[76] Ibid., p. 31.
[77] E. P. Thompson, "Patrician Society, Plebian Culture," *Journal of Social History* 7 (Summer 1974): 389.
[78] Ibid., p. 387.
[79] For example, see: Joseph W. Esherick and Jeffrey N. Wasserstrom, "Acting Out Democracy: Political Theater in Modern China," *Journal of Asian Studies* 49 (November 1990): 835–65.
[80] Clifford Geertz, *Local Knowledge: Further Essays in Interpretive Anthropology* (New York: Basic Books, 1983), pp. 142–3.

meaning in society, in the forging of a social unity that naturalizes and sustains states. This dimension involves informal interactions in public space.

The concept of public space or the public sphere has been much discussed during the last generation, in good part due to the influence of Jürgen Habermas.[81] His concern is with the debate on public issues by private people (as opposed to policymakers or others whose vocation make them part of political society or the state). Any number of practical discourses may proceed simultaneously on varied issues.

Habermas and those who followed him have been largely preoccupied with the quantity and quality of public debate and its effect on democratic politics. Nonetheless, some important presuppositions have gone into their thinking that raise questions related to our concern, the ability of states to remain intact. For one, the public sphere is understood to be an egalitarian space, that is, one in which "arguments and not statuses determine decisions."[82] Beyond that, the public sphere includes, not only the content of conversations on public issues, but also an understanding of how give-and-take should take place. Seyla Benhabib calls these conditions *"universal moral respect* and *egalitarian reciprocity."*[83] She goes on to say that "democratic debate is like a ball game where there is no umpire to definitively interpret the rules of the game and their application."[84] Somehow, without the state or other authoritative umpires, rules for conversation among strangers do develop, at least in some societies.

The kinds of rules of the game to which Benhabib refers have to do with social interaction geared toward civic engagement. She is certainly right that these sorts of rules are preconditions for conversations that can influence political decisions and that such influence is essential in a democracy. But it is not only democratic debate that is like a ball game without an umpire. All societies, democratic and nondemocratic alike, have broad dimensions of public life – life outside the walls of one's home – where social interaction is frequent and largely ungoverned by state law. And

---

[81] Jürgen Habermas, *The Structural Transformation of the Public Sphere: An Inquiry into a Category of Bourgeois Society* (Cambridge, MA: MIT Press, 1991); Craig Calhoun, *Habermas and the Public Sphere* (Cambridge, MA: MIT Press, 1996); Stephen Edgell, Sandra Walklate, and Gareth Williams (eds.), *Debating the Future of the Public Sphere* (Brookfield, VT: Avebury, 1995).

[82] Calhoun, *Habermas and the Public Sphere*, p. 1.

[83] Seyla Benhabib, *Situating the Self: Gender, Community and Postmodernism in Contemporary Ethics* (New York: Routledge, 1992), p. 105.

[84] Ibid., pp. 106–7.

these, too, require rules without the benefit of an umpire, in part to insure social tranquility but also to create a sense of unity or solidarity among those in society.

In the section on law above, I referred to these sorts of rules as a form of non-state law consisting of what various groups of people in society think is just and use as their guide to proper behavior. The arena outside one's private or family domain can be threatening and frightening, and state laws have been able to provide only a modicum of security there. No matter how effective or pervasive the state apparatus, it cannot alone provide the kind of security that Hobbes imagined. Indeed, the perceived *effectiveness of the state rests on how well other sorts of implicit law or rules guide proper behavior* and limit to some manageable level the deviance with which the state must deal.

Thinkers through the years have made reference to these non-state rules. Burke, for example, characterized them as the "human 'links', which, although having no legal status, act to constrain and restrict, as well as to give motion to the organised activity of a society."[85] Contemporary writers, too, continue to dwell on the issue of the rules of social engagement. Robert D. Putnam relates the amount of civic engagement, including such mundane things as membership in choral societies and football clubs, to the effectiveness of governance in different regions of Italy.[86] And he worries about the decline of "social capital" – "networks, norms, and social trust that facilitate coordination and cooperation" – in the United States.[87] He argues that "networks of civic engagement foster sturdy norms of generalized reciprocity and encourage the emergence of social trust."[88] In a similar vein, David D. Laitin stresses the importance of societies developing what he calls shared "points of concern."[89] These are a critical foundation for forging common understandings about what the public agenda should be and agreement on the proper ways to disagree.

How and why do strong social networks form in public space? Which societies manage to hammer out shared points of concern that determine

---

[85] Hindson and Gray, *Burke's Dramatic Theory of Politics*, p. 8.
[86] Robert D. Putamn, "What Makes Democracy Work?" *National Civic Review* 82 (Spring 1993): 101–7.
[87] Robert D. Putamn, "Bowling Alone: America's Declining Social Capital," *Current* 373 (June 1995): 4.
[88] Ibid., p. 4.
[89] David D. Laitin, *Hegemony and Culture: Politics and Religious Change Among the Yoruba* (Chicago: University of Chicago Press, 1986), p. 175.

what is up for discussion and what not, and which societies fail to do that? How do forms of engagement with others whom one encounters only fleetingly become established? All societies have multiple sites of jurisgenesis, law creation, but which ones have some dovetailing of the understanding of what is proper and appropriate public behavior? Unfortunately, we do not yet have answers to these questions, so essential for understanding the cohesion of states.

What we can say at this point is that the public space in modern times has been marked by three related characteristics, all of which have complicated the ability of societies to create and maintain a semblance of social solidarity. First, the *rules for engagement in the public space have been constantly renegotiated.* Urbanization, migration, tourism, mass media, and women's liberation, among other powerful processes, all have repeatedly introduced new groups and individuals into the public space as well as different ideas of proper modes of interaction. In short, the public space has continued to expand dramatically. That never-ending process has put tremendous pressure on social stability and solidarity. In some cases, the new faces in the public space have assimilated into existing conventions; at other times, they have successfully induced changes in the existing ways of doing things to accommodate them; and, in still other instances, they have precipitated fierce struggles over who should rightfully participate in the public sphere and whose conventions will prevail. These conventions may include everything from how to behave when two people are walking directly toward each other on the sidewalk (who gives way?) to how much emotion to display in a conversation.

Second, *the claim for egalitarianism has energized the entry of new groups into the public space.* Habermas emphasizes the importance of bourgeois society in the creation of the public sphere and the notion, mentioned earlier, that in egalitarian space, arguments and not statuses determine decisions.[90] Once introduced, the idea of equal claims on the right to participate in and shape the conventions of the public space is insidious. It did not end with the demands of the bourgeois stratum, by any means. Whatever a group's social basis for participation in the public sphere, whether class, gender, ethnicity, or some other, it has used the claim of equality to challenge others' feelings of entitlement to dominate public space. And that has been a very powerful demand indeed.

---

[90] Habermas, *The Structural Transformation of the Public Sphere*, p. 23.

Third, *egalitarian assertions have precipitated counterclaims, leading to contentious struggles about who properly belongs in the public space.* In some of the most intense struggles, such as the fight over slavery in the United States or the Taliban's campaign against women in Afghanistan or the mutual claims for exclusion among ethnic groups in the former Yugoslavia, the state actually did disintegrate in the process. In all cases of claims and counterclaims, severe pressure was put on the unity of society. Why some societies could reconstitute their public space and develop practices that could continue or reestablish social unity is a question that we cannot yet answer. But it is one that holds great import for states and their ability to remain intact.

Conclusion

International factors, such as the globalization of capital and the actions of United Nations agencies, have both buffeted and sustained the state. But any thoroughgoing explanation of why so many states have avoided collapse and stayed intact must deal with issues beyond these systemic, environmental factors. We must look to the actual relations between states and those they purport to govern. Organizational theorists point us toward social exchange, where individuals trade loyalty for selective access to public goods. Underlying this notion is an understanding that the state's efficient allocation of goods in that exchange will enhance its chances for survival. While that is a very helpful notion, it still leaves us wondering how so many grossly inefficient states continue to withstand disintegrative forces. How do states sustain loyalty and compliance even when their delivery systems falter?

Our answer starts with the dictum that "the heart has its reasons which the mind does not suspect."[91] The argument here has implied a realm of feelings and implicit understandings that go beyond rational calculation. Relying exclusively on provision of services or material goods to its population, whether directly through a complex bureaucracy or indirectly through an umbrella for patron-client ties, is a flimsy foundation for states. Their staying ability will ultimately rest on how well they tie into people's hearts.

Where states have tapped into the creation of shared meaning in society, they have become naturalized, and the thought of their dissolution or

---

[91] Shils, *Center and Periphery*, p. 135.

disappearance has become unimaginable. That shared sense that the state is as natural as the rivers and the mountains has gone far in combating the effects of disintegrative forces, including the states' own inefficiency. We have identified three areas in which changes in society and the nature of ensuing state-society relations can bolster or batter the cohesion of the state. The three are the generation of law in society, the sharing of public rituals between state and society, and the ongoing renegotiation of the rules of informal behavior in the public sphere.

What we cannot say at this point is under what conditions changes in these areas will work to keep the state intact. What we can suggest is how they can work to sustain the state. First, the three areas of state-society engagement can both *alert* state officials to important changes in society – to *who is participating*, to *what practices are emerging*, and to *what import or meaning the changes hold* – and *induce* the state to adapt to the reconstitution of society. Second, changes in *participants*, *practices*, and *meaning* can lead, at times, to more social solidarity or unity, enhancing the unquestioned presence of the state. More than that, states can provide symbols, forums, and institutions that can increase the chances that social changes will dovetail to create social solidarity. Third, these sorts of changes, when they do dovetail, can increase social stability. Informal practices in the public sphere and other forms of non-state law can lead to greater public civility and tranquility, further enhancing the state. Finally, these practices can seriously lighten the burden on the state. A state like one envisioned by Hobbes, responsible for all social security, would simply be stretched too thin. Where non-state practices provide security in their own right, the state is in a position to marshal and deploy its scarce resources more successfully.

Can we expect changes in informal practices and in the groups clamoring to be heard in the public space to help states remain intact or hurt them? From Habermas on, a dark pessimism has pervaded discussions of changes in the public sphere and the future of (democratic) states. In the United States, in particular, expressions of the deterioration of the public sphere have been commonplace.[92] One encounters

---

[92] For example, see: Ray Oldenburg, *The Great Good Place: Cafés, Coffee Shops, Community Centers, Beauty Parlors, General Stores, Bars, Hangouts and How They Get You Through the Day* (New York: Paragon House, 1989); Robert D. Putamn, "Tuning in, Tuning Out: The Strange Disappearance of Social Capital in America," *PS: Political Science and Politics* 27 (December 1995): 664–83.

foreboding book titles, like *The Fall of Public Man*,[93] or references to the "American trauma."[94]

My own inclination is to be more cautious about proclaiming an imminent apocalypse or even a slow deterioration of a public space that can produce social solidarity. It is tempting to view the public sphere as beleaguered, in part because it is an area of ongoing renegotiation, contestation, and struggle. Present-day clashes take on an ominous cast and precipitate a nostalgia for some idyllic past, when the public sphere was really a civil space.

It is doubtful that such a heartwarming past did exist in the period from the industrial revolution on. But, more than that, those characteristics of contestation and struggle also give the public space countless possibilities for rebirth and new vigor. Claims and counterclaims surrounding the public sphere signal and spur parts of the state to change themselves and to renegotiate their coalitions with segments of society. Encounters in the public space also goad some in the state to nudge diverse social changes in common directions, building complementarities rather than fostering divisions. Out of these processes may come reinvigorated states. Focusing on these sorts of state-society relations in the future should give us an indication of when that happens and when it does not.

[93] Richard Sennett, *The Fall of Public Man* (New York: Knopf, 1977).
[94] Martin E. Marty, *The One and the Many: America's Struggle for the Common Good* (Cambridge, MA: Harvard University Press, 1997).

PART IV

Linking Micro- and Macro-Level Change

6

Individual Change in the Midst of Social and Political Change

Scholarly writing about rapid political and social changes, especially in the Third World, has had a Janus-faced quality. Some scholars focused on macro-level topics, dealing with changes at the structural or organizational level. Much of the research labeled political development, social and political modernization, economic development, and dependency was pitched at this level. Others concentrated on the individual as the key to the direction and content of rapid societal change. Rarely did a single work seriously attempt to join the two levels of analysis.

Frequently authors writing on one level would do little more than acknowledge the problems and complexities on the other. More often than not, scholars dealing with macro-level topics shrouded the subject of individual change in implicit assumptions instead of explicit assertions. Or, at times, they put forth ideas of individual change based on purely mechanistic notions of individuals as rational actors, who engage in simple cost-benefit calculations.[1] Those focusing on the level of the individual likewise made simple assumptions about complex macro-level political and social changes.

Every theory of social and political change must have a corresponding model of individual change: There is no social change without individual change and vice versa. The gap between the two levels of analysis has led to some curious developments. Whereas the literature on macro-level change written in the several decades after World War II has come under severe attack leading to new approaches to the subject, the literature on individual change in the throes of rapid social and political

---

[1] See, for example, Samuel L. Popkin, *The Rational Peasant* (Berkeley: University of California Press, 1979).

transformation has suffered much less from such a relentless and wide-spread assault. As a result, models of change in the individual's outlook and motivation for action have not kept pace with knowledge about macro-level changes in societies in Africa, Asia, and Latin America since the 1950s.

This article has two purposes. First is to show the progression of thinking about, and the intellectual influences on, the subject of individual change in the context of third-world studies. The second is to demonstrate how that thinking failed to provide an adequate complement to what was learned about macro-level change. It will be argued that the abandonment of theories that divide types of societies and polities into simple dichotomies, such as traditional and modern, has not led to a corresponding reassessment of the nature of individual change. As a result, newer approaches to the study of rapid social and political change have rested on inadequate micro-theoretical foundations, ones that rely much too strongly on the concept of a unified personality.

Daniel Lerner and the Beginnings of a Model of Individual Change

One of the earliest and most influential books linking micro- and macro-level change in the Third World was Daniel Lerner's, *The Passing of Traditional Society*. In his path-breaking analysis, Lerner argued that virtually all "modernizing" societies have begun to copy the process of social and political change in the West.[2] What lay behind the West's modernization? To answer that question, Lerner turned to the character of Western man – what he termed the "mobile personality." People with such personalities "come to see the social future as manipulable rather than ordained and their personal prospects in terms of achievement rather than heritage."[3] The chief characteristic of "modern" people – those with mobile personalities – is empathy, the ability to perceive oneself in the situations of others. Empathy marks modern personalities, and a sufficient number of people with empathy lead society as a whole to be industrial, urban, literate, and participant.

Several key assumptions went into Lerner's understanding of the basis for change in people's outlook and motivation. These assumptions are

[2] Daniel Lerner, *The Passing of Traditional Society* (New York: Free Press, 1958), p. 46.
[3] Ibid., p. 48.

174

worth mentioning because they played a prominent role in many subsequent theories, too, as will be seen shortly.

(1) Individuals reach a *critical psychological threshold*, triggering massive changes in internal personal motivations. In essence, there are only two psychological states for the individual – in Lerner's case, empathetic and nonempathetic – and they are mutually exclusive. Either one has it or not. Just as Lerner saw change in the entire society as "systemic" (modernity as a "syndrome"), so too is change in the individual. People move from one syndrome of motivations to another. Reaching the critical psychological threshold triggers changes in all one's values and general outlook as well as behavioral changes in all aspects of one's life, including economics, family, politics, and so on.

(2) These psychological changes are *unidirectional*. Just as he could not conceive of whole societies becoming more "traditional," so too could he not imagine people becoming less empathetic. Once one reaches the critical threshold, there is no backsliding.

(3) Major psychological adaptation comes in only *limited periods* in people's lives. For most writers, this assumption simply meant that people are likely to change greatly in response to outside stimuli only when they are children, through childhood socialization.[4] Lerner rejected implicitly the idea that childhood is the only time one can change so drastically. But he did accept the idea of there existing only limited periods of adaptation. In Lerner's view, adults are capable of major internal change through massive exposure to new and different life-styles, usually via the mass media. In short, he saw "traditional man" as extremely malleable for a one-time, particular type of change, that is, gaining a mobile personality, when subjected to the proper stimuli.

(4) Lerner also differed with so-called behavioralists and those stressing childhood socialization in the way in which he divorced psychological change from people's individual life experiences. Instead of looking at the psychological impact of one's daily experiences, such as schooling, interaction with parents, occupational

---

[4] For eample, Easton and Hess argue that political socialization is largely completed by the time one is in the eighth grade. David Easton and Robert Hess, "Youth and Political System," in Seymour Martin Lipset and Leo Lowenthal (eds.), *Culture and Social Character* (Glencoe, IL: Free Press, 1961), p. 240.

experiences, or interaction based on social class, Lerner chose to focus on vicarious experiences. Lerner seemed to take very seriously the saying that the silver screen (and radio speaker?) is bigger than life. For Lerner, one's accumulated social history would make little difference in one's orientation to new values and modes of behavior. It is not surprising, then, that on a societal level Lerner had an acultural and ahistorical understanding of change. The structure of "tradition," whether in terms of certain patterns of beliefs and values or in terms of the way social life is organized, simply has no bearing on the direction, content, or rate of change. He saw saturation by the mass media, for all classes of people, as the important factor in precipitating change toward "modernity."

As a sociologist writing on individual change, Lerner drew on important intellectual trends in the field of psychology that gained preeminence in the 1950s and 1960s. Jean Piaget's work, for example, was first widely disseminated in the United States in the 1950s. Lawrence Kohlberg also began developing his theory in the mid-1950s. Both downplayed people's different life experiences in their writings on cognitive and moral development in favor of culturally universal processes.[5] Kohlberg portrayed individual moral change as unidirectional and teleological, coming in six specified sequential stages.[6]

[5] This is not to say that their theories are purely "maturational." They are not. They also reject the other extreme, a learning (behavioristic) model. Kohlberg stated that the cognitive developmental approach to socialization takes a middle position, emphasizing the interaction between innate structures and the environment. There is no doubt, however, that in concern for finding "developmental universals," the stress is on the "organism structuring tendencies," which are in stages and which assimilate the environmental inputs. See Lawrence Kohlberg, "Stage and Sequence: The Cognitive Developmental Approach to Socialization," in David A. Groslin (ed.), *Handbook of Socialization Theory and Research* (Chicago: Rand McNally, 1969), pp. 348–52. For a second critique of Kohlberg's notion that these changes take place during childhood only, see Todd Isao Endo, "The Relevance of Kohlberg's Stages of Moral Development to Research in Political Socialization," Ph.D. dissertation, School of Education, Harvard University, 1973.

[6] "There are six forms of thinking and they constitute an invariant sequence of stages in each culture." Lawrence Kohlberg, "Education for Justice: A Modern Statement of the Platonic View," in James M. Gustafson (ed.), *Moral Education* (Cambridge, MA: Harvard University Press, 1970), p. 70. Kohlberg did some work on a seventh stage as well. Also, he admitted to some temporary backsliding, but that is inconsequential to the larger process. Moral development, like political development, may be arrested, but there is a strong prescriptive element in Kohlberg, not unlike that found in Lerner and other writers in political development, that the highest stage is the best stage. See Ben Zingman, "Lawrence Kohlberg: Morality *sans* Community," unpublished paper, p. 18. Note a similar

Moral and cognitive development theories relied heavily in their assumptions on another important psychological theory of the 1950s, the theory of cognitive dissonance.[7] In simple terms, the dissonance one encounters in facing difficult moral or cognitive contradictions forces the person to a resolution at a higher stage of moral or cognitive development, if at the present stage one cannot resolve those contradictions.

Theories of cognitive dissonance include an important assumption about the human personality: that there is an overriding need for consistency of principles in the diverse aspects of an individual's life.[8] This assumption draws from John Dewey's notions of rationality, including the "office of deliberation" whose purpose "is to resolve entanglements in existing activity, restore continuity, recover harmony, utilize loose impulse and redirect habit."[9] For the sake of shorthand, one can term this the "unity of personality" principle. Note Kohlberg's statement:

There is a fundamental unity of personality organization and development termed the ego, or the self. While there are various strands of social development (psychosexual development, moral development, etc.), these strands are united by their common reference to a single concept of self in a single social world.[10]

A. H. Maslow, whose landmark book, *Motivation and Personality*, was published in 1954, also started with a premise of the unity of personality and a limited number of distinct personality levels or stages.[11] These fundamental needs or goals are in a hierarchical relationship so that a person

---

tendency to conceptualize in terms of mutually exclusive stages in theories of cognitive change in O. J. Harvey, David E. Hunt, and Harold M. Schroder, "Stages of Conceptual Development" in Edward E. Sampson (ed.), *Approaches, Contexts, and Problems of Social Psychology* (Englewood Cliffs, NJ: Prentice-Hall, 1964), pp. 16–26.

[7] Leon Festinger, *A Theory of Cognitive Dissonance* (Palo Alto, CA: Stanford University Press, 1957).

[8] See Ronald Duska and Mariellen Whelen, *Moral Development* (New York: Paulist Press, 1975), chap. 1. Festinger, *A Theory of Cognitive Dissonance*, p. 1, states that individuals strive for internal consistency. "In short, I am proposing that dissonance, that is, the existence of nonfitting relations among cognitions, is a motivating factor in its own right" (p. 3).

[9] John Dewey, *Human Nature and Conduct: An Introduction to Social Psychology* (New York: Henry Holt, 1992), p. 199.

[10] Kohlberg, "Stage and Sequence," p. 349 (Kohlberg's emphasis).

[11] Abraham H. Maslow, *Motivation and Personality* (New York: Harper, 1954). Maslow was much more careful than most other theorists in qualifying his notions about the integration of the person and the hierarchy of his levels. He specifically wrote that organisms usually behave as integrated wholes but that sometimes they do not (p. 75). Also, he said that most needs are satisfied in the sequence of levels he presented, but there also may be reversals of the hierarchy (p. 98).

does not seek a higher level goal until he has satisfied his needs at the next lower level.

Although in his development of the theory Maslow did not have available the concept of cognitive dissonance, he effectively worked out a similar concept himself in his own language. He talked of "a new discontent and restlessness" that characterizes a person who has satisfied his needs at the first four levels and feels impelled to move on to the next level.[12] Maslow, then, subscribed to the assumption of the importance of a critical threshold in the process of personal change. Once a person satisfies all his needs at any level, he reaches a new threshold that catapults him to the next motivational level. Maslow wrote, "Another peculiar characteristic of the human organism when it is dominated by a certain need is that the whole philosophy of the future tends also to change."[13] That is, one's total outlook reflects one's motivational level. And, finally, for Maslow personality development has a certain universality (or, as he writes, "relative unity") that minimizes the roles of social history and culture as important factors in understanding individual change.[14]

Lerner's understanding of the emergence of the mobile personality rested upon the same sorts of assumptions found in the schools of psychology of the period that Kohlberg and Maslow represented. Elements that go into making up a traditional person, Lerner implied, simply cannot coexist within an individual's mind with the elements of a modern person. Such coexistence would be anomalous, an unbearable contradiction in the individual's mind. Exposure to wholly different life-styles forces the individual to a resolution involving a new, higher state. Important changes in social-political life, then, come about when there are sufficient numbers of mobile personalities. These personalities, in turn, emerge once people reach the critical threshold where cognitive dissonance forces them to find new means of resolution. The unity of personality principle means that

---

[12] Maslow, *Motivation and Personality*, p. 91. Elsewhere, he expresses this concept for all the levels as "a hierarchy of relative prepotency" (p. 83).

[13] Ibid., p. 82.

[14] Ibid., p. 101. Erik H. Erikson, *Childhood and Society* (second edition; New York: W. W. Norton, 1963), was developing his psychosocial theory at the same time Maslow was writing *Motivation and Personality* (*Childhood and Society* was first published in 1950). Erikson was much more sensitive to historical factors and their effect upon personality development, but he shared some of the same assumptions of unidirectionality, stages, and thresholds. He wrote, "The human personality in principle develops according to steps predetermined in the growing person's readiness to be driven toward, to be aware of, and to interact with, a widening social radius" (p. 270).

people do not keep bits of their traditional personalities while assimilating new bits of a mobile personality; the modem personality reflects an integrated syndrome of principles, a "whole philosophy of the future."

Such a model of individual change has had some unfortunate results for the study of social and political change in the Third World. Scholars subscribing to Lerner's assumption all too often have viewed people caught in the bombardment of new stimuli, especially those emanating from the West, in rather undifferentiated terms – with little regard for social class or other factors (having to do with their day-to-day experiences and relationships). They have seen change as unidirectional, coming in a rather integrated package for individuals as they cross the critical threshold taking them from a lower stage (traditional) to a higher one (modern).

Lerner's important book set the tone in the late 1950s and 1960s for studies of the individual in the new fields of political development and social modernization: academics studied change as a process of diffusion, with the mass media (or other stimuli) triggering broad internal changes in individual after individual. The transformed individuals constituted the raw material needed for a modern, developed, participatory society. Diffusion implies no major obstacles; it implies no discontinuities, it leaves no room for violence or losers; it understands no differentiations among the different segments of society.

The Probelmatic Nature and Selectivity of Individual Change: Theories of Lucian W. Pye and David McClelland

By the mid-1960s, the mounting evidence on the unevenness and difficulty of individual change led to new theories stressing not the universality of individual change, but rather its problematic nature and its selectivity. Lucian W. Pye, for example, dealt with the psychological makeup of people who did not fit well into either of Lerner's categories of traditional or modern.[15] His Burmese administrators existed in a netherworld called transitional society – another of those huge residual categories the field seems to spawn. Pye dropped the assumption of a critical threshold and looked upon the dilemmas facing the individual, not in terms of an immediate resolution at a higher level, but as the basis for profound personal insecurities. He also dispensed with the assumptions of limited

---

[15] Lucian W. Pye, *Politics, Personality, and Nation-Building* (New Haven: Yale University Press, 1962).

periods of psychological adaptation and the separation of psychological change from people's individual life experiences. The administrators in postcolonial Burma faced two major contradictory processes of socialization: their socialization in the family, primarily childhood socialization, and that associated with their roles in the bureaucracy.

For Pye, the difficulties in personal change spelled trouble at the institutional level. The creation of effective organizations depends fundamentally upon the capacity of individuals to associate with one another.[16] It was personality traits that arrested "development" in Burma through their negative impact on people's ability to relate to co-workers. For Pye, lack of coherence in socialization patterns created a weakened sense of identity for the Burmese and thus an inability to lend direction and initiative to their roles.

Pye thus introduced a new complexity into the understanding of individuals and how personal change relates to larger social and political transformation. He no longer portrayed them simply in terms of two states, empathetic and nonempathetic, with a clear threshold separating them. Pye looked closely at the continuing life experiences of individuals, particularly their political recruitment and subsequent socialization. One's recruitment, training, and role as an administrator had important effects on personality and capacities for larger political and social change.

Nevertheless, Pye's very choice of language limited his divergence from some of the assumptions of the previous decade. The concept "transitional" strongly implies a way station between the traditional and the modern. It is transitory, impermanent. Only for the transitional stage did Pye relax the assumption of the unity of personality. And, even there, he represented that stage as one of psychological distress. The complexities and insecurities Pye described do not present a new path that must be studied in a new light, but simply a lag in the unidirectional, teleological process that was already familiar.

Whereas Pye focused on the problematic nature of individual change, David C. McClelland looked at its selectivity.[17] The obstacles to the rapid recasting of third-world societies along Western lines compelled writers to reexamine their assumptions about the inevitability and universality of such transformations. Two types of interpretations appeared in the late 1950s and early 1960s: some countries or groups within countries suffered from either a deficient economic structure or a deficient value

---

[16] Ibid., pp. 51–2.
[17] David C. McClelland, *The Achieving Society* (New York: The Free Press, 1961).

system.[18] McClelland is the paramount example of one who looked to a deficient value system. Although his concern was to explain the basis (or lack of a basis) for economic growth, McClelland saw the economic question as an indicator for the growth and decline of entire civilizations. Much in the vein of others who have looked at the individual to explain larger patterns of organizational capabilities, he wrote, "It would certainly not surprise us to discover that these forces lie largely in man himself – in his fundamental motives and in the way he organizes his relationships to his fellow man."[19]

Like Maslow, McClelland turned to motivations of behavior or personality "needs." But, rather than speaking of the total personality and broad integrative needs on different levels, as Maslow did, he looked at a narrower and less universal motivation, the "need for Achievement," or what he called *n* Achievement. His argument is that those societies that have succeeded at certain periods in achieving high economic growth are the ones that have inculcated in their children high *n* Achievement, that is, high motivation to achieve.

McClelland, while denying the inevitability or unidirectionality of change toward a high-growth, technologically sophisticated society, still maintained a number of the earlier assumptions. Psychological adaptation, for instance, is limited to a circumscribed period in the individual's life. In fact, McClelland focused almost entirely on childhood socialization and its decisive impact in shaping the individual.[20] Also, he continued to rely heavily on a critical threshold and two-state image of the individual – either one has the need to achieve or not – and he continued to assume the unity of personality so that traits in one state were seen as incompatible with traits in the other. He rejected out of hand the idea that "societies can *both* retain their traditional values *and* develop economically."[21]

Although McClelland cited numerous historical examples and stressed that different contexts are associated with different personal motivations, his theory turns out to be, in a disquieting way, very ahistorical. He did

---

[18] Daniel Chirot, *Social Change in the Twentieth Century* (New York: Harcourt Brace Jovanovich, 1977), p. 2.

[19] McClelland, *The Achieving Society*, p. 3.

[20] Ibid. In Chapter 10, "Accelerating Economic Growth," McClelland indicated a number of ways in which high *n* Achievement may be induced. Most of these are tied in to his stress on the main source of *n* Achievement he has identified, child-rearing practices (see Chapter 9), but a small number suggest the possibility of adult change under certain stringent conditions.

[21] Ibid., p. 394 (McClelland's emphasis).

not relate major changes in class relations, resources, and technology to changing motivations. In this sense, history is neutral. Instead, he resorted to "explaining" change in motivation in certain societies by pointing to changes in the will of groups to achieve: "What each generation wanted above all, it got."[22]

New and Unsettling Findings

New, empirical research sprouted in the late 1960s and the 1970s from practically all of the social sciences and dealt with nearly all of the areas of the Third World. A number of these researchers seemed unaware that their results were challenging some of the accepted tenets concerning the nature of rapid change, especially the models of individual change. Some went so far as to claim that they were supporting that body of literature, while, in fact, their results raised fundamental questions about the principles on which that literature was built. Many, certainly, were not focusing directly on the question of individual psychology, but their results pointed to the inadequacy of older theories, even those that had addressed the problematic nature and relativity of personal change. The use of their material as a basis for criticism of the dominant theories, then, must rest in large part on inferences. A few examples of the new research on different parts of the Third World will illustrate the problems that their findings raised for the existing models of individual change.

India's complex social structure and culture provide a rich hunting ground for discovering patterns of change that did not sit well with the dominant theories. As early as 1952, M. N. Srinivas, India's outstanding social anthropologist, introduced the concept of Sanskritization. In brief, "Sanskritization is the process by which a 'low' Hindu caste, or tribal or other group, changes its customs, ritual, ideology, and way of life in the direction of a high, and frequently, 'twice-born' caste."[23] It involves the adoption by lower castes of the customs and ways of life of higher castes, emphasizing ideas and values found in Sanskrit literature.

As Srinivas pointed out, one of the interesting contradictions following the advent of British colonial rule and its vast acceleration of social change was that, as the Brahmins became more and more "Westernized," the other

---

[22] Ibid., p. 437.

[23] M. N. Srinivas, *Social Change in Modern India* (Berkeley: University of California Press, 1966), 6.

castes became more and more Sanskritized.[24] Not only has change on a group level not seemed to be unidirectional or replicated from group to group in India, but even within individuals the pattern of change has seemed to be more complex than reflected in the theories surveyed above. Srinivas indicated, for example, that the Brahmins themselves became the filter through which Western traits were transmitted to the rest of the population, but those same Brahmins also found some of the Western ways difficult to accept.[25]

Srinivas's findings were path-breaking in several ways. Rapid environmental change after contact with the West, he found, could strengthen old social institutions, such as caste, rather than weaken them.[26] The breakdown of old social commitments by the individual was not a necessary result of rapid change in other spheres.[27] Collective behavior (as in collective social mobility), with its maintenance of strong ties to kinship and other so-called traditional groups could become more important than any process of individualization. Increased religiosity could result instead of secularization.

These findings could undermine notions of mutually exclusive syndromes of motivation and a critical threshold catapulting the person into a whole new philosophy of the future. Despite the fact that Srinivas wrote about his findings as early as the 1950s, they did not contribute to a challenge of models of personal or institutional change until the latter portion of the 1960s. And, even then, the challenge was largely to the usefulness of modernization theory at the structural and organizational level. Assumptions about individual psychology and change were only infrequently linked to these social findings. Only in 1966 did Joseph R. Gusfield, a sociologist studying India, begin to challenge modernization theories directly and to question the then accepted view that "tradition" and innovation are necessarily in conflict.[28] Even Gusfield, however,

---

[24] M. N. Srinivas, *Caste in Modern India and Other Essays* (Bombay: Asia Publishing House, 1962), Chap. 2.

[25] Ibid. For some analogies to Sanskritization in an Egyptian case, see Hussein M. Fahim, "Change in Religion in a Resettled Nubian Community, Upper Egypt," *International Journal of Middle East Studies* 4 (1973): 163–77.

[26] Srinivas, *Caste in Modern India*, Chap. 1.

[27] On the breakdown of old commitments, see Karl W. Deutsch, "Social Mobilization and Political Development," *American Political Science Review* 55 (1961): 493–514.

[28] Joseph R. Gusfield, "Tradition and Modernity: Misplaced Polarities in the Study of Social Change," *American Journal of Sociology* 72 (November 1966): 351–62. Also writing on this theme were Lloyd I. Rudolph and Suzanne H. Rudolph, *The Modernity of Tradition* (Chicago: University of Chicago Press, 1967).

looked only at fallacies on the level of structural and organizational analysis and not on the level of the individual.

Even more than with India, area specialists studying China seemed unconcerned with theories aimed at explaining universal processes of change.[29] Only in the early 1970s did several major works emerge that challenged directly some of the old assumptions in models of change. G. William Skinner's well-known article, "Chinese Peasants and the Closed Community," for example, led one to question the assumptions of the unidirectionality of change, of limited periods of psychological adaptation, and of the separation of individual change from people's life experiences.[30] Historically, Skinner asserted, peasant villages were not simply closed self-sufficient units but were responsive to external opportunities and dangers, leading them to become either more open or more closed. Skinner asserted that significant changes occurred in the normative sphere (the first sphere to be strengthened in the face of dangers, the last to be relaxed in the face of new opportunities).[31] In times of outside instability, people became less tolerant of normative deviations and more resistant to outside cultural influences. Individual openness to innovation, then, was not simply related to vicarious experiences (Lerner) or to cultural values acquired in childhood (McClelland) but also to one's changing life experiences. Moreover, individual change could be either in the direction of greater tolerance to innovations or in the direction of intolerance. People's outlooks and needs were not fixed.[32]

---

[29] G. William Skinner, "Chinese Peasants and the Closed Community: An Open and Shut Case," *Comparative Studies in Society and History* 13 (July 1971): 270–81. Skinner asked why students of China's peasantry were silent on the theoretical issues concerning peasantry: "In part, it is because we are so few and too preoccupied with our own peasants to have time for anybody else's. More to the point, however, the whole body of inherited anthropological wisdom concerning peasantries seems somehow alien and irrelevant to students of Chinese society" (270). A rule of thumb may be that the more difficult a language for area studies (and thus the more time social scientists have to devote language skills), the less likely are those area studies to be tied into broader theoretical thinking in the field.

[30] Ibid.

[31] Ibid., p. 278.

[32] For a look at the other end of China's social structure – the intellectuals – see Benjamin Schwartz, "The Limits of 'Tradition Versus Modernity' as Categories of Explanation: The Case of the Chinese Intellectuals," *Daedalus* 101 (1972): 83. Schwartz's line of thinking suggested that one reason individual change – whether of Indian Brahmins or Chinese intellectuals – occurred in such unexpected patterns was because there might be less real dissonance causing tension between the categories than previously believed.

Perhaps, of all the regions of the Third World, Africa presented some of the most unsettling evidence in terms of the accepted assumptions about the individual in the midst of rapid social change. J. Clyde Mitchell's essay on the Kalela dance is among the best works on personal change.[33] He found that in the mid-1950s, as southern African blacks urbanized, they did not adopt a broad territorial identity (as Europeans had presumably done previously), nor did they drop their tribal identities. On the contrary, tribalism seemed to be on the upswing as tribal dancing became a prominent feature of city life throughout southern Africa.

Much of the dancing was in the form of organized recreation in which teams of dancers competed weekly. Christian men, who often worked as unskilled laborers during the week, pulled together artifacts from two diverse worlds in their Sunday and holiday dances. They dressed for the dance in sharp European-style clothes. Their accompaniments were huge drums made out of forty-two-gallon oil drums covered with cowhide. At times the dancing was punctuated by the shrill blowing of a football whistle. Teams sang distinctive songs, not in their native languages, but in the language of the urban area. In the songs, they praised their own lands and origins and lampooned those of other tribes. The dancers on each team ignored the significant differences in their rural origins in order to assert their unity vis-à-vis all the other tribes of the urban area. Mitchell wrote of the situation:

In other words, we are presented with an apparent paradox. The dance is clearly a tribal dance in which tribal differences are emphasized but the language and the idiom of the songs and the dress of the dancers are drawn from an urban existence which tends to submerge tribal differences.[34]

The paradox is even stronger, for the Africans resorted at times to tribalism (as in the dance competitions) and at other times organized along more modern, social-class lines. Mitchell addressed the paradox by noting that "it is impossible to generalize operation of these principles without reference to the *specific social situation* in which the interaction takes place."[35] When dealing with Europeans, the Africans frequently ignored

---

[33] J. Clyde Mitchell, *The Kalela Dance*, Rhodes-Livingstone Papers No. 27 (New York: Humanities Press, 1956). Another author who dealt with issues in Africa challenging much of the dominant theory is C. S. Whitaker. See Whitaker, "A Dysrhythmic Process of Political Change," *World Politics* 19 (January 1967): 190–217.

[34] Mitchell, *The Kalela Dance*, p. 9.

[35] Ibid., p. 43 (emphasis added).

both social class and tribal differences and identified with others according to skin color. Within specific tribal associations, class differences played a major role. And, in the context of social interactions among urbanized Africans, tribal differences were paramount. "The fact that tribalism emerges as a significant category of interaction only in certain situations, may help to explain some of the apparent contradictions which acute observers have noted from time to time."[36]

Mitchell's findings, like those of Srinivas, did not have an immediate impact. Taken together, however, their work, combined with countless other empirical studies in all parts of the Third World during the 1960s and early 1970s, brought into question the established theories of social change, especially modernization theories. Unfortunately, critics most often ignored the implications of the evidence on models describing individual change in outlook and motivations. Yet, a close look at that evidence brought into question existing models, which simply did not allow for an interpretation of the individual that was as situational as Mitchell and others implied was necessary – where the individual utilizes different principles for interactions in different social situations. Certainly, the two-state, critical threshold assumptions seemed woefully inadequate. The fundamental assumption of the unity of personality – of a single self in a single social world – did not fit the wave of new accounts coming from all parts of the Third World. Neither were theories of "lag" very helpful. The tribes in Mitchell's study were not mere vestiges. They differed radically in function and organization from those that the urban laborers had left behind in the countryside. These new urban tribes were very much a part of the new semi-industrial city. A new individual seems to emerge who is very responsive and adaptive to his life experiences – in Mitchell's case to the unfortunate mixture of classes, tribes, and races – and who seems to be changing in ways inadequately explained by stages, threshold, unidirectionality, and limited periods of psychological adaptation.

Becoming Modern: Another Attempt at Understanding Individual Change

In the mid-1970s, after almost a decade of anticipation by the scholarly community, came the publication of *Becoming Modern* by Alex Inkeles and David H. Smith. The book was the culmination of perhaps the most

---

[36] Ibid., p. 43.

massive study of individual change ever undertaken. It reflected the monumental task of administering almost six thousand interviews in six countries and analyzing the mass of data that came from those interviews.[37] The aim of the book, as described by the authors, was deceptively simple: "*It seemed to us there was no more relevant and challenging task for social psychology than to explain the process whereby people move from being traditional to becoming modern personalities.*"[38]

The task was more than to reproduce on a grand scale the assumptions and principles of the earlier literature dealing with the individual in the midst of rapid social changes. It sought, rather, to overcome some of the shortcomings that had become increasingly obvious. Inkeles and Smith stressed the critical interaction between the person and essential components of his or her environment, especially as that environment changes. They found, for example, that the longer people are employed in factories or attend schools (regardless of the quality of education), the more likely they are to score highly on their scales of overall modernity (OM). They thus dropped or disproved a number of accepted assumptions including such beliefs as (a) the exclusive importance of childhood socialization, (b) the view of personal adaptation as coming only in limited periods, and (c) the understanding of personal change as divorced from real life experiences. In addition, there was no assumption that exposure to the diverse attributes of tradition and modernity creates lags or transitional types who are psychologically distressed individuals. They found, instead, "that the more modern the individual, the better his psychic adjustment."[39]

At first look, then, *Becoming Modern* not only did away with some of the earlier untenable assumptions in the field, but it presented a mountain of evidence to support its own approach. In fact, the authors, in their best performance, claimed to explain an incredible 62 percent of the variance in individual modernity.[40]

From the point of view of seeking a basis from which to understand complex individual change in the midst of rapid social change, however, there are fundamental problems in the design and findings of the project.

---

[37] Alex Inkeles and David H. Smith, *Becoming Modern* (Cambridge, MA: Harvard University Press, 1974). The six countries were Argentina, Chile, East Pakistan, India, Israel, and Nigeria.

[38] Ibid., p. 5 (emphasis in original).

[39] Ibid., p. 264.

[40] "The multiple correlation between our small set of basic explanatory variables and individual modernity scores went as high as 79." (Ibid., p. 7).

OM is a measure, based on a pool of 166 items from the questionnaire, which consists of twenty-four subthemes, ranging from political activism to religious-secular orientation.[41] The high intercorrelation of the items and subthemes reinforced the authors' belief that modernity is a syndrome. The syndrome of modernity carries with it all the baggage of the assumption of the unity of personality. Inkeles and Smith are back once more to a two-state psychological theory – in this case, traditional man and modern man – in which change is unilinear from one to the other. And, although change from modern to traditional is conceivably possible, Inkeles and Smith wrote of a single direction for individual change, from traditional to modern.

How is it possible that such an empirically grounded study seemed to contradict the new and unsettling evidence (collected in the decade and more before the book's publication)? How could it ignore the critique of the unity of personality principle, the idea of a single self in a single social world, implied by works that demonstrated the individual's use of different principles for different social situations? A possible answer is that Inkeles and Smith seem to have been unaware of practically all of that new material. Their bibliography, at least, indicates that they did not read Srinivas before going into the field in India; neither did they consult C. S. Whitaker's writings in their research on Nigeria; nor did they consider the implications of Weingrod's book in their work on Israel.[42] All these works (and many others) indicated not a tight "syndrome" but extreme heterogeneity and eclecticism in personal motivations, outlooks, and behavior. More recent works have all but taken the notion of multiple syndromes for granted: "Across the Middle East, any number of observers have noted patterns of multiple, seemingly conflicting, simultaneously held values, attitudes and professed beliefs."[43] Even when *Becoming Modern* was being formulated, however, there were

---

[41] The subthemes were generated by three "perspectives" that the authors took: the analytic (a coherent viewpoint on modernity, including such items as openness to new experience, orientation to time, etc.), the topical (views on assorted institutions and issues that may be obstacles to modernization such as kinship and family, women's rights, etc.), and the behavioral (behavior reported and behavior tested). Ibid., Chap. 2.

[42] C. S. Whitaker, *The Politics of Tradition: Continuity and Change in Northern Nigeria 1946–1966* (Princeton, NJ: Princeton University Press, 1970); Alex Weingrod, *Reluctant Pioneers* (Ithaca, NY: Cornell University Press, 1966).

[43] Jon W. Anderson, "Sentimental Ambivalence and the Exegesis of 'Self' in Afghanistan," *Anthropological Quarterly* 58 (October 1985): 204.

more than enough data available to suggest alternative understandings of individual change.

The design of the Inkeles and Smith project was simply ill-suited to test for anomalies in individual behavior and altitudes. The figure of 62 percent may explain variance of their test instrument more than actual personal traits. OM is overwhelmingly weighted toward subjective measurement – what people say they believe and what they say they do – rather than giving equal weight to how they really act in different situations. Even the behavioral items are simply what people reported they did on information tests given to them.[44] If individuals indeed do act on different sorts of motivational principles in different situations, then the extremely narrow (or nonexistent) base of observed behavior makes OM a wholly inadequate measure.

The interviews were administered mostly within private rooms in the factory or in similarly private settings wherever possible. The problem, it seems, is not the length of the interview (up to four hours) or the veracity of the answers but the appropriateness of the single research tool, the opinion survey administered in single settings. One reason that *Becoming Modern* was so disappointing is that, as the major work of the decade on individual change, its narrow, single-setting interview technique was unable to test whether individuals use different principles of reasoning – whether they activate different, even conflicting values and moral judgments – in varying situations.

In fact, it can be said that *Becoming Modern* was a major setback for developing a model of individual change that fits the rush of findings in the Third World at the institutional level. It fell back all too easily on worn assumptions of two stages, of unilinearity, of the unity of personality. Even in terms of their own goals, Inkeles and Smith faltered. In the end, the authors said nothing more than the clothes make the person, or, more to the point, one's principal setting determines his or her orientation. This is not to trivialize that finding, for it tells that the ways things are organized help determine the motivation, outlook, and behavior – a very important finding indeed. What it does not do is what Inkeles and Smith

---

[44] They also collected additional independent information on behavior. "However, these supplemental measures were not used systematically in the analysis reported in this book" (Inkeles and Smith, *Becoming Modern*, p. 34). More importantly, these additional measures were collected only on behavior in the factory and thus give us no hint whether there are, in fact, anomalies between behavior in the factory and behavior in outside institutions, such as family or tribe.

promised at the beginning of their book that it would, namely, give a model of individual change in which "thinking and feeling" (the level of the individual) tell things one would not know by looking only at "organizing and doing" (the level of social and political change). If anything, they showed that "thinking and feeling" are mere artifacts of institutional change. If institutions "need" modern people, the conclusion seems to be, then, they produce them – without the fuss of considering "thinking and feeling." The organizational setting – whether factory, school, or agricultural cooperative – is the best independent factor explaining change.[45]

Toward a New Understanding of the Individual and Individual Change

If scholars are to go beyond theories of individual change that give merely a passing nod to "organizing and doing," then they must first ask if there are some generalizations that they can make about the organization of life in societies undergoing rapid social change. In many third-world countries, individuals participate in a variety of organizational settings demanding different sorts of motivations and operating principles. These societies still face conflict among heterogeneous social organizations – from families and tribes all the way to large industrial organizations and the state itself. The environment of conflict within which individuals act is marked by tensions over the most basic values and norms – the rules of the game – that govern even the details of people's lives, including regulations on burials, dining, lending, and much, much more. Although political leaders may suggest that the state is the only legitimate source of authority to establish rules for social behavior, in fact other organizations may set the effective rules of the game in opposition to those put forth by the state.

In such bewildering and fragmented settings, individuals must respond not only to the constraints and opportunities posed by one organization but by many. Some of these organizations exist side by side peacefully, but others are struggling actively with one another over what the rules of the

---

[45] *Becoming Modern* is not the only example of a purported social psychological or cultural approach undermining its own basis for inquiry. For two other examples, see George M. Foster, "Peasant Society and the Image of Limited Good," *American Anthropologist*, 67 (April 1965): 293–315, and F. G. Bailey, "The Peasant View of the Bad Life," *The Advancement of Science* 23 (December 1966): 399–409.

game should be. Individuals thus confront a fundamental lack of coherence in their social worlds, with various organizations proposing contradictory values and modes of behavior. Models that assume a fundamental unity underlying one's actions, feelings, and thoughts are inadequate for explaining the diverse strategies people use in acting within these heterogeneous organizational settings. Many psychologists, at this time, are finding the unity of personality principle equally unsatisfying. "Much of the history of social and personality psychology can be understood as an unsuccessful quest for evidence of psychological unity."[46] In recent research in diverse branches of psychology, "disunity and lack of consistency [have] been a major theme."[47]

If personality unity fails as the basis for understanding individual motivations and behavior, so too does the simple aggregation of individual acts, each arrived at through rational calculation. As Ann Swidler wrote, "There has been an excessive emphasis on the 'unit act,' the notion that people choose their actions piece by piece, striving with each act to maximize a given outcome. Action is necessarily integrated into larger assemblages."[48]

This more complex view of change at the organizational or institutional level can now suggest new directions for understanding individual-level change. A model of individual change must account for how syncretic individuals respond to diverse situations or social worlds with a (limited) variety of concepts of self. As Swidler noted, "Both individuals and groups know how to do different kinds of things in different circumstances."[49] A new model of individual change must point to the conflicting sets of principles and values people call upon as states and other social organizations with different rules of the game battle in an environment of conflict.

---

[46] William B. Swann, Jr., John J. Griffin, Jr., Steven C. Predmore, and Bebe Gines, "The Cognitive-Affective Crossfire: When Self-Consistency Confronts Self-Enhancement," *Journal of Personality and Social Psychology* 52 (May 1987): 887.

[47] Ibid.

[48] Ann Swidler, "Culture in Action: Symbols and Strategies," *American Sociological Review* 51 (April 1986): 276.

[49] Ibid., p. 277.

PART V

Studying the State

7

*Studying the Politics of
Development and Change*

THE STATE OF THE ART

When Daniel Lerner surveyed Middle Eastern societies nearly half a century ago, the word that came to mind as he sought to make sense of the many images he encountered was "chaos."[1] It is not a term most social scientists would use very comfortably in describing any sort of situation. Lerner's initial bewilderment at the dizzying pace and scope of change was not atypical, however, nor was his response to societies seemingly engaged in a headlong rush into confusion. As Harry Eckstein put it, "The development theorists tried, in essence, to find patterns in pervasive novelty and seeming flux – to get bearings in a world devoid of all fixity and precedents."[2] Lerner's reaction, much like that of other social scientists, was to ferret out a pattern, a system – indeed, even to impose an intellectual order where social and political order could not be discerned. The term development came to denote the movement from social and political "chaos" in Africa, Asia, and Latin America toward some implicitly understood order.

From the beginning, the field of development and change was constitutive; it was the musings of scholars seeking the principles of political and social orders and the conditions initiating them. Although the study of formal constitutional process was already considered somewhat antiquated in political science by the end of the 1950s, writing on non-Western politics came to be nothing less than excursions into how societies and states might be constituted – or better yet,

---

[1] Daniel Lerner, *The Passing of Traditional Society: Modernizing the Middle East* (New York: Free Press, 1958).

[2] Harry Eckstein, "The Idea of Political Development: From Dignity to Efficiency," *World Politics* 34 (1982): 457.

reconstituted.[3] The field of development, in some senses, housed the new successors to Hobbes, Montesquieu, and the other political philosophers who had sought constitutive measures in a similarly chaotic Europe.

The flush of excitement associated with the changes in the world map from 1947 to 1965 gripped political scientists who were seeking to untangle the debris of the old to articulate new bases of order. Few scholars agreed on any one approach to this great challenge. Lucian Pye wrote an article enumerating the many meanings the term political development had already taken in the literature.[4] Half a decade later Samuel P. Huntington seemed to throw up his hands, saying that as long as there is a lack of a precise definition, the term political development can have no analytic value. All it does, he asserted, is describe some common field hoed by scholars.[5]

For all the intellectual diversity the field spawned, there were important shared perspectives about the nature of political and social change in the Third World. But, in the late 1960s and early 1970s, serious critics attacked some of these notions, including the teleology, unidirectionality, and evolutionary determinism in the development literature.[6] Those criticisms initiated a new era of vitality for the field, as many, but by no means all, older perspectives were jettisoned and new approaches blossomed.

In assessing the state of the field, it is worth looking back at some of the major shared notions. A number of these ideas continue to sway, even today, interpretations of how change occurs. I will then turn to three major currents that have greatly influenced research in recent years and close

[3] Very few authors acknowledged their debt to the earlier constitutional writers. An exception came in one of the very best books written on Africa – see Martin Kilson, *Political Change in a West African State: A Study of the Modernization Process in Sierra Leone* (Cambridge, MA: Harvard University Press, 1966).

[4] Lucian Pye, "The Concept of Political Development," *Annals of the American Academy* 358 (1965): 1–13.

[5] Samuel P. Huntington, "The Change to Change: Modernization, Development and Politics," *Comparative Politics* 3 (1971): 282–322.

[6] The most notable rejection of the idea of patterned change is found in C. S. Whitaker, Jr., "A Dysrhythmic Process of Political Change," *World Politics* 19 (1967): 190–217. Among other serious, critical articles are Dean C. Tipps, "Modernization Theory and the Comparative Study of Societies," *Comparative Studies in Society and History* 15 (1973): 199–240; Benjamin Schwartz, "The Limits of 'Tradition Versus Modernity' as Categories of Explanation: The Case of the Chinese Intellectuals," *Daedalus* 101 (1972): 71–88; Joseph R. Gusfield, "Tradition and Modernity: Misplaced Polarities in the Study of Social Change," *American Journal of Sociology* 72 (Jan 1967): 351–62.

with a discussion of how this new scholarship has affected the understanding of first principles.

Approaching the Study of Development and Change

Several landmark books, appearing within a few years of one another, inaugurated the fields of development and modernization across the social sciences.[7] The Gabriel A. Almond and James S. Coleman volume placed studies of developing areas firmly into the subject matter of comparative politics writ large. It gave birth to a highly touted nine-volume series, "Studies in Political Development," which spanned a fifteen-year period. Both the Almond and Coleman work and the subsequent series grew out of the prestigious Committee on Comparative Politics of the Social Science Research Council. Oddly, though, these works had only a muted impact on the burgeoning field in the 1960s and 1970s. Certainly, the volumes were read, discussed, and reviewed.[8] They did make political scientists take the politics embedded in kinship systems as seriously as those found in Western parliaments. But the volumes were also much ignored. No school developed; they did not shape ongoing research. An obligatory opening footnote citing the committee's work would be encountered in many monographs and articles, but there would be little evidence that it made a contribution to method or substance.

The work that played the role of midwife to the several branches of the field of political development was by the sociologist Lerner.[9] All of these new branches shared, in one way or another, a commitment to Lerner's system of modernity. The notion of a system rested on the belief that the seemingly diverse aspects of sociopolitical change are actually related in a pattern of high covariation.

By the mid-1960s, many scholars accepted three key features found in the Lerner book without necessarily endorsing Lerner's central hypothesis. First, a general research focus in those years was on domestic change.

---

[7] For example, see Gabriel A. Almond and James S. Coleman, *The Politics of the Developing Areas.* (Princeton, NJ: Princeton University Press, 1960); Max F. Millikan and W. W. Rostow, *A Proposal Key to an Effective Foreign Policy* (New York: Harper, 1957); Lerner, *The Passing of Traditional Society.*

[8] John D. Montgomery, "The Quest for Political Development," *Comparative Politics* 1 (1969): 285–95.

[9] In Lerner's concept of empathy, we find the basis for the "psycho-cultural school," which has included such notable scholars as David C. McClelland.

The herald of such change may have been the rapid transformation of the international environment, but the internal transformations siphoned off almost all of the interest of scholars. Second, at the macro-level, political scientists focused upon the creation of central institutions (the term "state" was not yet in vogue) and their ability to transform society. Third, at the micro-level, they used surveys and other research tools to assess the process of individual change, and its relationship to social processes, such as urbanization, industrialization, and the like. Karl Deutsch's concept of social mobilization, with its stress on the relationship between the breakdown of personal commitments and these near-universal social processes, became the byword for interpreting aggregated individual change.[10]

Understanding macrochange – the configuration of institutional transformations in an entire society – demanded a framework of a different order. Several such frameworks were employed, often differing only in terminology. The most popular was the modern traditional dichotomy used by Lerner and other important social scientists such as Almond and Coleman, David E. Apter, C. E. Black, S. N. Eisenstadt, Marian J. Levy, and Edward Shils.[11] Also widely employed was the metaphor of center and periphery.[12] Among the other concepts used to make fairly similar distinctions are: elite-mass;[13] diffracted-fused;[14] Great Tradition-little tradition;[15] and even, at times, urban-rural.[16] Some scholars added

[10] Karl W. Deutsch, "Social Mobilization and Political Development," *American Political Science Review* 55 (1961): 493–514.

[11] See for example: Lerner, *The Passing of Traditional Society*; Almond and Coleman, *The Politics of the Developing Areas*; David E. Apter, *The Politics of Modernization* (Chicago: University Press, 1965); C. E. Black, *The Dynamics of Modernization: A Study in Comparative History* (New York: Harper & Row, 1966); S. N. Eisenstadt, *Modernization: Protest and Change* (Englewood Cliffs, NJ: Prentice-Hall, 1966); Marian J. Levy, Jr., *Modernization and the Structure of Societies: A Setting for International Affairs* (Princeton, NJ: Princeton University Press, 1966); Edward Shils, "Political Development in the New States," *Comparative Studies in Society and History* 2 (1960): 265–92. This work also appeared as Edward Shils, *Political Development in the New States* (Paris: Monton, 1962).

[12] See for example, Daniel Lerner. "Some Comments on Center-Periphery Relations," in Richard L. Merritt and Stein Rokkan (eds.), *Comparing Nations* (New Haven, CT: Yale University Press, 1966); also see Edward Shils, *Center and Periphery*.

[13] Gaetano Mosca, *The Ruling Class* (New York: McGraw-Hill, 1939).

[14] Fred W. Riggs, *Administration in Developing Countries: The Theory of Prismatic Society* (Boston: Houghton Mifflin, 1964).

[15] Robert Redfield, *Peasant Society and Culture* (Chicago: University of Chicago Press, 1960).

[16] See for example: Gideon Sjoberg, *The Pre-industrial City* (New York: Free Press, 1960); Charles Tilly, *The Vendee* (New York: John Wiley & Sons, 1967).

intermediate terms, such as transitional or prismatic, but the endpoints of the continuum were the most theoretically important concepts. A formal theory of the relationship between the two sectors was never developed, but it is worth looking for a moment at some of the widely shared assumptions held by those employing such dichotomies. Although there may be variability in the size and strength of the two components of each dichotomy, the dichotomies themselves were meant to be enduring analytic tools not bound by time or space. The intent in the field of political development was to use the tool to depict a beachhead imagery; that is, in contemporary societies, the locus of "development" is the modern sector or center (or elite, Great Tradition, urban areas) – the beachhead of change – and the locus of the "underdeveloped" part of society is the traditional sector or periphery (or masses, little tradition, rural areas).

The modern sector or center was seen as activist and aggressive; its authority was the motor of social and political change. The strength of the center lay in its integration, a result of the high consensus among elites sharing modern values. (The meaning of "modern values" did not, for most authors, stray far from the instrumental side of Parsons's five pattern variables.) To political scientists, the array of public institutions – the state – should have been the most interesting component of the center. Yet, it was not until the latter 1960s and 1970s that the state qua activist organization, began to become a major subject of research.[17] Before then, a rather hazy image prevailed of interlocking authoritative institutions in the modern sector or center. But the importance of authority was clearly understood. The very need for authority implied a measure of resistance in the society. Values were not fully or equally shared throughout the society and did not impel everyone toward the same type of behavior; otherwise, there would have been no politics at all. Social and political control of imperfectly integrated parts underlay the use of the modern-traditional and center-periphery dichotomies.

The traditional sector or periphery consists, not of those parts of the population that exercise authority, but "of those strata or sectors of the society which are the recipients of commands and of beliefs which they do not themselves create or cause to be diffused, and of those who are lower

---

[17] See J. P. Nettl, "The State as a Conceptual Variable," *World Politics* 20 (1968): 559–92; and Charles Tilly, ed., "Western State-Making and Theories of Political Transformation," in *The Formation of National States in Western Europe* (Princeton, NJ: Princeton University Press, 1978).

in the distribution or allocation of rewards, dignities, facilities, etc."[18] Authority expands the modern sector into the traditional. The leadership is never satisfied to live and let live but wants everyone to obey and to accept the validity of its rules of the game. Rewards and punishments exercised through the modern sector's organizations are used by the elites to facilitate the acceptance of their decisions and views.

Indifference to the structure, resiliency, and autonomy of the traditional sector or periphery marked many of the earlier major political science works on development as well as many contemporary studies – although there have been, to be sure, important exceptions.[19] The periphery, while capable of change, took on in the 1950s and 1960s, and frequently continues to wear, a two-dimensional visage.

The European experience, in which nationalism has been the crucial component of the belief system and people have become increasingly attached to the larger territory in which they live, served for many writers as a model of change for the rest of the world. The Western experience, portrayed in grossly oversimplified terms, was seen as a process of change that involved the major centers winning over minor centers and a shift from unimposing bureaucratic empires and feudal systems to modern, dynamic, effective centers. And that process was then presumed to be universal. The direction of development, it was assumed, is away from the primordial (biological criteria of affinity) toward attachment to the larger territory; the form of development is away from weak, nonintrusive centers to active, dominant centers; the substance of development is toward a civil society, marked by modern values and procedures. It is true, a noted author suggested, that many states in Asia and Africa "have not yet become societies in a modern sense because they do not yet have effective centers."[20] Rulers face "a population which is not yet formed into a society but which consists of a number of proto-societies."[21] Even on these continents, however, the evolution seemed to be clear, and what must be overcome was the lag.

---

[18] Shils, *Center and Periphery*, p. 39.
[19] See for example, Robert A. Dahl, *Polyarchy: Participation and Opposition* (New Haven, CT: Yale University Press, 1971); Huntington, *Political Order in Changing Societies*; Fernando Henrique Cardoso and Enzo Faletto, *Dependency and Development in Latin America* (Berkeley: University of California Press, 1979).
[20] Shils, *Center and Periphery*, p. 44.
[21] Ibid., p. 89.

What is lacking currently, it was implied, are the key ingredients of authority and power. Huntington noted that in many cases in Asia, Africa, and Latin America "governments simply do not govern."[22] "Government implies power," wrote LaPalombara but "the most unequivocal and uncontestable statement one can make about most of the new nations today is how little power those at the center actually possess."[23]

If third-world societies, in fact, lack the authoritative element, if governments really do not govern, then the field of development may have been not very different from Alice in Wonderland. The ideas developed to analyze macro-level change – modern and traditional or center and periphery – were geared to explain the impact of the authoritative sector of society on those that are the recipients of commands. The analytic lenses filtered a pattern of change in which the primary struggle was that between a relatively united, institutionally strong elite against an undifferentiated mass. But were the institutions and elites really what they appeared to be? The questions posed by political scientists of those years tended to be directed more toward what these elites and their institutions had not yet become – that is, modern in targeted sectors or strong centers – rather than toward what they actually were. Without an authoritative center, with governments that did not govern, analysts seemed to be describing a nonexistent situation. The challenge for political scientists was made all the more imposing because in much of the Third World there was an adoption of institutional forms and names from the West (states, parliaments, parties, and the like). It was seductive to assume that there had been a convergence of elites and values in these institutions and that the outputs would eventually be those that were expected. It was tempting to assume that a state, any state, was tied into other central institutions sharing with it important values and that such a state was activist and powerful.

Huntington had a clear and lasting impact on the field largely because he took institutions seriously.[24] He looked at what the political institutions

---

[22] Samuel P. Huntington, *Political Order in Changing Societies* (New Haven, CT: Yale University Press, 1968), p. 2.

[23] Joseph LaPalombara, "Political Science and the Engineering of National Development," in Monte Palmer and Larry Sterns (eds.), *Political Development in Changing Societies* (Lexington, MA: D. C. Heath, 1971), p. 53.

[24] Huntington, *Political Order in Changing Societies*.

of societies actually were, not at what they had "not yet" become nor at what they formally were supposed to be. Questions concerning the real political capabilities of states, of the possibility of institutional decay or breakdown, now became central topics of concern. For political scientists, the political institutions were returned to the limelight, no longer subsumed within the broader category of center nor made the simple outgrowth of nonpolitical events, as they were in Lerner's work.

Huntington's analysis was in some ways a technical one. The guiding question was what specific kinds of mechanisms maintain political stability even in the face of increased political demands – potentially destabilizing demands growing out of the near-universal process of social mobilization. The effective mechanisms, he answered, were political institutions, especially political parties: institutions that are adaptable, complex, autonomous, and coherent. Still left to be answered, however, were the political-philosophical questions that had informed the field from the 1950s: What are the principles – rather than the mechanisms – of social and political order? Why have some societies generated effective constitutional principles and institutions while others have not? What are the processes of change involved in constituting new orders? If modern sectors or centers are not what they are supposed to be how can we explain order and change?

In the 1970s and 1980s the means chosen to answer these macro-level questions resulted in a number of startling changes in the development field. First, the field, which usually had been defined by a residual geographic area – non-Western, non-Communist, neither from the First nor Second worlds but from a heterogeneous Third World – was now extended into all other geographic regions, including the West. Second, in a subdiscipline that had regarded itself as au courant, that had concentrated on the subject of becoming modern in the post–World War II era, there was now an unexpected return to history. And such history was not simply the obligatory background preceding the "real" analysis but was a primary subject of research. Third, in a field that had restricted itself almost exclusively to domestic concerns, that had placed itself firmly under the heading of comparative politics,[25] there were now new frameworks that were as much international as comparative.

---

[25] Dankwart A. Rostow, "Modernization and Comparative Politics: Prospects in Research and Theory," *Comparative Politics* 1 (1968): 37–51.

Three Major Research Currents

From the Third World to the First (and Second)

An irony of the first change, the spreading influence of the development field beyond the Third World into Europe and North America, is that the study of non-Western societies has been saddled with so many handicaps compared to research elsewhere. Access is frequently limited. Government statistics are often haphazard and unreliable; other baseline materials are also scarce. Sampling is problematic because of the heterogeneity of the population. Nonetheless, the intellectual excitement of social scientists observing change in that momentous era of successful independence movements infected those studying other societies as well. Mark Kesselman, for example, toyed with Huntington's concept of institutionalization, weighing its usefulness for explaining French politics; Ronald Inglehart did much the same for Europe with Deutsch's notion of social mobilization.[26]

In one sense, Europe was part of the development field from the outset. The very connection of social change to development, as Robert A. Nisbet makes clear, goes back to the earliest European writings.[27] And the Western notion of development gathered special force in the theories of the late nineteenth and early twentieth centuries. When it came to giving substance to words such as "developed" or "modern" in the Third World, writers both implicitly and explicitly fell back on those patterns typical of the West. In addition, they used their understanding of the processes of change in Western history to project along which route non-Western states and societies would evolve. Not only did they assume the content of modernity but also the nature of the process – development or modernization – that would bring societies to modernity. Most interesting is how these Western cases were incorporated into development models, for it could be argued that the American and European "models" that were used bore little resemblance to the actual processes of change that had taken place in the United States and Europe. It was not until the 1970s, however, that the European experience began to be examined more closely

---

[26] Mark Kesselman, "Over-institutionalization and Political Constraint: The Case of France," *Comparative Politics* 3 (1970): 21–44; and Ronald Inglehart, "Cognitive Mobilization and European Identity," *Comparative Politics* 3 (1970): 45–70.

[27] Robert A. Nisbet, *Social Change and History: Aspects of the Western Theory of Development* (London: Oxford University Press, 1969).

to see what kinds of distortion had crept into the models used in understanding processes of change in the Third World.[28]

What some writers came to question was the utter confidence that infused the works of those who used the modern-traditional metaphor or other similar imagery. Had centers coalesced or states centralized in Western history as completely and smoothly as had been assumed? Have peripheries been as passive and malleable as has been thought? In an excellent monograph, Suzanne Berger found that even a state as highly centralized as France found itself faced with a peasantry and "its imperfect insertion into the body politic."[29] In France there had arisen "corporative organizations" characterized by their efforts to regulate peasant matters fully without tying these matters into the politics of the state. The corporative organizations were able to build a reservoir of political loyalty by assuming functions important to the peasantry. They then jealously guarded this arena of conflicts and interests that lay beyond the reach of the centralized state and, as a result, they inhibited "change in the political system by withdrawing from the domain of parties and the state those issues on which alignments of interests and values are formed."[30]

Berger's later work extended some of the conceptions that underlay this analysis to other European cases and to sectors besides the peasantry. Various segments of some European societies have continued to differ substantially from one another. These variations (or dualism) have not been "mere way stations to ultimate convergence" through the authority of centers or states. Rather "traditional" segments have endured "because of the ways in which [their] political and economic interests overlap with those of the modern sector."[31] In this, European societies differ little from non-Western ones: "The evidence from both developed and developing countries suggests the persistence, not the disappearance, of the traditional or informal sector."[32] As Ronald Rogowski and Lois Wasserspring put it, even in advanced industrial societies, "nothing compels individuals . . . to

---

[28] See for example, Stein Rokkan, "Cities, States, and Nations: A Dimensional Model of the Study of Contrasts in Development," in S. N. Eisenstadt and Stein Rokkan (eds.), *Building States and Nations* (Beverly Hills, CA: Sage, 1973).

[29] Suzanne Berger, *Peasants Against Politics: Rural Organization in Brittany 1911–1967* (Cambridge, MA: Harvard University Press, 1972), p. 2.

[30] Ibid., p. 168.

[31] Suzanne Berger and Michael J. Piore, *Dualism and Discontinuity in Industrial Societies* (Cambridge, MA: Cambridge University Press, 1980), p. 87.

[32] Ibid., pp. 4–5.

become atoms, bonded only by the nexuses of cash and self-interest."[33] Perhaps Europe looks more like the Third World than the Third World was thought to look like Europe.

Also reflecting the impact of third-world development literature on the understanding of the constitutive principles of European society and state is the growing corporatist literature. Although the term corporatism referred earlier in this century to the fascist states of Europe, in the postwar era it was applied almost exclusively to Iberian cultures and their offshoots, most notably in Latin America. Only after its elaboration in that context did the concept return to the advanced industrial states of Western Europe, now in a much more benign form.

Corporatism for most writers meant something quite different from Berger's corporative organizations. For Berger, the corporative organizations try "to acquire the power and authority to rule their own household" outside the orbit of the state.[34] In the Iberian and Latin American literature and later in the materials for other parts of Europe, the corporatist organizations are "recognized or licensed (if not created) by the state."[35] The state has moved to center stage.

Researchers working on postwar Spain, Portugal, and Latin America resuscitated the term corporatism almost reluctantly after the ignominy it suffered by the time of the Nuremberg trials. Even revived, it at first retained a negative taint. Corporatism, after all, was the historical antithesis of liberalism, placing the group – with its special bonds and rights – over the individual. It was thought to exclude the ambrosia of the twentieth century, industrialization and modernization. Corporatism was an atavistic survival in a world of more dynamic "isms": "The Iberian and Latin American political systems have retained a mausoleum-like appearance."[36] As Ronald C. Newton put it, "In the experience of the Atlantic world the corporate state is an anachronism, and a faintly tawdry one at

[33] Ronald Rogowski and Lois Wasserspring, "Does Political Development Exist? Corporatism in Old and New Societies," *Comparative Politics Series 2* (Beverly Hills, CA: Sage, 1971), p. 44.

[34] Berger, *Peasants Against Politics*, p. 9.

[35] Phillippe C. Schmitter, "Interest Intermediation and Regime Governability in Contemporary Western Europe and North America," in Susan Berger (ed.), *Organizing Interests in Western Europe: Pluralism, Corporatism and the Transformation of Politics* (New York: Cambridge University Press, 1981), p. 93.

[36] Howard J. Wiarda, "Transcending Corporatism? The Portugese Cooperative System and the Revolution of 1974," *Institute of International Studies Essay Series 3* (Columbia: University of South Carolina, 1976), p. 5.

that."[37] The term corporatism came to be associated with states and societies mired in habits and institutions ill-fitted to the twentieth century. "Corporatism and the corporatist tradition," wrote Howard J. Wiarda, "are a natural, almost inherent part of the Iberic-Latin political culture."[38]

By the mid- to late 1970s, practically all of these associations began to die. Rather than the antithesis of Iberalism and democracy, corporatism began to appear in titles such as "Liberal Corporatism and Party Government," "The Development of Corporatism in Liberal Democracies," and "Corporatism, Parliamentarism, and Social Democracy," no longer associated exclusively with Iberic and Latin American cultures, corporatism blossomed into a tool of analysis for other parts of Europe, Japan, and elsewhere.[39] And, instead of being the scourge of industrialization, corporatism has been heralded as the foundation for advanced industrial growth and adaptation.[40] More and more, writers came to accept "that corporatism, like liberalism or socialism, may take a variety of forms, both as between nations and within a single nation over time."[41] The new authoritarianism in Brazil following the coup of 1964, Salazar's old Portugal, the Portuguese shift toward socialism after the 1974 coup, Japan's corporatism without labor, along with many other cases, all became subjects of corporatist analysis.[42] The difficulty with the concept's success is that without proper specification and disaggregation, it may become little more than a

---

[37] Ronald C. Newton, "Natural Corporatism and the Passing of Populism in Spanish America," in Federick B. Pike and Thomas Stritch (eds.), *The New Corporatism: Social-Political Structures in the Iberian World* (Notre Dame, IN: University of Notre Dame Press, 1974), p. 35.

[38] Howard J. Wiarda, *Corporatism and Development: The Portuguese Experience* (Amherst: University of Massachusetts Press, 1977), p. 4.

[39] Gerhard Lehmbruch, "Liberal Corporatism and Party Government," in Philippe Schmitter and Gerhard Lehmbruch (eds.), *Trends Towards Corporatist Intermediation* (Beverly Hills, CA: Sage, 1979); Leo Panitch, "The Development of Corporatism in Liberal Democracies," ibid; Bob Jessop, "Corporatism, Parlimentarism, and Social Democracy," ibid.

[40] See examples: T. J. Pempel, "Japanese Foreign Economic Policy: The Domestic Bases for International Behaviui," in Peter J. Katzenstein (ed.), *Between Power and Plenty: Foreign Economic Policies of Advanced Industrial States* (Madison: University of Wisconsin Press, 1978).

[41] Wiarda, *Corporatism and Development*, p. 5.

[42] See for example: Alfred Stepan, *Authoritarian Brazil: Origins, Policies, and Future* (New Haven, CT: Yale University Press, 1973); Schmitter, "Interest Intermediation and Regime Governability in Contemporary Western Europe and North America"; Wiarda, *Corporatism and Development*; T. J. Pempel and Keiichi Tsunekawa, "Corporatism Without Labor? The Japanese Anomaly," in Schmitter and Lehmbruch (eds.), *Trends Towards Corporatist Intermediation*.

residual category that is used to explain nearly all state-society relationships. Such fears have already been expressed by some.[43] As Phillippe C. Schmitter noted, "It has become such a vaguely bounded phenomenon that, like clientelism, it can be found everywhere and, hence, is nowhere very distinctive."[44]

For political scientists, the return of corporatism has had a welcome by-product, the return of politics to the limelight. The field of development has been overshadowed from the beginning by economic issues and by the economists (although within the discipline of economics, development has been fairly low in status of late). At the same time, sociologists from Talcott Parsons and Edward Shils, in the Weberian tradition, to Barrington Moore and Immanuel Wallerstein, in the Marxist mode, had dominated macro-level approaches. Corporatism identified as central to both economic change and societal structure two interrelated types of organizations that lie clearly in the domain of the political scientist.

The first type of organization is that of interest representation. Corporatist analysis thus became part of a larger body of work within political science. It stood as one kind of interest representation among the several different sorts familiar to the discipline, pluralism being the most identifiable. Schmitter played an important role in "restricting the concept, so to speak, to refer only to a specific concrete set of institutional practices or structures involving the representation (or misrepresentation) of empirically observable group interests."[45]

The second type of organization within corporatist analysis that falls within the political scientist's bailiwick is the state. Corporatism was not the only concept that reintroduced the state into analyses in the 1970s and 1980s, but it did follow in Huntington's path of extricating political institutions or processes from more general social phenomena. Of the criteria that Huntington gave for assessing the capabilities of political institutions, none so grabbed the imagination of political scientists as that of autonomy. A major focus of attention came to be the autonomous or semi-autonomous state.[46]

---

[43] See Nedelmann and Meier, "Theories of Contemporary Corporatism: Static or Dynamic?" and Pempel and Tsunekawa, "Corporatism without Labor?"

[44] Schmitter, "Still the Century of Corporatism," p. 86.

[45] Ibid., p. 87.

[46] See, for example, Eric Nordlinger, *On the Autonomy of the Democratic State* (Cambridge, MA: Harvard University Press, 1981) and Nicos Poulantzas, *Political Power and Social Class* (London: NLB, 1975).

What role does corporatism demand of the state? Here, scholars divided according to their regional interests. Those writing on Western Europe disentangled corporatism from its illiberal and antidemocratic past. Now corporatism – sometime used with qualifiers such as neo, liberal, or societal[47] – became a political-economic tool or structure that coexisted with, indeed, integrated into, parliamentary government. It was viewed almost exclusively in the industrial sector as that mechanism that could assure survival and even growth in a fast-paced, open international economy.[48] Corporatism's great advantages for advanced industrial democracies are that it promotes tranquility in industrial and political relations and adaptation in sector investment in response to changing international economic circumstances. A corporatist political structure enables the state to advance domestic tranquility, at least in the short run, by negotiating among self-seeking groups that are at odds with one another and co-opting them into collaborative policy arrangements. Labor and capital, especially, participate in national economic planning and incomes policy bodies.[49] As Schmitter noted, "The relative ruliness and effectiveness of the outcome is impressive."[50] Corporatism furthers industrial adaptation through national planning as the state modifies "the free operation of the market by incorporating into the public decision-making apparatus those groups that are affected by the unhampered operation of the market."[51]

Those working on Latin America started from a different understanding of corporatism, one laced with political authoritarianism. In these cases, the state does not merely negotiate with interest organizations in order to preserve social peace nor simply license and incorporate them into the policymaking apparatus so as to ensure smooth industrial adaptation. Here, regimes incorporate, even reshape, groups to deal with the near-impossible task of maintaining political ossification, the continued operation of an antiquated elite system of rule along with class harmony, in the face of rapid

---

[47] Claus Offe, "The Attribution of Public Status to Interest Groups: Observation of the West German Case," in Suzanne Berger (ed.), *Organizing Interests in Western Europe: Pluralism, Corporatism, and the Transformation Politics* (New York: Cambridge University Press, 1981).

[48] But see John T. S. Keeler, "Corporatism and Official Union Hegemony: The Case of French Agricultural Syndicalism," in Berger (ed.), *Organizing Interests in Western Europe.*

[49] Leo Panitch, "Recent Theorization of Corporatism: Reflections on a Growth Industry," *British Journal of Sociology* 31 (1980): 160.

[50] Schmitter, "Interest Intermediation and Regime Governability in Contemporary Western Europe and North America," p. 318.

[51] Gudmond Hernes and Arnie Selvik, "Local Corporatism," in Berger (ed.), *Organizing Interests in Western Europe*, p. 104.

industrial growth. These are states "within which populist interests and participatory politics are reduced in scope, distributional concerns ignored or placed in low priority, and the maximization of economic growth and rapid industrialization given a top priority."[52] In the corporatist structure, the state does not just mediate within voluntarist arrangements among existing functional groups, as in Western Europe. In Latin American corporatism, the state creates these groups or, at the very least, imposes firm control over them. The tensions of social and economic change, then, have demanded substantial changes in politics as well, leading to a new sort of political system characterized by the bureaucratic authoritarian regime.

Ruth B. Collier and David Collier attempted to bridge the gap between European-style and Latin American–style corporatism by viewing the two types not as a dichotomy but as part of a continuum with considerable variation within each one.[53] Their argument is that corporatism can be categorized for different societies by classifying the inducements and constraints employed by the state with respect to group representation. Nonetheless, the thrust of the literature on Latin America emphasizes the authoritarian character of the state. I will return to this literature, especially that on bureaucratic authoritarianism, later in the essay when considering how some in the field have moved away from such dichotomous paradigms as modern and traditional.

Here, it is worth noting that the revival of corporatism and the development of bureaucratic authoritarianism in Latin America had reverberations for study far beyond Western Europe. Daniel Chirot, for example, wrote an essay entitled "The Corporatist Model and Socialism."[54] Although the article dealt largely with the case of Romania, it did raise the point that corporatism offers the same advantage of social and political stability to socialist states driving toward rapid industrialization that it provides for those in the Third World. Corporate structures have emerged to deal with the immediate problems generated by rapid social and economic change, despite the ideal of the Communist party to create a unitary society.

---

[52] Douglass H. Graham, "Mexican and Brazilian Economic Development: Legacies, Patterns, and Performance," in Sylvia Ann Hewlett and Richard S. Weinert (eds.), *Brazil and Mexico: Patterns in Late Development* (Philadelphia: Institute for the Study of Human Issues, 1982), p. 14.

[53] Ruth B. Collier and David Collier, "Inducements Versus Constraints: 'Disaggregating Corporatism,'" *American Political Science Review* 73 (1979): 978–9.

[54] Daniel Chirot, "The Corporatist Model and Socialism," *Theory and Society Journal* 9 (1980): 363–81.

Corporatism's application to Communist Eastern Europe followed the spread of third-world development literature to other aspects of socialist politics. Indeed, Jan F. Triska and Paul M. Cocks noted "a growing need to integrate Communist studies more closely within a broader comparative politics framework."[55] They focused their volume on political development, and a small but growing number of other scholars did likewise.[56] The Latin American materials also had an impact on work about socialist and nonsocialist states in Asia. A workshop on the political economy of Taiwan run by Columbia University's East Asian Institute in 1980, for example, focused on the relevance of a model of Latin American–style authoritarianism for Taiwan. Bruce Cumings wrote an essay, "Corporatism in North Korea," and another on the relationship of politics and economics in the four industrial states of Northeast Asia: Japan, North Korea, South Korea, and Taiwan. For the latter two, Cumings suggested dropping the recently fashionable acronym NICs (Newly Industrialized Countries) for one that includes and reflects the similarity to Latin American cases. That acronym is BAIRs, or Bureaucratic-Authoritarian Industrializing Regimes.[57]

All in all, the influence of development literature beyond the specific regions to which it had originally applied has been truly dramatic. The impact has come unexpectedly from the study of areas considered to be world peripheries, the non-Western world, to shape the way social scientists have viewed those regions thought of as world centers, the Socialist bloc and especially Western Europe. Cumings noted that the entry on "corporatism" in the *International Encyclopedia of the Social Sciences*, published in 1968, read simply, "see fascism."[58] Since then, the term has gained considerable renown, transcending its earlier association with European fascism. It has been transformed from a term concerned parochially with

---

[55] Jan F. Triska and Paul M. Cocks, eds., *Political Development in Eastern Europe* (New York: Praeger, 1977), p. xv.

[56] See for example: Ken Jowitt, *Revolutionary Breakthroughs and National Development: The Case of Romania, 1944–1965* (Berkeley: University of California Press, 1971); Jan F. Triska and Paul M. Johnson, "Political Development and Political Change in Eastern Europe: A Comparative Study," *University of Denver Monograph Series in World Affairs 13*, Book 2 (1975); Walter D. Connor, "Revolution, Modernization, and Communism: A Review Article," *Studies in Comparative Communism* 8 (1975): 389–96; David W. Paul, *The Cultural Limits of Revolutionary Politics: Change and Continuity in Socialist Czechoslovakia* (Boulder, CO: East European Quarterly and Columbia University Press, 1979).

[57] Bruce Cumings, "Corporatism in North Korea," Working paper presented at the annual meeting of the American Political Association (New York, 1981).

[58] Ibid., p. 11.

traditional Iberian and Latin American societies to one dealing with the dynamics of change in a number of regions. The decline of static conceptions associated with "the end of ideology" and "postindustrial societies" opened the door in the West for theories and frameworks stressing social and political transformation. It was this new emphasis on change that enabled approaches dealing with the Third World to have such a telling effect elsewhere.

The Return to History

Also influencing the Europeanists' newfound interest in third-world studies was the reconsideration of European history mandated by the development literature. Through the 1950s and 1960s, notions about where changes in the Third World were heading rested upon implicit assumptions about the previous course of "development" and "modernization" in Western Europe and the United States. Beginning in the late 1960s, there were voices of dissent against some of those suppositions, paving the way for a later reorientation of the field. Huntington gave a telling critique of the use of the United States as a model for the Third World,[59] and Moore's landmark study was to serve as an example of macro-level historical analysis that looked closely at state-society relations.[60]

It was not until the 1970s, though, that a concerted reexamination of European historical development got underway. As Peter H. Merkel put it, "While taking maximal advantage of available historical – especially European – scholarship, we must attempt to bridge the gulf between this historiography and theories of development."[61] Until then, ideas about cohesive centers and steady centralization in Europe used by those studying the Third World went largely unquestioned.

Some of the most influential books joining theories of development with European history were edited volumes.[62] Almond was the most intent

---

[59] Huntington, *Political Order in Changing Societies*.

[60] Barrington Moore, Jr., *Social Origins of Dictatorship and Democracy: Lord and Peasant in the Making of the Modern World* (Boston: Beacon Press, 1966).

[61] Peter H. Merkel, "The Study of European Political Development," *World Politics* 29 (1977): 463.

[62] See: Gabriel A. Almond, Scott C. Flanagan, and Robert J. Mundt, *Crisis, Choice, and Change: Historical Studies of Political Development* (Boston: Little Brown, 1973); Charles Tilly, ed., *The Formation of National States and Western Europe* (Princeton, NJ: Princeton University Press, 1975); and Raymond Grew, ed., *Crisis of Political Development in Europe and the United States* (Princeton, NJ: Princeton University Press, 1978).

on maintaining the continuity of the field, even with its new departure into Europe and into history. He wrote in a matter-of-fact manner:

The logic of our undertaking was elementary. As the Western nations were in some sense modern, and the non-Western ones were in almost all cases not modern but seeking to become so, the historical experience of the modern nations had some relevance for our understanding of the problems and prospects of modernizing efforts among the new nations.... Our search for a cure in history now took a more modest, empirically grounded, form. The logic of our inquiry was simple. Since the development that we were seeking to explain occurred in history, why not select several historical episodes, examine them in great detail, try out our varieties of developmental explanation, and see how they fit?[63]

The volumes edited by Charles Tilly and Raymond Grew demonstrated more skepticism about the ability to skip back and forth easily between development theories and actual historical circumstances and between the West's past and the Third World's present. The irony of the questioning attitude one encounters in these two books is that they are the last of the Social Science Research Council (SSRC) Committee on Comparative Politics series "Studies in Political Development." That series, after all, had canonized some of the most important notions now questioned by the Tilly and Grew books. Perhaps the doubts stemmed from the fact that Tilly is a sociologist and Grew, a historian; indeed, almost all of the authors in Grew's volume are historians. The commissioning of the Grew book by the SSRC committee in the latter part of the 1960s may have reflected not only a renewed interest in history but also an attempt to confirm the universality of the members' latest schema, the so-called crisis approach. Be that as it may, the results of both the Grew and Tilly volumes did little to support the committee's earlier works.

Tilly departed from the Gabriel A. Almond, Scott C. Flanagan, and Robert J. Mundt book in two important ways. First, Tilly and his coauthors used the volume as an opportunity to debunk "misconceived models of Western experience as the criteria of political development."[64] This reexamination of the European experience challenged some sacred assumptions about the nature of change. For example, the dichotomous model of change (e.g., center versus periphery) was brought into serious

---

[63] Gabriel A. Almond, "Approaches to Developmental Causation," in Almond et al. (eds.), *Crisis, Choice, and Change*, pp. 2, 22.

[64] Charles Tilly, "Reflections on the History of European State-Making," in Tilly (ed.), *The Formation of National States in Western Europe*.

question by the finding that "the Europeans of 1500 and later did not ordinarily expand from a highly organized center into a weakly organized periphery."[65] Second, the Tilly volume raised doubts about the relevance of European political change for current third-world states. At best, it argued, some broad inferences may be drawn and some generalizations made about comparative processes of state building.

What seems to have been less obviously pursued after the appearance of the Almond, Flanagan, and Mundt volume is the quest for a universal theory of development that could explain European history as well as events in the contemporary Third World. More and more, one sees a focus on specific historical forces – whether in a single country or, as is increasingly the case, in world historical terms linking the fate of nations – in order to explain the root causes of differing types of social and political change.

There are, however, several promising paths that have been pursued seriously in the last few years to get at such causes. The distant and not-so-distant past, even outside Europe, now has become increasingly acceptable as part of the purview of political scientists; the horizons of the field have widened considerably. Excellent studies such as those by David Vital on Zionism or Elizabeth J. Perry on China seek to understand the political changes that have had deep ramifications in the postwar period by examining events in the nineteenth and early twentieth centuries.[66] Jorge I. Dominguez took a longer look back at the insurrections that brought the end of Spanish rule in the Americas. In his introduction, he was explicit about the need for a dialogue between history and the viewpoint of contemporary political science.[67]

Another path came directly from the questioning by some that a universal model of development could be created. As Almond and others recognized, the concepts and classification schemes of the 1950s and 1960s were Western in character.[68] Grew noted, "To argue that modernization is a new type of "Great Tradition" pointing toward a worldwide civilization is at the same time to admit that the roots of the process lie in Western

[65] Ibid., p. 24.
[66] See David Vital, *The Origins of Zionism* (Oxford: Clarendon Press, 1975) and *Zionism: The Formative Years* (Oxford: Clarendon Press, 1982); Elizabeth J. Perry, *Rebels and Revolutionaries in North China 1845–1945* (Stanford, CA: Stanford University Press, 1980).
[67] Jorge I. Dominguez, *Insurrection or Loyalty: The Breakdown of the Spanish American Empire* (Cambridge, MA: Harvard University Press, 1980), pp. 1–2.
[68] Almond, "Approaches to Developmental Causation," p. 2.

Europe."[69] Scholars, especially in the Third World, have responded by creating alternative, indigenous models of change. These models, wrote Wiarda "represent serious and fundamental challenges to many cherished social science assumptions and understandings and even to the presumption of a universal social science of development."[70] Among the works cited by Wiarda are those by Vrajanda Raj Mehta and Claudio Viliz.[71] One could add Goran Hyden's impressive work on Tanzania, among others.[72]

The cure in history that Almond mentioned had an additional result linking European and third-world processes of change, even in the absence of a universal theory. The result was a revival of Alexander Gerschenkron's notions about late development found in his famous essay on economic backwardness. Gerschenkron's major premise ruled out a simple replication from country to country of historical processes – his own interest as an economist was industrialization – because the environment within which change has taken place has varied so markedly in different periods. Late developers, to achieve the same industrialization, had to apply "institutional instruments for which there was little or no counterpart in an established industrial country."[73] Grew pointed to the notion of late development as the most important link between European history and change in the Third World:

Most European nations thought of themselves as late developers; many felt they had too long been a cultural or economic colony of others (Italy, Germany, Poland); nearly all experienced the contradictions between efficiency and equality, change and stability. More than the older monarchies or pressured states to the east, the centralized republics of southern Europe . . . have had an experience comparable to that of the Third World.[74]

Gerschenkron's ideas had never gone completely out of fashion. Albert O. Hirschman had applied them imaginatively to Latin American cases,

---

[69] Grew, *Crisis and Political Development in Europe and the United States*, p. 5.

[70] Howard J. Wiarda, "Toward a Non-Ethnocentric Theory of Development: Alternative Conceptions from the Third World," Working paper presented to the American Political Science Association (1981), p. 2.

[71] See Vrajendra Raj Mehta, *Beyond Marxism: Towards an Alternative Perspective* (New Delhi: Manohar, 1978); and Claudio Viliz, *The Centralist Tradition in Latin America* (Princeton, NJ: Princeton Univeristy Press, 1980).

[72] Goran Hyden, *Beyond Ujamaa in Tanzania: Underdevelopment and an Uncaptured Peasantry* (Berkeley: University of California Press, 1980).

[73] Alexander Gerschenkron, *Economic Backwardness in Historical Perspectives: A Book of Essays* (Cambridge, MA: Harvard University Press, 1962), p. 7.

[74] Grew, *Crisis of Political Development of Europe and the United States*, p. 35.

speaking of their "late, late" industrialization.[75] In recent years, however, there has been an increased interest in notions of late development, still mostly in Latin America. James R. Kurth, for example, drew the analogy between European and Latin American cases.[76] Sylvia Ann Hewlett and Richard S. Weinert's volume on Brazil and Mexico focused specifically on the implications, largely political, of late development.[77] In that book, the article by Douglass Bennett and Kenneth Sharpe is the most explicit about the need to understand the peculiar role of the state as banker and entrepreneur in terms of Gerschenkron's outlook.[78] The late, late development in Latin America, they argued, had created problems greater in scope than those faced by the late developers in Europe and, therefore, has elicited different state responses.

One of the interesting outcomes of the cure-in-history perspective, still largely inchoate, is a broad outlook emerging in the development literature on the nature of institutional change. The standard perspective on institutional change has been expressed best by the neoclassical economists.[79] Institutions are simply the established systems of rules within which people deal with one another. An institution changes, according to the neoclassical formulation, at the margins. That is, when certain parameters or environmental conditions change – the appearance of people with different abilities or a shifting capital stock due to varying population numbers and human knowledge – there is a corresponding adjustment process in the rules.

Thus, institutions change incrementally; with each new benefit or cost accorded by varying conditions, rules for human behavior and interaction are transformed. People are willing to change the rules when the expected benefits of the new institutional arrangements outweigh the

---

[75] Albert O. Hirschman, "The Political Economy of Import-Substituting Industrialization in Latin America," *The Quarterly Journal of Economics* 82 (1968): 2–32.

[76] James R. Kurth, "Industrial Change and Political Change: A European Perspective," in David Collier (ed.), *The New Authoritarianism in Latin America* (Princeton, NJ: Princeton University Press, 1979).

[77] Sylvia Ann Hewlett and Richard S. Weinert, *Brazil and Mexico: Patterns in Late Development* (Philadelphia: Institute for the Study of Human Issues, 1982).

[78] Douglas Bennett and Kenneth Sharpe, "The State as Banker and Entrepreneur: The Last Resort Character of the Mexican State's Economic Intervention 1917–1970," in Hewlett and Weinert (eds.), *Brazil and Mexico*.

[79] See Douglass C. North, *Structure and Change in Economic History* (New York: W. W. Norton, 1981); Lance E. Davis and Douglass C. North, *Institutional Change and American Economic Growth* (Cambridge, UK: Cambridge University Press, 1971).

expected costs. A system of rules, or an institution, included innumerable, individual prescripts, so that the system as a whole, bound by written laws as well as moral codes, will change slowly and at the margins. Long-term institutional structure and change, in Douglass C. North's own view, derive from the tension between the benefits to be gained through organizational specialization of institutions and the costs coming from such specialization – as in setting up specialized bureaus.[80] Nonetheless, North did not seem to deviate from the neoclassical perspective of institutional change taking place incrementally, along a fairly smooth curve, at the margins.

Implicitly, at least, it is precisely this view, that has been brought into question in the return to history by political scientists. In the field of international relations, a new concern with long waves or long cycles drew from an earlier literature of economic thought, represented by N. D. Kondratieff and Joseph Schumpeter, and from an even longer philosophical tradition in Western civilization.[81] Others in international relations developed interesting notions about change in international regimes – a regime being none other than an international institution. Over time, Stephen D. Krasner argued, regimes face pressures that, contrary to the neoclassical vision, may build without bringing corresponding adjustments in the rules.[82] A lag exists until the pressure is so great that there is a sudden, massive change. This image is not at all one of smooth curves and changes at the margins.

The development field, too, has begun to diverge from the neoclassical outlook in ways very similar to those set out by Krasner. Here, the word most often used to convey the inducement of sudden, massive change has been "crisis." The Social Science Research Council Committee on Comparative Politics introduced the term as a central concept in the field in 1971 with the publication of the seventh volume in the series, "Studies in Political Development."[83] Crises, though, had an odd meaning in this book. They are not necessarily "critical, episodic, political upheavals";

---

[80] North, *Structure and Change in Economic History*, pp. 201–9.

[81] See George Modelski, "The Long Cycle of Global Politics and the Nation-State," *Comparative Studies in Society and History* 20 (1978): 214–35; N. D. Kondratieff, "The Long Waves in Economic Life," *The Review of Economic Statistics* 17 (1935): 105–15; Joseph Schumpeter, *Business Cycles* (New York: McGraw Hill, 1939); Nisbet, *Social Change in History*, p. 211 ff.

[82] Stephen D. Krasner, "Regimes and the Limits of Realism: Regimes as Autonomous," *International Organization* 36 (1982): 497–510.

[83] Leonard Binder, "Crises of Political Development," in Binder, Pye, Coleman, Verba, Sidney, LaPalombra, Joseph, Weiner, and Myron (eds.), *Crises and Sequences of Political Development* (Princeton, NJ: Princeton University Press, 1971).

rather they denote "the functional requisites of a modern or developed political system."[84] In fact, Sidney Verba preferred the term "problem area" to "crisis."[85] In any event, crisis implied little more in this volume than the movement from the traditional to the modern along a series of dimensions reminiscent of Parsons's pattern variables. There seemed to be no quarrel yet with the neoclassical interpretation of institutional change. Leonard Binder wrote that the crises are likely to appear as recurrent issues that "may be coped with by the gradual arrangement of certain standardized patterns of response."[86]

Although the concept of crisis has continued to be vague in meaning,[87] it has been applied in recent years in ways that make it a promising complement to the neoclassical approach. Studies on the Third World,[88] on Western Europe,[89] and on Europe and the Third World[90] focus on the consolidation of new institutional arrangements as a result of historical crises that erupted from building pressures. In all of these cases, the model of institutional change was not a continuous curve representing incremental alterations at the margins. It was, rather, an image of history as discontinuous, as bursting at rare moments with catastrophic suddenness. Some of these authors emphasize elite actions in response to environmental change. Alfred Stepan, for example, wrote of

corporatism primarily as an elite response to crisis, a response that involves the attempt by elites who control the state apparatus to restructure the relationship

---

[84] Ibid., pp. 69, 67.

[85] Sidney Verba, "Sequences and Development," in Binder et al. (eds.), *Crises and Sequences of Political Development*.

[86] Binder, "Crises of Political Development," p. 69.

[87] Richard Sandbrock, "The Crisis in Political Development Theory," *Journal of Development Studies* 12 (1975): 163–85.

[88] For example, see Alfred Stepan, *The State and Society: Peru in Comparative Perspective* (Princeton, NJ: Princeton University Press, 1978); Joel S. Migdal, *Peasants, Politics, and Revolution: Pressures Towards Political and Social Change in the Third World* (Princeton, NJ: Princeton University Press, 1974); see Migdal's essay "Capitalist Penetration in the Nineteenth Century: Creating Conditions for New Patterns of Social Control," in Robert Wheeler and Scott Guggenheim (eds.), *Power and Protest in the Countryside: Studies of Rural Unrest* (Durham, NC: Duke University Press, 1982).

[89] See for example: Berger, *Peasants Against Politics*; Peter Gourevitch, "The Second Image Reversed: The International Sources of Domestic Politics," *International Organization* 32 (1978): 881–912; Peter J. Katzenstein, *Corporatism and Change* (Ithaca, NY: Cornell University Press, 1984).

[90] Theda Skocpol, *States and Social Revolutions: A Comparative Analysis of France, Russia and China* (New York: Cambridge University Press, 1979).

between sectors of civil society and the state. This "crisis response" explanation of the existence of corporatism competes with one in which corporatism is viewed as a function of historical continuity.[91]

Others are more interested in the response of nonelites, especially the peasantry, to important changes in their environment.[92] No one has as yet culled from this material a theory or set of generalizations as formal as those in neoclassical economics. How and when new compacts emerge, creating whole classes of rules, is still shrouded in mystery. Nonetheless, the use by scholars of a still implicit, alternative interpretation of institutional change in diverse regions in itself suggests how attractive a more developed theory might prove to be.

Adding an International Perspective

"Is the traditional distinction between international relations and domestic politics dead?" Peter Gourevitch, surveying the literature on the influence of international factors on domestic politics, opened his essay with this question.[93] Certainly, if the mushrooming of research on the merging of these fields is any indicator the answer is yes. Along with the two topics surveyed above – the geographical extension of development studies into areas other than the Third World and the growing importance of history – interest in the impact of international elements on domestic change has marked a major departure for the development field.

Gourevitch noted two aspects of the international system that have powerful effects on the character of domestic regimes: the distribution of power in the state system and the distribution of economic activity and wealth in the international economy. "Put more simply, political development is shaped by war and trade."[94] While some very interesting material has appeared on the distribution of power,[95] the real burgeoning of inter-

---

[91] Stepan, *The State and Society*, p. 47.
[92] See James C. Scott, *The Moral Economy of the Peasants: Rebellion and Subsistence in Southeast Asia* (New Haven, CT: Yale University Press, 1976) and Joel S. Migdal, "Why Change? Toward a New Theory of Change Among Individuals in the Process of Modernization," *World Politics* 26 (1974): 189–206.
[93] Gourevitch, "The Second Image Reversed," p. 881.
[94] Ibid., p. 883.
[95] See Perry Anderson's *Lineages of the Absolutist State* (London: NLB, 1974) and Skocpol's *States and Social Revolutions*.

est has come in the effects of international economic influence and control on domestic structures.

Unlike practically all other streams in the development field – indeed, in the social sciences generally – the dependency literature has not been an American invention, packaged and shipped off to eager academic consumers in the Third World. Latin American scholars, following in the footsteps of economist Raul Prebisch, created dependency explanations against the current of accepted works in development. The standard writings had anchored the field securely in the waters of comparative politics: domestic, immanent factors lie at the heart of any causal explanation of systemic political change, or lack of change. Only in the 1970s and 1980s, did the ideas and concerns of the dependency theorists begin "creeping into mainstream North American social science"[96] on Latin America and, to a much more limited degree, on Africa and Asia.[97] Peter Evans summarized the thrust of the dependency literature:

The starting point is still relations with the external world. A dependent country is one whose development is "conditioned by the development and expansion of another economy." Dependent countries are classically those whose histories of involvement with the international market have led them to specialize in the export of a few primary products. While the income from these few products is absolutely central to the process of accumulation in the dependent country, for the center each product represents only a tiny fraction of total imports, and can usually be obtained from several different sources. The development of the dependent country, however, requires the continued acceptance of its products in the center. Therefore, economic fluctuations in the center may have severe negative consequences for the periphery, whereas an economic crisis in the periphery offers no real threat to accumulation in the center.[98]

Complementing and often underlying dependence based on trade relations is dependence based on foreign ownership of the productive apparatus of the dependent country. When the principal aspect of dependence

---

[96] Richard R. Fagen, "A Funny Thing Happened on the Way to the Market: Thoughts on Extending Dependency Ideas," *International Organization* 32 (1978): 287.

[97] It is interesting to note that dependency literature included the first serious challenge by Marxist and Neo-Marxist works to the dominant approaches in the United States to development and change. For a review of this literature and its relationship to modernization literature in the United States, see Richard Higgott, "Competing Theoretical Perspectives on Development and Underdevelopment: A Recent History," *Politics* 13 (1978): 26–41.

[98] Peter Evans, *Dependent Development: The Alliance of Multinationals, State, and Local Capital in Brazil* (Prinecton, NJ: Princeton University Press, 1979), pp. 26–7.

is that key sectors of the local productive apparatus are integral parts of capital that is controlled elsewhere, then accumulation in the dependent country is externally conditioned more by the "development and expansion of center-based capital" rather than by the "development and expansion of another country." The asymmetry is there nonetheless.

Dependence is then defined most simply as a situation in which the rate and direction of accumulation are externally conditioned.[99]

The danger of dependency is that it can become the residual variable that explains anything and everything, much the same as the role played by the term "traditional" in earlier models of development. The temptation of making international inequality a deus ex machina that explains the true causes of all poverty can lead to neglect of the complex linkages between outside pressures and internal mechanisms. To be sure, the writing on dependency has been extremely uneven, much of it suffused with tendentious arguments. Andre G. Frank, for example, went beyond existing notions about dualistic societies in seeing underdeveloped sectors as a modern creation ("the development of underdevelopment")[100] and as products of international relationships. But he squeezed Latin American events and anomalies into his framework and, even more so in his subsequent book, mercilessly bent worldwide cases to the needs of his theory.[101]

Nonetheless, a body of research and theory has appeared under the dependency heading that has been very provocative. Fernando Enrique Cardoso's work on associated-dependent development, as a case in point, took account of the phenomenal industrial growth accompanied by immense foreign investment in countries such as Brazil.[102] The restructuring of politics after the 1964 coup in Brazil must be understood, he argued, as an outgrowth of the new economic realities there and their relationship to external capital. Evans took up much the same subject in an insightful analysis, trying to untie the three strands of a Gordian knot, the multinational corporations, local private entrepreneurs, and state-owned

[99] Ibid.
[100] Andre G. Frank, *Capitalism and Underdevelopment in Latin America* (New York: Monthly Review Press, 1967).
[101] Andre G. Frank, *Crisis: In the Third World* (New York: Holmes & Meier, 1981).
[102] Fernando Enrique Cardoso and Enzo Faletto, "Associated-Dependent Development: Theoretical Practical Implications," in Alfred Stepen (ed.), *Authoritarian Brazil: Origins, Policies and Future* (New Haven, CT: Yale University Press, 1973).

enterprises.[103] In a somewhat confusing book, Cardoso and Enzo Faletto made a valiant effort to tackle the difficult problem of analytically incorporating different domestic structures in Latin American societies as more than the mere playthings of international forces. The political struggles in a society, they stressed, must be weighed alongside political-economic structures of domination, both internal and external.[104] Although an overwhelming share of the literature has concerned First World–Third World relations, several pieces have begun to explore the dependent role of some Socialist countries.[105]

Probably the most valuable contribution of the dependency literature was that it put the question of the change of social and political institutions into a world capitalist context: "The dependency framework, in other words, explicitly rejects the unified state as actor as a useful conceptual building block of theory."[106] Many of the works in the 1960s and early 1970s were not concerned with what model might replace the one based on states as building blocks. On the whole, scholars simply assumed a bilateral relationship between the United States and/or American-based multinational corporations, on the one hand, and dependent Latin American societies, on the other.

In the mid-1970s, the notion of a world system did offer an alternative to the perspective of single societies or states as individual building blocks. The paradigmatic shift, as some have called it, owed much not only to dependency literature but also to work in the field of international relations. An important volume edited by Robert O. Keohane and Joseph S. Nye marked a shift away from seeing international relations solely as the interaction of independent states – the billiard ball model or what they termed the state-centric view of world affairs.[107] They built on another, neglected tradition, that of transnational relations. Here, interactions are as likely to be peaceful as conflictual and lead to sorts of interdependence in a single transnational society undreamed of in the state-centric model.

[103] Evans, *Dependent Development*.
[104] Cardoso and Faletto, *Dependency and Development in Latin America*.
[105] See, for example, Hendenrik-Jan A. Reitsma, "Development, Geography, Dependency Relations, and the Capitalist Scapegoat," *The Professional Geographer* 34 (1982): 125–30.
[106] James A. Caporaso, "Introductions to the Special Issue of International Organization on Dependence and Dependency in the Global System," *International Organization* 32 (1978): 2.
[107] Robert O. Keohane and Joseph S. Nye, Jr., *Transnational Relations and World Politics* (Cambridge, MA: Harvard University Press, 1970).

The new literature on international regimes has been only one product of the paradigmatic shift. George Modelski drew specifically on the transnational literature and on the "cure in history" to develop an approach to international relations based on the idea of the modern world system.[108] A world system perspective in the field of development and change also borrowed from other disciplines, such as Eric R. Wolf's anthropological work dealing with the effects of nineteenth-century capitalism on peasant societies.[109] Most important of all, however, was the flowering of world-systems theory in sociology, especially in the work of Wallerstein, but also in that of others.[110] Their macrosociological views built on the point raised by the dependency theorists: that is, it is misleading to assume that once external "factors impinge on a society, the main consequences occur through the internal structural processes that maintain the coherence of the society as a bounded system."[111] They rejected

the intellectual tradition [that] emphasizes the treatment of societies as real units of analysis. . . . This is clearly naive. The economies, states, and cultural systems of almost all national societies are historical creations of the European political economy. . . . Further, the current evolution of most national societies is greatly affected by the economic, political, and cultural events which occur entirely outside their boundaries. Economic developments in Africa, the Near East or Latin America are clearly resultants, for better or for worse, of dominant world markets and technologies. Similarly, political events in such areas (e.g., the Nigerian civil war, the creation of an independent Angola) are also creations of the world system.[112]

[108] George Modelski, *Transnational Corporations and World Order: Readings in International Political Economy* (San Francisco, W. H. Freeman, 1979) and his working paper presented at the annual meeting of the American Political Science Association, "Long Cycles of World Leadership" (New York, 1981).

[109] Eric R. Wolf, *Peasant Wars of the Twentieth Century* (New York: Harper & Row, 1969).

[110] See Immanuel Wallerstein, *The Modern World-System: Capitalist Agriculture and the Origins of the European World Economy in the Sixteenth Century* (New York: Academic Press, 1974) and *The Modern World System II: Mercantilism and the Consolidation of the European World Economy, 1600–1750* (New York: Academic Press, 1974). For other world-systems theories, refer to: Daniel Chirot's, *Social Change in a Periphery Society: The Creation of a Balkan Colony* (New York: Academic Press, 1976) and his *Social Change in the Twentieth Century* (New York: Harcourt Brace Jovanovisch, 1977); John W. Meyer and Michael T. Hannan, *National Development in the World System: Educational, Economic, and Political Change, 1950–1970* (Chicago: University of Chicago Press, 1979); Barbara H. Kaplan, *Social Change in the Capitalist World Economy* (Beverly Hills, CA: Sage, 1978); Walter L. Goldfrank, *The World System of Capitalism: Past and Present* (Beverly Hills, CA: Sage, 1979); Skocpol, *State and Social Revolution*.

[111] Meyer and Hannan, *National Development and the World System*, p. 3.

[112] Ibid., pp. 11–12.

The advance by world-systems theorists beyond the dependency framework is illustrated by the term "system" itself. It denotes an entity, other than a single society, within which there is an established set of rules for human interaction – what some have referred to as an ongoing division of labor. The term "world" signifies that the area of such an entity extends beyond individual societies or culture groups; it does not mean necessarily that such a system blankets the entire globe. Most world systems historically have been world empires, such as the Roman Empire. One world system, the one we live in, has had no unifying political structure but has maintained its rules or division of labor through market exchanges (capitalism); it is a world economy. This modern world system "flourished, expanded to cover the entire earth (and thereby eliminated all remaining mini-systems and world empires), and brought about a technological and ecological 'explosion' in the use of natural resources."[113]

World systems have beginnings and all besides ours have had ends. The momentary events and relationships in any society can be understood only in terms of the life history of the system as a whole. This premise of the world-systems theorists has dovetailed with the return to history by many political scientists to produce a growing trend counter to the cross-sectional analyses so common in comparative politics.

The level-of-analysis problem has bedevilled political scientists for decades, and the world-systems approach has only complicated matters by rejecting all the levels commonly used by comparativists. It is not surprising, then, that political scientists have shown rather cautious interest in the new theories. Wallerstein's economic determinism and his relegation of the state to secondary status have created concern. Uneasiness has also surfaced since Wallerstein's theory neglects any independent role for domestic institutions and culture in processes of change. Nonetheless, despite these and other reservations, a number of political scientists have begun to use the world system rather than single states or societies, as their point of departure.[114] It is likely that in the coming decade the level-of-analysis debate will intensify and that the old

---

[113] Immanuel Wallerstein, "A World System Perspective of the Social Sciences," *British Journal of Sociology* 27 (1976): 349.

[114] See, for example, Modelski, "The Long Cycle of Global Politics and the Nation-State," and Aristide R. Zolberg, "Origins of the Modern System: A Missing Link," *World Politics* 33 (1981): 253–81.

distinctions between comparative politics and international relations will continue to erode. The world-systems field is now a growth industry with its own journal (*Review*), an institute headed by Wallerstein (the Fernand Braudel Center), a series of annuals, and more. With this sort of infrastructural support, one can expect a paradigmatic battle, which may bring new vigor into the field.

Back to First Principles

For close to a decade, the field of development and change has undergone a rejuvenation, overcoming the inertia brought on by sterile definitional battles and, later, by the loss of faith in the United States as the model of the first new nation. Scholarship has been freed from the Procrustean notions that the future of the Third World is faithfully reflected in the mirror of Western history. Has the new vitality in the field also led toward some acceptance of new constitutive principles? Have the recent forays into the uncharted waters of history, new geographic regions, and international politics challenged the assumptions of the earlier theorists and their dichotomous models about the nature of order and the causes of change? The answer to both questions seems to be a qualified yes: qualified because so many of the ramifications coming from the new work are still inchoate and because important connections to past assumptions do survive.

The issue of authority has been at the heart of the field's concerns. Those relying on center-periphery or other such dichotomies to comprehend the twists and turns of political changes made suppositions about the source and direction of authority. They assumed flows from a society's central elites and their integrated institutions to the rest of the population, which was often seen as rather undifferentiated. Dependency and world-systems theorists departed from an essential tenet of that premise, the integrity of the society itself as a basis for interpreting the source and direction of authority. They construed the most important movements of authority to be those across national boundaries. In world-systems analysis, the flows lie in the unequal exchanges consantly reproducing the worldwide division of labor, enforced when necessary by strong states. Order and change depend not primarily on the mix of values, institutions, and elites in a society but on the niche of that society in a much larger configuration. The values, the institutions, and the elites reflect a world pattern and act to ensure in their small corner, at least, the conditions necessary for the constant reproduction of the world division of labor.

Ironically, world-systems theory, inspired by an even earlier borrowing of terms by Prebisch and others,[115] used the same center-periphery metaphor. Now, however, the center, or core as some call it, signifies the portion of the world that appropriates the lion's share of world surplus through the international market, with the added backing of strong state mechanisms. The periphery includes the weakest political entities, where populations are organized to produce commodities needed by the center. Like earlier models the internationalized version construes change in largely dichotomous terms (though Wallerstein adds an intermediate category, the semiperiphery). The international model treats the periphery in much the same way as the earlier conception: the periphery is passive and malleable in the face of a strong, integrated center. The center is the repository of authority.

Even for those who have accepted the shift away from a single society to transnational society, the conditions of order and change in an individual society still are created at that society's center – now because of the local center's ties to the world core. Political scientists from both sides of the paradigmatic divide have given special attention to the state as the storehouse of authority. As Charles W. Anderson put it, "There is a predisposition to see state action as a primary factor in the process of economic development" and, one could add, in countless other processes as well.[116] "Many contemporary notions about development," Anderson added, "seem to posit government as a kind of 'omnipotent given' that could if it would set matters right."[117]

Oddly, this state-centered view runs directly counter to a perspective that has been described as maintaining "a pervasive grip upon citizens, journalists and scholars alike."[118] This alternative outlook depicts authority flowing from society to state, not vice versa. Eric Nordlinger calls this view society centered. It includes both pluralism and Marxism, which portray state officials as subject to the desires, even control, of interest groups or social classes embedded in civil society. One might account

[115] United Nations, *The Economic Development of Latin America and Its Principal Problems* (New York: United Nations, 1950).

[116] Charles W. Anderson, *Politics and Economic Change in Latin America: The Governing of Restless Nations* (Princeton, NJ: D. Van Nostrand, 1967), p. 3.

[117] Anderson, *Politics and Economic Change in Latin America*, p. 5.

[118] Nordlinger, *On the Autonomy of the Democratic State*, p. 1.

for the contradictions between state-centered and society-centered perspectives by pointing to the state-centered portrayals largely as ones of non-Western countries while the society-centered descriptions are of democratic, industrial countries. Even so, it might also be noted that the pendulum for scholars studying the West has also swung toward a state-centered interpretation, emphasizing the autonomy, or at least the relative autonomy, of the state.

In the third-world literature, bureaucratic authoritarian interpretations have, if anything, strengthened Anderson's observation; the state remains at the foundation of many causal theories of order and change. This conclusion is not as true of much of the empirical on-site literature, which often has stressed the disarray in many states. But, in the general theories, civil society has most often been presented as the clay in the hands of the potter, the state. The premises of the dichotomies in which strong, integrated centers mold weak, diffuse peripheries, seem as popular as ever.

The most influential of the writers on bureaucratic authoritarianism has been Guillermo O'Donnell.[119] He contended that increasing industrialization in Brazil and Argentina activated the popular sector, inducing more rigidity by other sectors and, eventually, unregulated conflict. These tensions combined with weakening political institutions to create a crisis alleviated only by a "coup coalition" that excluded the popular sector and established a bureaucratic authoritarian regime. The new military-led governments adopted "a technocratic, bureaucratic approach to policy making (as opposed to a more political approach through which policies are shaped by economic and political demands from different sectors of society, expressed through such channels as elections, legislatures, political parties, and labor unions)."[120] In the bureaucratic authoritarian literature, the state looms larger than before, more shielded from societal pressures and inputs.[121] And, in this respect, this literature has blended in effortlessly with the corporatist works discussed earlier. In both sorts of studies, the state "is characterized by strong and relatively autonomous governmental structures that seek to impose

---

[119] Guillermo O'Donnell, "Tensions in the Bureaucratic-Authoritarian State and the Question of Democracy," in David Collier (ed.), *The New Authoritarianism in Latin America* (Princeton, NJ: Princeton University Press, 1979).

[120] Ibid., p. 4.

[121] Ibid.

on the society a system of interest representation based on enforced limited pluralism."[122]

It remains highly questionable whether states are indeed so formidable. Indeed, one question is whether corporatist and bureaucratic authoritarian theories portray accurately the roots of change and the maintenance of order. Like the nineteenth-century German philosophers, such as Fichte and Hegel, who saw the state as the guide to social transformation, these theories assume all too glibly the endless capacity of the state to shape society. Some recent and some not so recent literature has implied that such state-centered perspectives may veil important elements of change and order. These same works, however, would not give heart to theorists using pluralist, Marxist, or other society-centered outlooks mentioned by Nordlinger.[123] What may be hinted at in these other writings is a new understanding of the causes of change and the nature of constitutive principles, rejecting the notion of the state or center as the sole repository of authority and also spurning the traditional society-centered approaches of the comparative politics field.

Merilee S. Grindle conducted a fascinating study of public policy in Mexico, a state noted for its bureaucratic authoritarianism and corporatism. The results of the state's efforts in creating and pursuing a new rural development policy were less than glowing. At every step in the policy process formidable obstacles appeared, thwarting the intent of central policymakers. Grindle noted one community worker's response:

Going out and meeting with peasants can be a dangerous business in Mexico. It threatens a lot of people. In some remote areas, the caciques [local bosses] were considered to be an unassailable force, even by the party. In one state, the reaction of such local influentials had caused the governor to request that CONASUPO [the state agency] completely remove the Field Coordination Program from his state.[124]

Influence or authority here does not appear to be the exclusive domain of the state at all. This conclusion echoes a point made by Anderson a decade earlier. In his research on Latin America, he found "limited

---

[122] James M. Malloy, "Authoritarianism and Corporatism in Latin America: The Modal Pattern," in James M. Malloy (ed.), *Authoritarianism and Corporatism in Latin America* (Pittsburgh, PA: University of Pittsburgh Press, 1977), p. 4.

[123] Nordlinger, *On the Autonomy of the Democratic State*.

[124] Merilee S. Grindle, *Bureaucrats, Politicians, and Peasants in Mexico: A Case Study in Public Policy* (Berkeley: University of California Press, 1977), p. 160.

government, limited not so much by constitutional arrangements, as that term is conventionally used, as by the resources which government has at its disposal, and the relations between its role and function in the social order and that of other institutions."[125] Drawing heavily on African cases, another work portrayed political conditions not greatly different from those described by Anderson for Latin America. Gerald A. Heeger depicted the "chronically weak [political] institutions which hinge on fragile bargaining relationships between elites in the center and the periphery."[126] He was deeply critical of studies on political consolidation, which

mistook the organizational aspirations of the political elites for reality and posited a cohesion that simply was not there. . . . Elite-mass consolidation was viewed as being comprehensible in terms of but a single successful linkage between center and periphery–charisma, the party, etc. To put this in another way, where such linkages were seen to exist, the relationships they were seen as establishing were given more coherence than they possessed in reality. The actual multiplicity of such links and their possible contradiction were either obscured or ignored altogether.[127]

One article addressed directly the corporatist literature on Latin America and its premise that states are capable of molding societies. The consensual order at the center so important to dichotomous models of change, Linn A. Hammergren suggested, is largely absent in Latin America, but corporatist writings persist in picturing "the convergence of political power at the center and top of corporations."[128] Hammergren went on to note, "The tradition of local *caudillos*, *caciques*, or *gamonales*, especially in more isolated areas of the country, the presence of regional elites even in more developed areas, the maintenance of economic ties between internal and external groups with minimal participation by the state, all point to a very limited penetration of society by the national center."[129]

All this should not lead one to dismiss the state too quickly. These criticisms do not necessarily lead us back willy-nilly to society-centered perspectives in which the state is little more than a stage for playing out conflicts among the factions and segments of society. The state is limited,

---

[125] Anderson, *Politics and Economic Change in Latin America*, p. 5.
[126] Gerald A. Heeger, *The Politics of Underdevelopment* (New York: St. Martin's Press, 1974).
[127] Ibid., p. 49.
[128] Linn A. Hammergren, "Corporatism in Latin American Polities: A Reexamination of the 'Unique' Tradition," *Comparative Politics* 9 (July 1977): 443.
[129] Ibid., p. 449.

to use Anderson's term, but it is surely not dead. It has tremendous resources available from international sources in the form of foreign aid, direct investment of foreign capital, and international loans, as well as, in some cases, political-military support. Internally, its ability to mobilize resources, to regulate society, indeed even to reshape society may be substantial in specific sectors, regions, or policy arenas. Theorists of corporatism and bureaucratic authoritarianism rightly highlight the state's "elimination of a whole network of intermediary groups and actors."[130]

It is an exaggeration of many cases to say governments do not govern,[131] as it is misleading to dismiss the Third World simply a consisting of proto-societies or of no societies at all. These are societies with distributions of authority that do not fit existing state-centered or society-centered models very well. And, one may add, if the authors quoted above – Tilly on the limits of European centers in history and Berger and Piore on the bounds of state authority in Europe today – are right, then these models are equally misleading for some cases outside the Third World. What we need to know is how to describe and assess these distributions of authority and how to understand the changes that brought them about. What caused different distributions of authority in different societies? In which areas can states use their extraordinary powers and in which areas may they be all but helpless against other authoritative bodies? If the state is not all-powerful, if elites in the periphery may at times predominate, what becomes of the dichotomous models of change and order? Where do we turn for constitutive principles?

Anderson wrote that the state "is not synonymous with the social order, but is one institution among the many that make up organized human life. Government has an impact on other social institutions and in turn is affected by them."[132] Social organizations of all shapes scattered throughout society may be repositories of authority. In many countries, varied groups have managed to maintain rules of behavior and ways of life in direct conflict with the codes of the state or the norms of the center. They have held onto their ways with leechlike tenacity despite the greater resources and the substantial determination of state leaders, and despite the international norms that have mandated these leaders' active role in fostering social change. Berger and Piore described the European situation: "Various segments of society organize around different rules,

---

[130] Ibid., p. 456.   [131] Huntington, *Political Order and Changing Societies*.
[132] Anderson, *Politics and Economic Change in Latin America*, p. 5.

processes, and institutions that produce different systems of incentives and disincentives to which individuals respond."[133]

States are in conflict with a heterogeneous flock of other social organizations that do not share the rules of the state. Whether and to what degree states can successfully triumph in their conflict with such organizations varies. These variations are rooted in the different ways in which world historical forces have been played out. Incisive studies on the United States and Europe treat states, not as "omnipotent givens," but as variable in their ability to effect social policy and reshape society.[134] The specific types of order and change in a society are the outcomes of the struggles over the rules of the game among social organizations, including the organization that is usually the weightiest of all, although not always strong enough to end the struggle altogether – the state. How that struggle has developed and how it will proceed depend not only on domestic factors but on important historical and contemporary actions and alliances originating in the larger world system.

[133] Berger and Piore, *Dualism and Discontinuity in Industrial Societies*, p. 2.
[134] See: Stephen D. Krasner, *Defending the National Interests: Raw Materials Investments and U.S. Foreign Policy* (Princeton, NJ: Princeton University Press, 1978), P. 57; Peter J. Katzenstein, "Conclusion: Domestic Structures and Strategies of Foreign Economic Policy," in Katzenstein (ed.), *Between Power and Plenty: Foreign Economic Policies of Advanced Industrial States* (Madison: University of Wisconsin Press, 1978).

8

Studying the State

Over the course of the twentieth century, comparative political scientists' core questions have changed very little. From Weber and Gramsci to Almond, Verba, and Skocpol, their concerns have centered on why people obey and on what sorts of structures and cultures facilitate obedience and conformist behavior.[1] The elements that political scientists have singled out for investigation as the key to understanding obedience and conformity have included the usual suspects: parliaments, bureaucracies, governmental leadership, courts and law, and police and military. These form the constituent parts and parameters of that complex and somewhat elusive structure called the modern state – the mountain that all political scientists sooner or later must climb.

In the pages ahead, I will make several central points. First, in the next section, I will argue that, despite the assault on the state from a number of directions, it will remain central to the study of comparative politics well into the twenty-first century. Second, in part due to the overwhelming influence of Weber on the study of the state, various perspectives – culturalist, rationalist, and institutionalist – have tended to isolate it as a subject of study, peering into its innards and poring over its organization in order to understand how it succeeds in gaining obedience and conformity from its population. This sort of analytic isolation of the state,

[1] See for example Max Weber, *Theory of Social and Economic Organization* (New York: Free Press, 1964); Antonio Gramsci, *Selections from the Prison Notebooks*, ed. Quitin Hoare and Geoffrey N. Smith (New York: International Publishers, 1971); Gabriel A. Almond and Sidney Verba, *The Civic Culture: Political Attitudes and Democracy in Five Nations* (Princeton, NJ: Princeton University Press, 1963); Theda Skocpol, *States and Social Revolutions: A Comparative Analysis of France, Russia and China* (New York: Cambridge University Press, 1979).

I will claim, has led to a mystification of its capabilities and power. Finally, if we are to develop a more useful way to approach the state, we will need to recognize it as the "limited state." To accomplish that will mean blending the largely ignored culturalist perspective with the more dominant institutionalist approach, as well as shifting the analytic focus from the state as a freestanding organization to a process-oriented view of the state-in-society.

Rhetoric and Reality of Modern States

That the state became so central to the study of comparative politics in the nineteenth and twentieth centuries is not so surprising. While global and transnational challenges to state authority have been evident throughout this period, particularly at the end of the twentieth century, the state – that sprawling organization claiming territorial sovereignty – has been the dominant form for organizing political power. Certainly, by the beginning of the nineteenth century, states had become "the sole constitutive elements of the international system at the exclusion of others,"[2] and that is still largely true today.[3] The state's very existence was part and parcel of the great transformation bringing modernity, which preoccupied Marx, Weber, and so many other major thinkers.

What makes the modern state modern? Serving both the ideals of the Enlightenment and the needs of modern capitalism, the modern state has been constructed to create a uniformity or universality to life within its borders. Weber fretted about just that dimension of states in his lament on the iron cage. Unlike most premodern political structures, the state has aimed to impose uniform and ultimate conformity on social life within far-reaching (but still circumscribed) boundaries: its leaders have sought obedience in even the most personal realms of social interaction from whom one might sleep with to how one must bury the dead. Compliance to these sorts of social norms was not new, but the claims of a single centralized organization to enforce such norms over huge territorial expanses were novel almost everywhere they were made. And, indeed, one can point to real cases in which this kind of microregulation has been successfully

---

[2] Hendrik Spruyt, *The Sovereign State and Its Competitors: An Analysis of System Change* (Princeton, NJ: Princeton University Press, 1994), p. 3.
[3] Robert H. Jackson and Alan James, eds., *States in a Changing World: A Contemporary Analysis* (Oxford: Clarendon Press, 1993), pp. 6–11.

achieved. Astonishingly, some states have been able to garner from people's yearly earnings a share equivalent to all their work performed through April or May or, sometimes, even June of that year and to sequester their children for thirty or so hours a week in a state institution. Premodern political leaders could not have imagined such audacious goals.

Now, whether one feels high taxes and compulsory public education are justified or not, the ability of some states to accomplish these acts over expansive territories in fairly uniform ways is truly remarkable. For that reason alone, states should remain centerpieces in the study of comparative politics well into the twenty-first century. Other important factors also suggest that scrutiny of the state will continue to hold sway in the decades ahead but most likely with a different sort of research agenda. In Western Europe, the very birthplace of the state, debates have raged over the proper distribution of powers between long-standing states and the European Union. Elsewhere, in what used to be the Third World and the Communist bloc, the late 1980s and the 1990s have brought the simultaneous disintegration of existing states and the birth of new ones.

The demise of old states has included rock-solid ones, as in the case of the Soviet Union, as well as flimsy reeds, such as Somalia, Liberia, and Afghanistan. The last decade has been the first time in more than half a century that some states have simply disappeared from the world map. At the same time, we have witnessed the creation of a gaggle of new states, the most proclamations of independence since the end of the colonial era about thirty-five years ago. From Kyrgyzstan to Croatia, from Eritrea to Palestine, new states and state wannabees have imposed themselves on the existing international system. The leaders of new states have made the same claims of territoriality, sovereignty, autonomy, and independence that marked the rhetoric of earlier states. And they have made similar calls for the obedience of their populations, for governing the minutiae of personal life, as did their forerunners. At the very moment that officials have been proclaiming the inviolability of their new states' sovereignty, however, global forces have cut into the prerogatives of even the well-established ones.[4] From the formal constraints imposed by the International Monetary Fund or international environmental conventions to the subtle (or sometimes not-so-subtle) pressures stemming from the vast increases in capital flows, new forces have emerged that have given the word

---

[4] David J. Elkins, *Beyond Sovereignty: Territory and Political Economy in the Twenty-First Century* (Toronto: University of Toronto Press, 1995).

sovereignty a shop-worn look.[5] All of these late-twentieth-century changes will force political scientists to look much more closely at states.[6] Old definitions of states as having a monopoly over coercive means or as shaping the public domain or as coherent actors with vast autonomy will come under close scrutiny. One certain conclusion is that most states, if not all, have failed to live up to earlier promises or even to scholars' characterizations of them. The grand rhetoric of states, even the most unsteady ones, as well as the expectations about state capabilities generated in the scholarly literature, have obscured the failures of public institutions and policies. The presumptions of political leaders, and even of political science theories – that states could impose a uniform and universal law, induce economic development, deal with abuse of women and children, shape the everyday behavior of those in society through public policies, and much, much more – have not simply eliminated the problem of achieving conformity and obedience. If anything, by setting the bar so high in terms of what states should and could properly demand of those they rule, leaders and scholars have succeeded in bringing the disparity between state goals and state accomplishments into sharp relief.

That gap is the scab that comparative political scientists will pick at as they explore subjects ranging from economic liberalization policies to the regulation of immigration to the prevalence of civic attitudes in a given population. As the twenty-first century unfolds, the state will remain center stage, but increasingly it will be the state's difficulties in achieving conformity and obedience that should attract the interest of compara-

---

[5] See for example: Joseph A. Camilleri and Jim Falk, *The End of Sovereignty? The Politics of a Shrinking and Fragmenting World* (Brookfield, VT: Edward Edgar, 1992); Ivo D. Duchacek, Daniel Latouche, and Garth Stevenson, *Perforated Sovereignties and International Relations: Trans-Sovereign Contacts of Subnational Governments* (New York: Greenwood Press, 1988); Julie A. Erfani, *The Paradox of the Mexican State: Rereading Sovereignty from Independence to NAFTA* (Boulder, CO: Lynne Rienner, 1995); Gidon Gottlieb, *Nations Against State: A New Approach to Ethnic Conflicts and the Decline of Sovereignty* (New York: International Publishers, 1971); Edmond J. Keller and Donald Rothchild, *Africa in the New International Order: Rethinking State Sovereignty and Regional Security* (Boulder, CO: Lynne Rienner, 1996); Thom Kuehls, *Beyond Sovereign Territory: The Space of Ecopolitics* (Minneapolis: University of Minnesota Press, 1996); Gene M. Lyons and Michael Mastanduno, eds., *Beyond Westphalia? State Sovereignty and International Intervention* (Baltimore, MD: John Hopkins University Press, 1995); Michael J. Shapiro and Hayward R. Alker, *Changing Boundaries: Global Flows, Territorial Identities* (Minneapolis: University of Minnesota Press, 1996).

[6] Philosophers, too, have come back to the question of the state. See John T. Sanders and Jan Narveson, eds., *For and Against the State: New Philosophical Readings* (Lanham, MD: Rowman and Littlefield, 1996).

tive political scientists. If they are to understand the yawning gap between state rhetoric and performance, their old ideal-typical images of states as able to successfully impose uniformity, as capable of building an iron cage, need to be replaced by theories that start with the limitations of actual states.

For two decades now, political scientists have isolated the state as a subject of inquiry.[7] Through a variety of lenses and approaches, they have studied this distinctive structure of the modern age intensively. The literature has been most prominent in research on the non-Western world, in large part because of the appearance of so many new states in Asia and Africa after World War II. Much of the research has focused on what some political scientists have called the developmental state, looking especially at state building or state capabilities. But books such as Krasner's *Defending the National Interest* mined the field for North American and European cases, as well.

My contention in the coming pages is that these sorts of inquiry – ones that isolate the state as a subject of study, focusing on its structure first and only then on how it fits in a world of other structures – have led too often to a mystification of the state and its capabilities. In the next section, I will review how political scientists using a variety of perspectives have approached the structure of the state. I will note here how the culturalists' and rationalists' approaches were fairly marginal to the study of state structure as it emerged in the late 1970s and early 1980s. Rather it was the system-dominant structural perspective that swept political scientists off their feet two decades ago. But the gap between rhetoric and reality, between an image of powerful states and the diversity in practices of actual states, has led to disillusionment with this approach, too. Increasingly, comparativists have moved to an "institutions" perspective on the state that is much less deterministic and more open to a diversity of outcomes.

I will go on to argue in the following section that a focus on structure, on the state in isolation, is insufficient. If we are to understand the inherent limitations of states we must develop a focus on *process*, one that starts with the web of relationships between them and their societies. At the heart

---

[7] In this regard, they have been influenced heavily by Weber who emphasized repeatedly the need to study the "power of command." In his discussion of Weber, Rodney Barker notes that "authority stems from an author who is both its possessor and its source." Barker, *Political Legitimacy and the State* (New York: Oxford University Press, 1990), p. 50. It was authority of the state, as seen through its structure and practices, toward which Weber pointed us.

of the modern state's successes and failures, especially with respect to its ability to gain obedience, is the nature of its relationship to those it claims to rule. The battering of states by global economic and information systems, by the challenges of supranational organizations like the European Union, by the disintegrative effects of virulent ethnic and tribal forces, all have deeply affected the relationship between states and their populations.

The point of departure in looking at process in this essay is the engagement of the contemporary state with those people within its boundaries. Again using different colored lenses, particularly those of culturalists and institutionalists, I will review how scholars have conceived states and their relationship to their populations. The argument will center on how a basic paradox in that relationship demands a move toward a different understanding of the state, one that starts with its hamstrung and limited qualities. Only by adding a culturalist approach to the prevailing "institutions" perspective can the study of states move in the twenty-first century to theories that explain the varieties of limited sovereignty and capabilities that we find in actual cases.

Explaining How the State Is Constituted

The Culturalist Perspective

Of the three lenses commonly used in studies of comparative politics – culturalist, rationalist, and institutionalist – the culturalist perspective has had, by far, the smallest impact on the study of why states turn out as they do. Only a limited number of political science works have used this approach in research on state building or state capabilities. As one researcher put it, "In every way 'culture' is the poor relation of 'structure.'"[8] Another stated, "The systematic study of politics and culture is moribund."[9] In Marc Ross's survey of politics and culture, one finds very little mention of the state.[10] None of the five contributions he sets out, in which culture has contributed to comparative political analysis, tackles the issue of the

---

[8] Margaret S. Archer, "The Myth of Cultural Unity," *British Journal of Sociology* 36 (September 1985): 333.

[9] David D. Laitin, *Hegemony and Culture: Politics and Religious Change Among the Yoruba* (Chicago: University of Chicago Press, 1986), p. 171.

[10] Marc Ross, "Culture and Identity in Comparative Political Analysis," in Mark Lichbach and Alan Zuckerman (eds.), *Comparative Politics: Rationality, Culture, and Structure* (New York: Cambridge University Press, 1997).

construction of the state. Indeed, the most interesting cultural approaches to studying the state have come from outside the discipline of political science.

Despite its marginality in previous political science research on the construction of the state, I want to spend a bit of time on this perspective now because of its potential to help us move toward a new agenda for research in the twenty-first century. Three related points coming out of this literature are very important for the study of the state. The first, often an implicit point, is, that everything else being equal, organizations (especially complex organizations like states) tend to disintegrate because their parts are pulled in so many different directions. Second, culture offers a centripetal antidote to those centrifugal tendencies. And, third, the rituals associated with the state, often undertaken as ends in themselves rather than simply as means to increase power, represent much of the cohesive power that culture offers.

Outside of political science, the work of the renowned anthropologist Clifford Geertz has been the most influential. While much of Geertz's thought on the topic stems from his research on the Balinese state of precolonial Indonesia, others have extended his work into the contemporary period. Geertz's specific case, Negara, differed from modern states most notably in its leaders' indifference to actual governing, in their hesitancy in regulating people's everyday actions, and in their lack of interest in territorial sovereignty.

Their attention pointed "toward spectacle, toward ceremony, toward the public dramatization of the ruling obsessions of Balinese culture: social inequality and status pride. It was a theatre state in which the kings and princes were the impresarios, the priests the directors, and the peasants the supporting cast, stage crew, and audience."[11] Geertz's culturalist perspective turned the study of the state on its head – "power served pomp, not pomp power."[12] All the elaborate ceremonies that one associates with states – from inaugurations to press conferences – might not be, as usually thought, means toward an end. They might, as in the Balinese case, be ends in themselves.[13]

---

[11] Clifford Geertz, *Negara: The Theatre State in Nineteenth-Century Bali* (Princeton, NJ: Princeton University Press, 1980), p. 13.

[12] Ibid.

[13] Similar attention to the ceremony of the state is made by other anthropologists. A. I. Richards for example, notes the deference paid in Buganda to the Kabaka, or king.

In this view the court and capital "is not just the nucleus, the engine, or the pivot of the state, it *is* the state. . . . It is a statement of a controlling political idea – namely, that by the mere act of providing a model, a paragon, a faultless image of civilized existence, the court shapes the world around it into at least a rough approximation of its own excellence."[14] Geertz does not hide from interests and institutions. He sees a constant tension between the integrative effects of the state provided by ideals or the master narrative – what he calls the "controlling political idea" – and the disintegrative forces of the "power system composed as it was of dozens of independent, semi-independent, and quarter-independent rulers."[15]

Implicitly, Geertz's notion takes issue with political scientists who simply assume the coherence that rationality or structure and institutions provide or to those who pay lip service to the role of "values and norms" while actually devoting themselves to studying the ins and outs of the organization of the state. His assumption is the opposite: we cannot look at the bricks of the state without understanding the mortar. We should expect that a complex of organizations would be pulled in a hundred different directions; only a controlling idea, a cultural glue, could keep them from doing that. A century ago Gaetano Mosca made reference to a similar notion in his analysis of the "political formula," the legal and moral principle that sustains the ruling class.[16] A comment made by one writer on Geertz concerning rulers and ruled might serve as a yellow flag for political scientists: master narratives "operate as the unchallenged first principles of a political order, making any given hierarchy appear natural and just to rulers and ruled."[17]

A political scientist, David Laitin, modified Geertz's insights and adapted them to political science. He also tried to break down the notion of master narratives to more workable subunits, what he called shared "points of concern." Here is how Laitin interpreted Geertz:

Richards, "Authority Patterns in Traditional Buganda," in L. A. Fallers and A. I. Richards (eds.), *The King's Men: Leadership and Status in Buganda on the Eve of Independence* (New York: Oxford University Press, 1964). "Loyalty had to be expressed formally and constantly." (p. 274).

[14] Geertz, *Negara*, p. 13.   [15] Ibid., p. 19.

[16] Gaetano Mosca, *The Ruling Class* (New York: McGraw-Hill, 1939), pp. 70–2.

[17] Sean Wilentz, *Rites of Power: Symbolism, Ritual and Politics Since the Middle Ages* (Philadelphia: University of Philadelphia Press, 1985), p. 4.

Social systems are not rigid. Subsystems have their own internal dynamics that influence the wider social system. Exogenous change puts pressures on different subsystems and ultimately the social system as well. Social systems are therefore adaptive; they accommodate change as subsystems mutually adjust their values so that there will be a homeostatic equilibrium in the society.[18]

Laitin allows for more discord than Geertz in saying that the points of concern, rather than simply values or preferences, represent sets of values that people share on what is worth worrying about: "A symbol system will provide a clue to what is worth fighting about and also to what is so commonsensical that attempts to change it seem pointless."[19] In other words, the cultural glue does not necessarily mean the existence of a broad consensus about some master narrative but can refer to common understandings about what the agenda should be and agreement on how and when to disagree.

Even in cases in which we are not talking about precolonial entities, Geertz's prescription resonates. Modern states are made up of multiple agencies and bureaus with widely different tasks and interests. The forces pulling them in different directions – regional demands, interest group leverage, international pressures – are tremendous. A focus on culture, whether it refers to some master narrative or simply points of concern, directs researchers toward the beliefs and shared meanings that prevent institutional chaos. Geertz's understanding of culture and the state differs from some of the more common cultural approaches in sociology, which zero in on the integration and disintegration of *society* as an indirect means of applying the notion of culture to the state or which focus on the interaction of culture and the state, including the manipulation of culture by the state (where the state is seen largely in structural or institutional terms).[20] Geertz also goes beyond common cultural approaches found in political science, such as that in an influential book like *The Civic*

---

[18] Laitin, *Hegemony and Culture*, p. 175.   [19] Ibid.

[20] See: Edward Shils, *The Constitution of Society* (Chicago: University of Chicago Press, 1972); Michael Schudson, "Culture and Integration of National Societies," *International Social Science Journal* 46 (February 1994): 63–82; Archer, "The Myth of Cultural Unity"; Gilbert M. Joseph and Daniel Nugent, "Popular Culture and State Formation," in Gilbert M. Joseph and Daniel Nugent (eds.), *Everyday Forms of State Formation: Revolution and the Negotiation of Rule in Modern Mexico* (Durham, NC: Duke University Press, 1994); Helen Siu, "Recycling Rituals and Popular Culture in Contemporary China," in Perry Link, Richard Madsen, and Paul G. Pickowiez (eds.), *Unofficial China: Popular Culture and Thought in the People's Republic* (Boulder, CO: Westview Press, 1989).

Culture, where the actual construction of the state plays a negligible role and the focus, instead, is on how broadly held values affect politics. Geertz examines directly the "concrete social institution"[21] of the state, and he devises a cultural explanation for its ability to stay together and shape its society.

E. P. Thompson, who seemingly came to the idea of the state as theater independently of Geertz, ended up at much the same point, although in the end he gave even more credence to the bricks that make up the state than Geertz. "A great part of politics and law," Thompson observed, "is always theater; once a social system has become 'set,' it does not need to be endorsed daily by exhibitions of power . . . ; what matters more is a continuing theatrical style."[22] To note that control is "cultural," he wrote, "is not to say that it was immaterial, too fragile for analysis, insubstantial. To define control in terms of cultural hegemony is not to give up attempts at analysis, but to prepare for analysis at the points at which it should be made: into the images of power and authority, the popular mentalities of subordination."[23]

Others have picked up on the idea of theater states and have tried to apply it to more contemporary cases.[24] Even Geertz makes no secret of his belief that an approach stressing theater and master narratives should be applied to modern examples, too. In another essay, he wrote, "Now, the easy reaction to all this talk of monarchs, their trappings, and their peregrinations is that it has to do with a closed past, a time in Huizinga's famous phrase, when the world was half-a-thousand years younger and everything was clearer. . . . Thrones may be out of fashion, and pageantry too," he continued, "but political authority still requires a cultural frame in which to define itself and advance its claims, and so does opposition to it."[25]

Culture for Geertz is not the cults and customs but the master narratives that give shape to people's experience. The problem for him and for

---

[21] Geertz, *Negara*, p. 19.

[22] E. P. Thompson, "Patrician Society, Plebian Culture," *Journal of Social History* 7 (Summer 1974): 389.

[23] Ibid., p. 387. Thompson borrowed the concept of cultural hegemony from Gramsci.

[24] See for example: Joseph W. Esherick and Jeffrey N. Wasserstrom, "Acting Out Democracy: Political Theater in Modern China," *Journal of Asian Studies* 49 (November, 1990): 835–65.

[25] Clifford Geertz, *Local Knowledge: Further Essays in Interpretive Anthropology* (New York: Basic Books, 1983), 142–3.

others seeking to apply this approach to the study of today's states is how to do that. Geertz himself notes, "One of the things that everyone knows but no one can quite think how to demonstrate is that a country's politics reflect the design of its culture."[26] Perhaps that is why the flurry of excitement with Geertz's approach, which rippled through the scholarly community in the 1970s and early 1980s, could not sustain itself.[27] We know that culture is important, that the state is more than a configuration of roles or an interchangeable structure; we just cannot quite figure out how to study it comparatively, how to make it much more than a giant residual category.

The System-Dominant Structuralist Perspective

While those who viewed the state from the culturalist perspective remained on the margins of political science, the structuralist approach swept comparativists by storm in the 1970s. In part, they were affected by the rebirth of realism (now as neorealism) in international relations. Many, too, were influenced by the reemergence of comparative historical sociology, led by key figures who spanned the disciplines of sociology and political science and by the rush to "bring the state back in."[28] Most commonly, this approach treated states as integral, coherent units whose actions could be understood by looking at the alignment of forces (domestic or international) in their environment. This is a system-dominant perspective in which structuralists see states as interchangeable to the degree that they expect them to act similarly if facing the same array of forces (the systemic element). Researchers could, then, understand a state's actions based on the its interests as an integral unit within a configuration of other forces.

In assuming the coherence of the state in following its own set of interests, political scientists, such as Eric A. Nordlinger and Stephen D.

[26] Clifford Geertz, *The Interpretation of Cultures: Selected Essays* (New York: Basic Books, 1973), p. 310.

[27] See for example, Wilentz, *Rites of Power*.

[28] See: Michael Mann, *The Sources of Social Power* (New York: Cambridge University Press, 1986); Barrington Moore, Jr., *Social Origins of Dictatorship and Democracy: Lord and Peasant in the Making of the Modern World* (Boston: Beacon Press, 1966); Skocpol, *States and Social Revolution*; Immanuel Wallerstein, *The Modern World System: Capitalist Agriculture and the Origins of the European World Economy in the Sixteenth Century* (New York: Academic Press, 1974); Peter B. Evans, Dietrich Rueschemeyer, and Theda Skocpol, *Bringing the State Back In* (Cambridge, UK: Cambridge University Press, 1985).

Krasner, touted its autonomy.[29] Indeed, autonomy became a kind of buzz-word in the state-building literature, especially with growing numbers of studies on the success stories of East Asia.[30] The oddity, from our perspective at the turn of the century, is how quickly the system-dominant structuralist approach faded, becoming nearly as rare as cultural interpretations of the state. As Ira Katznelson indicates, this approach has lost its energy, imagination, and leadership.[31]

One of the last monumental works on the state from the system-dominant structuralist perspective was Jack A. Goldstone's *Revolution and Rebellion in the Early Modern World*.[32] His direct concern is not with state building as much as with state breakdown. While attentive to a variety of historical forces, Goldstone's powerful theory allows him to treat a multiplicity of states across several centuries as interchangeable parts in his equation. The theory is so attractive because it is both simple and general.

According to Goldstone, states crack when they are hit simultaneously by three sorts of crises – a state financial emergency, severe elite divisions, and a potential and propensity for popular groups to mobilize. What is the underlying structural condition that leads to these crises occurring simultaneously in different places and in varying periods? The answer can be found in demographic patterns – a worsening in the ratio of resources to population size sets the stage for the problems that undermine the state. What draws us to such theories is also what repels us. The general, abstract quality of the argument is spellbinding. Goldstone does nothing less than give us a grand narrative plan for understanding history. But the theory is troubling nonetheless. Culture rears its head but as a mere byproduct of the three crises. Once those occur, he argues, we will see an increase in heterodox cultural and religious ideas. The actual content of these ideas does not seem to matter

[29] Eric A. Nordlinger, *On the Autonomy of the Democratic State* (Cambridge, MA: Harvard University Press, 1981); Stephen D. Krasner, *Defending the National Interest. Raw Materials Investments and U.S. Foreign Policy* (Princeton, NJ: Princeton University Press, 1978).

[30] Meredith Woo Cummings, *Race to the Swift: State and Finance in Korean Industrialization* (New York: Columbia University Press, 1991); Stephen Haggard, *Pathways from the Periphery: The Politics of Growth in the Newly Industrializing Countries* (Ithaca, NY: Cornell University Press, 1990).

[31] Ira Katznelson, "Structure and Configuration in Comparative Politics," in Lichbach and Zuckerman (eds.), *Comparative Politics: Rationality, Culture, and Structure*.

[32] Jack A. Goldstone, *Revolution and Rebellion in the Early Modern World* (Berkeley: University of California Press, 1991).

much at all. Nor do the different institutional paths that widely varying states and societies have taken. His theory has removed agency, the power of people to affect the course of history, from both state and society. In the end, we remain with an overly determined portrait in which the differing institutional histories, contrasting systems of meaning, and the initiatives of groups or individuals count for very little in the unfolding of history.

The Rationalist Perspective

At the same time that system-dominant structuralist theories were in their glory, some rational choice writers also turned their attention to the state, although that subject was certainly not central to the emerging rational choice paradigm. No book was more influential here than *Markets and States in Tropical Africa.*[33] Robert H. Bates begins his inquiry by noting a fundamental paradox: African state rulers knew quite well what sorts of economic policies were needed to spur economic success, yet they pointedly avoided those policies and chose pathological others. The resolution he comes to in his research starts with the interests of these leaders. Their precarious political stand dictated to them a path of behavior that left their economies in shambles. Through an examination of the actions and choices of key individuals, Bates could tell us about the pathologies of entire states.

In a subsequent book *Beyond the Miracle of the Market*, Bates extends his rational choice analysis by stressing the importance of institutions, particularly political institutions.[34] Drawing on Douglass C. North[35] and others working on new institutional theories in economics, he notes that the particular institutional milieu within which policymakers find themselves creates the incentive structure that guides their choices. In other words, the preferences that politicians hold and that establish the goals they rationally aim to achieve are not simply random. His implication is that such preferences cannot remain exogenous to rational choice theory but must be endogenized, that is, theoretically accounted for. Bates's clear aim is to

---

[33] Robert H. Bates, *Markets and States in Tropical Africa: The Political Basis of Agricultural Policies* (Berkeley: University of California Press, 1981).

[34] Robert H. Bates, *Beyond the Miracle of the Market: The Political Economy of Agrarian Development in Kenya* (New York: Cambridge University Press, 1989).

[35] Douglass C. North, *Structure and Change in Economic History* (New York: W. W. Norton, 1981).

contribute to the growing literature on the state by giving the rationale for the choices made by "autonomous" states. Or, in his words, his theory "provides the micro-foundations for the macro-themes dominating the statist literature."[36] Those microfoundations derive from interests – "interested actions of private parties who bring their resources to bear upon politically ambitious politicians and the political process."[37] In the case of Kenya, the subject of Bates's research, the dominance of a social class geared toward accumulation rather than redistribution explains that country's policy choices and consequently its higher economic growth rates than its neighbors. We can explain the Kenyan outcome on the basis of its "structure of political institutions and the incentives they generate for politicians."[38] He goes on:

People see clearly where their interests lie. They invest in the creation of institutions in order to structure economic and political life so as better to defend their position within them. They invest in institutions so as to vest their interests. . . . Institutions influence subsequent actions. They may have been created for economic reasons; or they may have been founded as to enhance the fortunes of particular economic interests. But once created, they generate positions of political power and systems of political incentives. They define strategic possibilities and impose constraints.[39]

The rationalist approach merged nicely with the reemergence of the state as a subject of study. It moved political scientists away from exclusive concern with extremely broad, often slippery macrostructures or master narratives to a much more manageable level of research. As Margaret Levi notes, rational choice theory drew on its experience with voting and electoral politics to provide a grounded, empirical approach to broad comparative questions.[40] This orientation led to a concern with hard evidence, too often sloughed off in the structuralist or culturalist perspectives.

By specifying leaders' goals clearly, it allowed researchers to deduce their actions – and, as a result, political outcomes – from those goals and from the specific configuration of circumstances that the rulers faced. In that sense, like structuralism, one could treat the units of study as largely coherent actors that were theoretically interchangeable. It lent great

---

[36] Bates, *Beyond the Miracle of the Market*, p. 6.
[37] Ibid., p. 5. [38] Ibid., p. 140. [39] Ibid., pp. 151–2.
[40] Margaret Levi, "A Model, a Method, and a Map: Rational Choice in Comparative and Historical Analysis," in Lichbach and Zuckerman (eds.), *Comparative Politics: Rationality, Culture, and Structure*.

parsimony to the study of states, even if it threatened the understanding of the state with an unbending reductionism. Bates went beyond system-dominant structuralism by putting politics squarely back into the analysis of the state. By incorporating institutions into the analysis, Bates succeeded in contextualizing interests (the dominant interests in Kenya differed from those in nearby countries) while still using a universal method (all politicians use the same rational calculations to deal with those varying interests). Levi writes, "As comparative and historical rational choice develops, it has increasingly become a form of institutional analysis."[41]

But, again, as with the structuralists, culture plays an entirely derivative role. Unlike the structuralists, the rationalists did try to account for different institutional paths. But Bates's effort to endogenize the institutional dimension was problematic. While his discussion of the historical development of social structure in Kenya through an analysis of class formation is very well informed, it takes place outside the parameters of the theory itself. The rationalists have not yet found a way to incorporate the institutional configuration, the particular array of interests that dominate in Kenya or elsewhere, within the elements of their theories. And, while the rational actor is the agent of change (unlike in the system-dominant structuralist theories), his or her agency is entirely utilitarian, predicted and determined by exogenous forces.

The Historical Institutionalist Perspective

It would be a gross exaggeration to say that culturalist, system-dominant structuralist, and rationalist perspectives on state building disappeared at the end of the twentieth century. Indeed, the rationalist orientation has prospered in many subfields of political science, and the comparative study of the state is no exception. Nonetheless, in surveying contemporary literature on the state, one comes away with the feeling that comparative political science has been left with a kind of default approach to the study of states, that of institutionalism. Or, more precisely, as Katznelson notes, the study of states has been subsumed under the heading of historical institutionalism.[42] This perspective is a close kin to structuralist, culturalist, and rationalist perspectives, and it absorbs elements from all of these. Like system-dominant structuralism, it is interested in how the parts are put

[41] Ibid., p. 149.   [42] Katznelson, "," in Lichbach and Zuckerman, *Comparative Politics.*

together so as to channel the choices available to individuals. But, as it emerged in the late 1980s and the 1990s, institutionalism's central premise was that the distinctive ways of doing things today will matter tomorrow, as well; states facing the same circumstances will not behave similarly, as the system-dominant structuralists would have it. In other words, the particular configuration of institutions determine, modify, and order individual motives.[43] Distinctive roles, relations, and procedures that mark how the parts of the state interact with one another and how they tie into groups both inside and outside society are critical for understanding state actions.

While culture plays an important role in coming to terms with institutional ties – after all, those roles, relations, and procedures are underwritten by shared subjective interpretations of how to behave – the emphasis by most institutionalist political scientists has been less on symbols and meanings than on the ordering of relations and the understanding of political institutions "as acting autonomously in terms of institutional interests."[44] Similarly, as we shall see, rationality is key to institutionalism, as individuals' choices are made within a socially formed context and, as in the case of Bates's policymakers, are understood by the interests that stand behind them. Indeed, the newer rational choice writings on the state, such as Levi's highly regarded book or that of Barbara Geddes[45] or, as we have seen, Bates's more recent work, have in effect merged rationalism with North's theories of institutionalism. These works have had a significant impact on yet another type of institutionalism, historical institutionalism.

An early work that used this approach was Karl Polanyi's monumental *The Great Transformation*,[46] a work that has greatly influenced me and a fair number of others.[47] The book provided a model of scholarship for

---

[43] James G. March and Johan P. Olsen, *Rediscovering Institutions: The Organizational Basis of Politics* (New York: Free Press, 1989), p. 4.

[44] Ibid., p. 4.

[45] Barbara Geddes, *Politician's Dilemma: Building State Capacity in Latin America* (Berkeley: University of California Press, 1994).

[46] Karl Polanyi, *The Great Transformation: The Political and Economic Origins of Our Time* (Boston: Beacon Press, 1944).

[47] Kathleen Thelen and Sven Steinmo have distinguished historical institutionalism from rational-choice institutionalism. Thelen and Steinmo "Historical Institutionalism in Comparative Politics," in Sven Steinmo, Kathleen Thelen, and Frank Longstreth (eds.), *Historical Institutionalism in Comparative Analysis* (New York: Cambridge University Press, 1992). Another key formative figure in historical institutionalism, who will not be discussed here, is Gerschenkron.

those who were dissatisfied with behavioralist and (mostly Marxist) system-dominant approaches and who were interested in developing a historically grounded perspective. Behavioralists' concerns with the characteristics, attitudes, and behavior of individuals and groups tended to minimize historical factors and miss the important impact that varying forms of organization could have. At the same time, Marxism's determinism seemed to deny the importance of institutional diversity.

The subtitle of Polanyi's book, "The Political and Economic Origins of Our Time," hints not only at Polanyi's own ambition but at a more general belief that such an approach need not devolve into small-scale idiographic studies and explanations. While Polanyi wove numerous threads through his narrative, in the end his preoccupation was with the demon that had turned his own world on its head, fascism. In dealing with that dreaded political form, he had to come to terms with the material interests approach that had so influenced his thinking and still find a way to steer clear of Marx's propensity to overdetermine outcomes. Note the fine line that Polanyi walks:

If ever there was a political movement that responded to the needs of an objective situation and was not a result of fortuitous causes it was fascism. At the same time, the degenerative character of the fascist solution was evident. It offered an escape from an institutional deadlock which was essentially alike in a number of countries, and yet, if the remedy were tried, it would everywhere produce sickness unto death. This is the manner in which civilizations perish.[48]

The deadlock to which he refers stemmed from the uneasy cohabitation in the liberal state of the needs of capitalism (institutionally expressed through the self-regulating market and adherence to the gold standard) and democracy. Here, as in Geertz, Goldstone, and Bates, the emphasis is first on the essential character of the state, on its makeup and decision making, and only then on the environment within which that structure operates. On one side, for Polanyi, the state served capitalism and the market, which subordinated society's expression of multiple needs and desires – as he writes, "It means no less than the running of society as an adjunct to the market."[49] The market, that "satanic mill," mercilessly disposed of the physical, psychological, and moral qualities of human beings and left them with no safety net into which to fall.

---

[48] Polanyi, *The Great Transformation*, p. 237.   [49] Ibid., p. 57.

At the same time, the state, through the pressure put on it by labor groups in parliament, became the basis for "paternalistic regulationism."[50] Groups organized a countermovement, "a reaction against a dislocation which attacked the fabric of society."[51] This bundle of contradictions in the state, the clash of economic liberalism and social protection, caused deadlock. The Alexander who could cut this Gordian knot was a new institutional configuration, fascism. Its solution was both to transform the market and to eliminate democracy.

Polanyi's goal was a delicate one. He at once wanted to show how a particular array of forces could explain the emergence of the fascist state (just as a good system-dominant structuralist would) and to leave open the possibility of other outcomes. Neither Britain nor the United States where he sat writing his book during the dark days of World War II had succumbed to the fascist solution. Institutions adapt to the real environment within which they are embedded – for Polanyi that environment was a world economy marked by the gold standard and a system of states within a balance of power. But that is not an infinitely replicable process. Different states and societies could respond in varying ways.

In the postwar era, Samuel P. Huntington stressed the same lesson: different sorts of political actions and varying types of engagement by social groups with the state produce disparate political results. His immediate attention was with the proliferation of new states that came out of the decolonization process and with the fond hopes that they would lead their societies to the promised land of modernity and prosperity. He observed rather dourly that political decay and instability were as likely an outcome as political development.[52]

Huntington did not use the word "state" – it was not fashionable yet – but it was very much present in his analysis. In fact, if anyone could be credited with bringing the state back in, it is Huntington; without the word at hand to encompass it, he described how the actions and characteristics of the array of public institutions in a country (the state) made a vast difference for society. He returned public institutions to center stage. Indeed, his theory implies that if we focused exclusively on how well the state developed its institutions, we would not have to look much further. His thesis is simple: only where the level of political institutionalization outstrips the

---

[50] Ibid., p. 125.   [51] Ibid., p. 130.
[52] Samuel P. Huntington, *Political Order in Changing Societies* (New Haven, CT: Yale University Press, 1968).

level of political participation can there emerge stable politics working in the public interest. Although his conservative outlook regarding U.S. foreign policy induced many to minimize his theory's impact on them, I would venture to say that no work surpassed Huntington's in its influence on a generation of comparative political scientists studying the state.

Huntington's impact went beyond academics. One former high-level Ethiopian official told me of the military coup against Emperor Haile Selasse in 1973. When the young officers burst into the room where the emperor's aides ran the affairs of state, one political official looked up and asked, "Where did we fail?" At that point, an army officer took a copy of Huntington's book and slid it across the table. "You should have read this." Now, whether that story is apocryphal or not, it gives some glimpse of how influential the work has been.

A host of important publications in the 1990s fed off of the insights of Polanyi and Huntington. The same balancing of environmental pressures and the variety of responses to those factors that one finds in Polanyi and the attention to political capacity and autonomy of a Huntington mark the best of the contemporary works on the state by historical institutionalists doing crossnational studies and by those doing in-depth country studies.[53] Peter Evans, for example, attempts to unravel why some states have so successfully tweaked industrial transformations of their societies while others' records have been so abysmal. His answer lies in the particularity of institutional arrangements: "States are not generic. They vary dramatically in their internal structures and relations to society. Different kinds of state structures create different capacities for state action."[54] This

---

[53] See for example: Ruth B. Collier and David Collier, *Shaping the Political Arena: Critical Junctures, the Labor Movement, and Regime Dynamics in Latin America* (Princeton, NJ: Princeton University Press, 1991); Peter B. Evans, *Embedded Autonomy: States and Industrial Transformation* (Princeton, NJ: Princeton University Press, 1995); Robert H. Jackman, *Power Without Force: The Political Capacities of Nation-States* (Ann Arbor: University of Michigan Press, 1993); John Waterbury, *Exposed to Innumerable Delusions: Public Enterprise and State Power in Egypt, India, Mexico, and Turkey* (New York: Cambridge University Press, 1993); Catherine Boone, *Merchant Capital and the Roots of State Power in Senegal* (New York: Cambridge University Press, 1992); Frances Hagopian, *Traditional Politics and Regime Change in Brazil* (New York: Cambridge University Press, 1996); Atul Kohli, *Democracy and Discontent: India's Growing Crisis of Governability* (New York: Cambridge University Press, 1990); Vivienne Shue, *The Reach of the State: Sketches of the Chinese Body Politic* (Stanford, CA: Stanford University Press, 1988); Robert Vitalis, *When Capitalists Collide: Business Conflict and the End of Empire in Egypt* (Berkeley: University of California Press, 1995).

[54] Evans, *Embedded Autonomy*, p. 11.

statement comes a long way in allowing for the diversity of actual states. But like the works of those using the culturalist, structuralist, and rationalist perspectives, it still reflects the emphasis on looking first and foremost at the state as a freestanding structure, as an entity that can be isolated in inquiry.

The Limited State: Engagement of State and Society

The modern state has posed itself as the ultimate authority, standing above society and demanding wide-ranging obedience and conformity. But the engagement of social groups with the state, and the mutual transformation that entails, have tempered those broad claims to be the ultimate authority. Appearances to the contrary, states may be badly fractured and weakened through the particular nature of their encounters with other social forces. By understanding how the state's sails have been trimmed through its engagement with such social forces, we begin to build a basis for a twenty-first century research agenda, one that starts with process rather than structure, a blueprint that focuses on a limited state. Such an agenda will allow us to escape from the stifling effects on clear thinking of national ideologies stressing the complete sovereignty of the state and from academic theories, beginning with Weber's ideal-typical state, that underscore the monopoly over coercive means and legitimate authority.

National ideologies create master narratives that may well be suited to dealing with issues such as the consolidation of power or the collective expression of identity. They are far less useful as guides to the capabilities and limitations of actual states. Theories such as those of Weber and political scientists following in his footsteps create different sorts of problems. Their understanding of the state as a stand-alone organization with firm boundaries between it and other social forces leads to inquiries that zero in on its makeup, into how it is constructed. The effect is to essentialize the state and overstate its capabilities. An approach that focuses on the state in society, on the process of state engagement with other social forces highlights the mutual transformation of the state and other social groups, as well as the limitations of the state. Mitchell elaborates this point very well. He writes:

Statist approaches to political explanation present the state as an autonomous entity whose actions are not reducible to or determined by forces in society. . . . The customary Weberian definition of the state, as an organization that claims a monopoly over the legitimate use of violence, is only a residual characterization. It does

250

not tell us how the actual contours of this amorphous organization are to be drawn.
... The state appears to stand apart from society in [an] unproblematic way.[55]

The twenty-first century state, buffeted by the winds of globalization, supranational entities, and divisive ethnic conflict, must be stripped of its myths of unity and omnipotence. With new states abounding and old states struggling with disintegrative challenges, more than ever political scientists will need ways of unraveling the relationship between states and those within their borders. They will need ways of studying the fractious process of redrawing social boundaries, of creating coalitions with some and excluding others.

That is a tall order. It will mean avoiding structural views that portray the state as largely determined by a grand historical narrative and/or that present it as a gargantuan coherent and unified "actor" in history.[56] It will entail improving the institutionalist tools for analyzing the states that have proliferated in the last decade, focusing increasingly on the institutional junctures of state and society, even where the boundary between them is blurred beyond recognition. And it will involve serious attention to cultural understandings of the state, which have made little headway so far in the political science literature.

The connection between the state and its population has been particularly complex, if for no other reason, as noted earlier, than the modern state in its rules and laws has demanded so much from people. If in premodern empires rulers might have aimed for little more than collecting revenue from many peasants, modern officials have devised legal codes – specifications of what individuals can and cannot do – whose volumes take up endless shelves. And they have constructed centralized bureaucracies to press their regulations on large populations. Of course, coercion and the threat of coercion, by most definitions, lie at the center of the meaning of the state and its demands for compliance by its population. Both Marx and Weber made that clear a century ago, and others, such as Cover, have regularly restated it.[57]

---

[55] Timothy Mitchell, "The Limits of the State: Beyond Statist Approaches and Their Critics," *American Political Science Review* 85 (March 1991): 82.

[56] Mitchell, "The Limits of the State."

[57] Martha Minow, Michael Ryan, and Austan Sarat, eds., *Narrative Violence and the Law: The Essays of Robert Cover* (Ann Arbor: University of Michigan Press, 1993), pp. 211–14; see also Charles Tilly, "War Making and State Making as Organized Crime," in Peter Evans, Dietrich Rueschemeyer, and Theda Skocpol (eds.), *Bringing the State Back In* (New York: Cambridge University Press, 1985).

But it is simply impossible for a state to achieve tractability by relying exclusively on its judges and jailers.[58] No matter how vaunted the bureaucracy, police, and military, officers of the state cannot stand on every corner ensuring that each person stop at the red light, drive on the right side of the road, cross at the crosswalk, refrain from stealing and drug dealing, and so on. Modern state leaders could easily find their institutions quickly overwhelmed by the enormity of the task of enforcement, even with vast bureaucracies.[59]

What have modern states done to ensure that each subject toes the line, even without a police officer at every corner? Their response has come on two additional levels, one addressed most cogently by those using an institutionalist outlook with strong rationalist overtones and the other, by researchers using a culturalist perspective. Both indicate a process-oriented approach in which states and societies are in a mutually transformative relationship.

For historical institutionalists the emphasis has been on rules and procedures, on routine. Those same weighty code books that spell out the do's and don'ts for individuals also implicitly address people's needs to have a road map explaining how to navigate an increasingly convoluted world. State rules have insured the viability of agreements into which one enters, protected the water one drinks, assured the terms for receiving credit, provided schools as a means of mobility for one's children, and much more. As the division of labor has become increasingly elaborated, state laws have given assurance to the individual concerning products and services about which one has meager knowledge or skills. Far more than in the premodern era, states have gone beyond defense of the realm to offer a large chunk of the *strategies of survival* that people construct for themselves.[60] Obedience and conformity, then, have been trade-offs accepted by individuals who see the state as a large piece of their personal life puzzles.

---

[58] "Political life centers on the exercise of power, and that, unlike physical force, power is intrinsically relational. Although all states have the capability to inflict physical sanction, their ability to exercise power is the key element of their political capacity. In this context, the prolonged use of force reflects a loss of power and is fundamentally apolitical, because it indicates a deterioration in the relationship between rulers and the ruled." Jackman, *Power Without Force.*

[59] In fact, the overburdened state (as seen, for example, in the mushrooming prison population in the United States) is one important part of the puzzle explaining the disparity between state goals and achievements.

[60] Joel S. Migdal, *Strong Societies and Weak States: State-Society Relations and State Capabilities in the Third World* (Princeton, NJ: Princeton University Press, 1988).

In their inquiries into the state, historical institutionalists have tended to spotlight this sort of calculation, merging their interest in structure with a rationalist perspective. But they have also gone to some lengths to differentiate themselves from rational choice theories. Historical institutionalism has emphasized the organizational milieu in which people do such reckoning. In other words, scholars using this approach favor looking at habit in any given situation more than at utility maximization. Thomas A. Koelble notes:

When making decisions, individuals do not ask the question "how do I maximize my interests in this situation?" but instead "what is the appropriate response to this situation given my position and responsibilities?". In the majority of situations, rules and procedures (that is, institutions) are clearly established, and individuals follow routines. They follow well-worn paths and do what they think is expected of them.[61]

Historical institutionalist works note that those paths are forged through the engagement of groups, such as labor or merchants or capitalists from certain sectors, with parts of the state. Indeed the nature of that engagement often underpins those writers' analyses. For Evans, the kinds of connections that states have had to certain industrial sectors and firms have determined whether they could induce sustained industrial growth.[62] While Evans focuses on the rosy question of state-led development, Robert Vitalis hones in on a far seamier side of state action, the creation of rent havens.[63] His inventive book challenges the grand narrative that places late (or failed) industrialization – in his case, Egypt – in "an overarching struggle between imperialism and the nation."[64] Rather, it is the variety of alliances between specific business groups and fractions of the state that explain Egypt's (and others') paths. Indeed, one of the great advantages of Vitalis's work is his willingness to go beyond analyzing the state as a single coherent actor (or as represented entirely by one of its agencies) to a view in which parts of the state operate quite differently, often in conflict with one another.

Other important works analyze different dimensions of the engagement of states with social groups. Frances Hagopian's innovative work examines

---

[61] Thomas A. Koelble, "The New Institutionalism in Political Science and Sociology." *Comparative Politics* 27 (January 1995): 233.
[62] Evans, *Embedded Autonomy*.
[63] Vitalis, *When Capitalists Collide*.
[64] Ibid., p. 5.

the ironic reliance of Brazil's military leaders on traditional oligarchic elites.[65] These soldiers took over the state in 1964 and professed a belief in technocratic rule rather than reliance on the old politicians but ended up depending on those they had spurned. In Ruth B. Collier and David Collier's research on Latin America, the key is the variety of ways in which labor was incorporated by states.[66] Senegal's state is seen by Catherine Boone as consisting of key political actors whose standing comes from their individual patron-client ties with constituencies in the country.[67] Her aim is to explain the impotence of the state despite all the trappings of power. Like Vitalis, her analysis does not presume the state to be a single actor. In fact, one could understand the Senegalese state only by taking account of its fractured core. She writes:

Regime consolidation was a political process that involved not only creating new structures and relations of power, but also tying existing structures of societally based power to the state. Modes of governance and exploitation were shaped by social forces that could subvert or strengthen these underpinnings of state authority, as well as by societally based competition for advantage within and through the institutions of government.[68]

The engagement of the state, or parts of it, with individuals and groups in society so aptly emphasized by the historical institutionalists has been not a static process but a mutually transformative one. One criticism of the rational choice institutionalists' approach has been its acceptance of goals, strategies, and preferences as given (and often fixed) rather than as changing over time in meaningful ways.[69] We might add that the very process of interaction of ruler and ruled, looked at so convincingly by a rational choice institutionalist, such as Levi, substantially changes both. This mutual transformation may limit the usefulness of rational choice methodology. The engagement of state and society involves the creation of alliances and coalitions and, for each side of the bargain, the incorporation of a new material basis as well as new ideas and values into its constitution. That process of incorporation of new constituencies and their ideas transforms the preferences and bases for action

---

[65] Hagopian, *Traditional Politics and Regime Change in Brazil*.
[66] Collier and Collier, *Shaping the Political Arena*.
[67] Boone, *Merchant Capital and the Roots of State Power in Senegal*.
[68] Catherine Boone, "States and Ruling Classes in Postcolonial Africa: The Enduring Contradictions of Power," in Joel S. Migdal, Atul Kohli, and Vivienne Shue (eds.), *State Power and Social Forces* (New York: Cambridge University Press, 1994), p. 133.
[69] Thelen and Steinmo, "Historical Institutionalism in Comparative Politics," p. 9.

of the original actor. What rational choice theorists assume is fixed may very well be a moving target. Beyond coercion, then, why have people obeyed state rules and dictates? The historical institutionalists, as we saw, respond by pointing to the calculation of individuals within the confines of rules and procedures and the routinization of their behavior within the possibilities that existing institutions afford. They picture the actions of the state's subjects as running on a treadmill to create viable strategies of *survival* (not maximization) – or to "satisfice," in James G. March and Johan P. Olsen's terms.[70] Institutions create routines, and, even with coercion only a distant threat, those routines ensure significant obedience.[71]

Another answer as to why and how states can avoid stationing police every fifty meters is much trickier. To understand it fully, comparative political scientists must turn to the culturalist approach and develop new tools within that genre. The answer rests on the premise that in individuals, as Shils wrote, there is a "state of consciousness which includes an awareness of a self residing in them, including them, and transcending them."[72] That is, humans are not only animals who run in packs, creating institutions for themselves. They also have conceptions about themselves as members of the pack and of the pack as something with a life beyond their personal existence. Those "packs" are societies, which in human history have come in all shapes and sizes – that is, with different institutional configurations.[73]

How have societies taken form? Lauren Berlant wrote that "the accident of birth within a geographical/political boundary transforms individuals into subjects of a collectively-held history. Its traditional icons, its metaphors, its heroes, its rituals, and its narratives provide an alphabet for a collective consciousness."[74] That shared alphabet imposes a discipline upon people, molding their discourse and action. Like Geertz's theater state, Berlant's subjects are drawn into props and pomp, into stories and metaphors, which mark them off from others outside. The formation of societies leads, again in Shils's words, to some degree of "authority and the

---

[70] March and Olsen, *Rediscovering Institutions*.

[71] Ruth Lane, *The Art of Comparative Politics* (Boston: Allyn and Bacon, 1997), 114–22.

[72] Shils, *The Constitution of Society*, p. vii.

[73] There is no sense in asking how individuals come to be associated. They exist and operate in association." John Dewey, *The Public and Its Problems* (New York: Henry Holt, 1927).

[74] Lauren Berlant, *The Anatomy of National Fantasy: Hawthorne, Utopia and Everyday Life* (Chicago: University of Chicago Press, 1991), p. 20.

maintenance of order," or, in our terms, to some modicum of obedience and conformity.[75]

This understanding of society, Shils noted, "could not be reduced to a marketlike equilibrium of interests or to a product of coercion."[76] In other words, neither police at every intersection nor trade-offs by calculating individuals, who are figuring out their strategies of survival, can fully explain obedience and conformity. For Shils, a big part of the explanation lies in people's internalization of society, their "collective self-consciousness." People obey, in this view, because their personal identities are inextricably tied to the existence of a bigger unit; their identities depend on the viability of the rules, written and unwritten, that maintain that larger group.[77]

Submission to the group's rules thus supports not only the collectivity but the individual whose identity rests on the continuing existence of the group; obedience and conformity are integral to establishing and maintaining one's identity. In society, any number of groups or organizations could ensure continuing compliance – "the household, the kinship group, the neighborhood association, the market community, and other loose associations formed for some specific purpose."[78] One's identity rests upon the continuing viability of one's family (or some other group), so individuals conform in ways that keep that group alive and thriving. In the twentieth century and for several centuries before that, it has been the state that has demanded such compliance, taking the lead in authority and the maintenance of order.

But the state has created some special problems in this regard. One key distinction of the modern era, as I noted, has been the broad claims of state leaders and officials – if not to demand all obedience and conformity directly, then at least for the state to be the umbrella under which other groups or organizations may gain and ensure their authority. Yes, families can exercise authority over their members, especially children and (often) women, or businesses can make rules for their workers. But they must do

---

[75] Shils, *The Constitution of Society*, p. vii.

[76] Ibid., p. xii.

[77] "Identities . . . produce societal boundaries allowing individual members as groups and collectivities, in actual or desired, existing or imaginary communities, to make sense of 'us' versus 'them.'" Dahlia Moore and Baruch Kimmerling, "Individual Strategies of Adopting Collective Identities: The Israeli Case," *International Sociology* 10 (December 1995).

[78] Max Weber, *Max Weber on Law in Economy and Society*, ed. Max Rheinstein (Cambridge, MA: Harvard University Press, 1954), p. 342.

so, state leaders assert, within the parameters set by the state. If a family exercises its authority by abusing its children, or a business sets discriminatory rules, the state steps in, even to the point of disbanding the family. In a fundamental sense, then, the state appears to stand above and apart from the rest of society. Even if the actual image of states standing above society is flawed, as Mitchell notes, at the very least state leaders aim for a "ghost-like effect,"[79] where the state appears to be standing above society, with a finger in every pot. In John Breuilly's terms, there exists a "distinction, peculiar to the modern world, between state and society."[80]

But, as important as the private-public marking (or its appearance) is in establishing the special status of state authority, it also has created enormous problems for state officials in demanding obedience. The appearance of a gulf separating the state from the rest of society makes it difficult for its leaders to tap into a basis of authority beyond coercion or "a marketlike equilibrium of interests" for calculating individuals. As an entity appearing to stand *apart* from society and its individuals, it has difficulty gaining conformity through individuals tying their personal identities to a collective of which they self-consciously felt *a part*. This is the paradox of the modern state, one that theoretically and practically leads us to the conception of the limited state.

The challenge for political leaders has been how to remain *apart* from society – the state as the ultimate authority – while somehow still benefiting from people's "collective self-consciousness," their sense of belonging to something bigger than themselves of which they are an integral *part*.[81] Or, to pose the problem differently, state leaders and their agencies have sought ways to change those they rule from disconnected *subjects* of state rule to some other status that would connect their personal

---

[79] Mitchell, "The Limits of the State," p. 91.

[80] John Breuilly, *Nationalism and the State* (Chicago: University of Chicago Press, 1994), p. 390.

[81] The problem for states is related to that posed by Habermas, regarding the legitimation crisis of the state. He writes, "The state must preserve for itself a residue of unconsciousness in order that there accrue to it from its planning functions no responsibilities that it cannot honor without drawing its accounts. . . . This end is served by the separation of instrumental functions of the administration from expressive symbols that release an unspecific readiness to follow." Jürgen Habermas, *Legitimation Crisis* (Boston: Beacon Press, 1975), pp. 69–70. But in the end he notes, "The state cannot simply take over the cultural system" (p. 73). The administrative (authoritative) role of the state does not sit easily with a cultural role, no matter how much theater is employed (as examples of such theater, Habermas offers symbolic use of hearings, juridical incantations, and others).

identities to the continued existence and vitality of the state. And state rulers have sought to establish this connection while all the while having state institutions, such as courts, remaining the ultimate authority and arbiter, standing in a continuing object-*subject* relationship with them.

Officials have dealt with the paradox of the state appearing to be above society but needing to seem an integral component of society in a number of ways, each of which aims to transform society. One has been the Communist path, to abolish society entirely. In that case, the individual's new status is that of state functionary, a role reserved not for a select subset of the population (public officials) but applicable to everyone. The population is not a society in the sense that its parts have been largely stripped of authority and it does not play an active role in people's collective consciousness. Those who by dint of class background are deemed unworthy of the new status may be resocialized into it during a transition period or, at worst, eliminated altogether. The new identity of individuals (such as the "new Soviet man and woman") indicates a collective self-consciousness revolving entirely around the state; no separate society, characterized by its own "authority and the maintenance of order," exists. Through raw power and through an impressive array of theatrical symbols, Communist leaders sought the extraordinarily ambitious goal of making the state the single authoritative entity and thus the only one with which people could ground their own identities.

A far more common route of transforming society involves, as Breuilly puts it, abolishing the distinction between state and society altogether through the use of nationalism.[82] In that case, the transformation of society comes by creating a subset of it, the *nation*, and a special status for those defined as nationals. Nationalist state leaders have aimed to eliminate the perception that the state stands above society and to foster an alternative view, that the state and the society are indistinguishable in purpose, if not in form.

Here is not the place to review the voluminous and growing literature on nationalism. But it is important to note that nationalism has been used to nibble at the state-society divide; states have sought added obedience and conformity through the merging of personal identity first and foremost with the collective self-consciousness of the nation. As the expression of the nation's sovereignty, the state has aimed to gain compliance beyond what it could expect from coercion and appealing to the calcula-

[82] Brecilly, *Nationalism and the State*, p. 390.

tions of individuals working out their strategies of survival.[83] Its authority can be accepted willingly if it is an extension or source of one's identity. The state, then, becomes the embodiment of the nation, and people who identify themselves primarily as nationals see their well-being and the well-being of the state as indistinguishable.

This perspective comes out strongly in culturalists' analyses of nationalism. Writers as opposed as Anthony D. Smith and Benedict Anderson note how nationalist myths have bound individuals to one another and to the *nation*-state.[84] "Nationalism's peculiar myth of the nation," writes Smith "may be seen as a particularly potent and appealing dramatic narrative, which links past, present and future through the character and role of the national community."[85] While Smith minimizes modernity as a formative influence in the creation of the nation, Anderson sees the nation as integrally related to the modern rise of capitalism. But Anderson, too, emphasizes the same cultural links: "The members of even the smallest nation will never know most of their fellow-members, meet them, or even hear of them, yet in the minds of each lives the image of their communion."[86] And that communion is related to the state: "Nations dream of being free. . . . The gage and emblem of this freedom is the sovereign state."[87] As Berdun Guibernau indicates, "The state favours nationalism as a means to increase the links existing among its citizens"[88] – and, it can be added, to link them to the state itself.

Perhaps the preceding paragraph makes the entire enterprise of creating the nation-state seem all too manipulative. The deep interpenetrations of state officials and certain social groups and the assimilation of icons, narratives, and metaphors into the theatrics of governing transform both rulers and ruled. The resultant political culture, which melds individual identities into a collective, state-focused identity, may become an unquestioned set of assumptions (a cultural hegemony) for state officials as much as for others in society. The notion of conscious manipulation of

---

[83] Paul C. Stern, "Why do People Sacrifice for Their Nations?" *Political Psychology* 16 (1985): 217–35.

[84] See: Anthony D. Smith, "Myth of the 'Modern Nation' and the Myths of Nations," *Racial Studies* 11 (January 1988): 1–26; Benedict Anderson, *Imagined Communities: Reflections on the Origin and Spread of Nationalism* (London: Verso, 1991).

[85] Smith, "Myth of the 'Modern Nation' and the Myths of Nations," p. 2.

[86] Anderson, *Imagined Communities*, p. 6.

[87] Ibid., p. 7.

[88] Berdun Guibernau and Maria Montserrat, *Nationalisms: The Nation-State and Nationalism in the Twentieth Century* (Cambridge, MA: Harvard University Press, 1996), p. 70.

such culture by state officials may lend too rationalist a perspective to this phenomenon.

Neither Communist states' attempts to abolish society nor nationalism's purported effect of eliminating the state-society distinction have freed the state from its paradoxical bind. Nowhere, not even in Stalin's Soviet Union, has a society with its own authority disappeared entirely.[89] And the total elimination of the boundary between state and society through nationalism has been impossible, as well.

Certainly states have reshaped societies with some success, refashioning societal boundaries to conform to the borders of the state (or to its desired borders). As Michael Schudson wrote, "The modern nation-state self-consciously uses language policy, formal education, collective rituals, and mass media to integrate citizens and ensure their loyalty."[90] Those using a culturalist perspective have pointed out how state leaders have used ritual and other means to blur the distinction between state and society and to have individuals develop a stake in the well-being of the state. Rituals have linked individuals to society and one another,[91] and to the state as the putative representation of society.[92] David Kertzer, an anthropologist, sees this connection as essentially nonrational: "Political reality is defined for us in the first place through ritual, and our beliefs are subsequently reaffirmed through regular collective expression."[93] We can add that the nonrational dimension may apply to state officials, too; they may be expressing deeply inculcated cultural mores of their own as much as a well defined plan to use symbols as the route to effective social control.

In short, the culturalists – from Geertz to those writing on nationalism – provide us with an image of the state as using and representing a master narrative. This narrative has multiple functions in their formulations. First, it serves as the basis to hold the state together, to prevent its multiple parts from flying off in different directions. Second, it links citizens to

[89] Kenneth Jowitt, *New World Disorder: The Leninist Extinction* (Berkeley: University of California Press, 1992), p. 54.
[90] Michael Schudson, "Culture and the Integration of National Societies," *International Social Science Journal* 46 (February 1994): 64.
[91] Emile Durkheim, *The Elementary Forms of the Religious Life* (London: Allen & Unwin, 1915); and David Kertzer, *Ritual, Politics and Power* (New Haven: Yale University Press, 1988), p. 10.
[92] Wilentz, *Rites of Power*; Siu, "Recycling Rituals: Politics and Popular Culture in Contemporary China."
[93] Kertzer, *Ritual, Politics and Power*, p. 95.

one another and to the state, subverting other narratives and thus the possibility of other autonomous, authoritative structures. And, third, the master narrative creates the limits and possibilities of the institutions involved in social control.

This image of the master narrative, however, needs modification. It, too, looks first and foremost at the state and its construction as stand-alone phenomena (rather than at the state in society) and consequently tends to overstate the power of the state or even the appearance of that power. Master narratives that eliminate other narratives are impossible to sustain, as Cover has argued.[94] At best, at a moment of epiphany, such uniformity can exist. But that quickly gives way to the creation of alternative and dissenting narratives. Perhaps in ancient societies, such dissonance could be handled by exile, secession, or death. But modern societies cannot avoid the existence of multiple narratives; they are irrevocably multicultural.

Some culturalists have noted this process of the creation of multiple narratives. They argue that the distinction between state and society – the state's aim to stand apart, as the ultimate authority – does quite the opposite from strengthening social control. It creates openings for opposition and distinction. Nicholas B. Dirks makes this point powerfully: "Because of the centrality of authority to the ritual process, ritual has always been a crucial site of struggle, involving both claims about authority and struggles against (and within) it. . . . Resistance to authority can be seen to occur precisely when and where it is least expected."[95] He adds, "At the same time that representation, in discourse or event, makes ritual claims about order, representation itself becomes the object of struggle."[96]

Dirks writes on India. Others writing theoretically or about different countries also take issue with the notion of the cultural unity implied in the works of Durkheim and Shils.[97] In Mexico, Gilbert M. Joseph and Daniel Nugent note, "The power of the state, especially the capitalist state, has been of signal importance in providing some of the idioms in terms of

---

[94] Minow, Ryan, and Sarat, eds., *Narrative, Violence and the Law.*

[95] Nicholas B. Dirks, "Rituals and Resistance: Subversions as a Social Fact," in Nicholas B. Dirks, Geoff Eley, and Sherry B. Ortner (eds.), *Reader in Contemporary Social Theory* (Princeton, NJ: Princeton University Press, 1994), pp. 487–8.

[96] Ibid., p. 502.

[97] Archer, "The Myth of Cultural Unity"; Schudson, "Culture and the Integration of National Societies"; and Siu, "Recycling Rituals."

which subordinated groups have initiated their struggles for emancipa-tion, particularly in the twentieth century."[98] William Roseberry refers in Mexico to "the problematic relationship between the talking state and the distracted audience."[99] The uniformity or universality that under-lies an image of the absence of a distinction between state and society falls victim to all sorts of refraction and diversity "as the laws, dictates, programs, and procedures of the central state are applied in particular regions, each of which is characterized by distinct patterns of inequality and domination."[100]

Conclusion

Returning to my earlier question – what makes the modern state modern? – I can now add that it has not been only the sheer magni-tude of the state's claims upon individuals it governs in terms of taxes, personal and social behavior, and the like. It also has been the effect of states through their practices to lay claim above all others to collective consciousness, that is, to the identity of the nation. Again, in Berlant's terms, the state has been at the center of struggles for people's collectively held history, "its traditional icons, its metaphors, its heroes, its rituals, and its narratives." In so doing, state leaders and agencies have been at the center of redrawing societal boundaries to coincide with the actual or desired political borders, a process as exclusive (in separating out those outside the physical or metaphorical boundaries) as it is inclusive (in creating an overarching collective self-consciousness). In short, through symbols and institutions states have been at the core of the reinvention of society.

But even where states have successfully sequestered youth for thirty hours per week, they have by no means guaranteed victory in the ambi-tious endeavor of defining collective consciousness. Both global factors outside of the state's control and internal elements of the society have worked to thwart or modify the emergence of a state-drawn collective consciousness. Because so much of the ability to get people to do what one

[98] Joseph and Nugent, "Popular Culture and State Formation," p. 13.
[99] William Roseberry, "Hegemony and the Language of Contention," in Gilbert Joseph and Daniel Nugent (eds.), *Everday Forms of State Formation: Revolution and the Negotiation of the Rule in Modern Mexico* (Durham, NC: Duke University Press, 1994), p. 365.
[100] Roseberry, "Hegemony and the Language of Contention."

wants them to do rests on the authority deriving from collective consciousness, it is not surprising that tremendous contestation has existed
over who defines and taps into it. Those struggles within states and
between states and other social forces, and their different outcomes in
various places and times, are of primary interest to political scientists. At
times, those struggles can lead to social and political disintegration, even
uncontrolled slaughter of the population. In other instances, while no
master narrative can be said to exist, Laitin's notion of shared "points of
concern" indicates that some cultural glue does exist. We must analyze
such points if we are to understand the continuing existence of state and
society and their particular patterns of interpenetration.

In the contemporary world, individuals have inhabited a number of
crucial social formations – nations, states, ethnic and other sub-national
groups, civil society, the global economy, and so on. All of these have
established authority, or at least have tried to, making powerful demands
upon the behavior and psyche of people. Sometimes those demands have
been complementary, even reinforcing shared points of concern, and in
other instances their stipulations have clashed head-on. In creating the
categories of citizen or member of the nation, state leaders, in effect,
have attempted to domesticate those other social formations, neutralizing their impact or subordinating their authority or eliminating them
altogether. These state efforts certainly are not new; they have gone on
for half a millennium and constitute the push by states to create
sovereignty.

State sovereignty has been elusive, however. While the efforts at Westphalia in the seventeenth century acted to codify and institutionalize a
continent of sovereign states in Europe, ever since then states have continued to face challenges along two paths. Both forces originating outside
the boundaries that the state claims for itself and those within its borders
have contested state efforts to monopolize the exercising of authority. The
result has been the limited state.

States have been unable to transform societies sufficiently so as to solve
the paradox of being simultaneously apart from society and a part of
society. More than that, the engagement of the state with society, which
has created sites of struggle and difference in society subverting the state's
efforts at uniformity, has also transformed the state. The mutual transformation of state and society has led to contending coalitions that have cut
across both and blurred the lines between them. It is within these dynamic
institutional arrangements that one must now approach the study of the

state – an organization divided and limited in the sorts of obedience it can demand. We must abandon approaches that isolate the state as a unit of analysis. To do that, we must develop the means to forge the efforts of the historical institutionalists and culturalists, who until now have worked mostly in splendid isolation from one another.

Bibliography

Ahrne, Göran. *Social Organizations: Interaction Inside, Outside and Between Organizations.* Thousand Oaks, CA: Sage Publications, 1994.

Almond, Gabriel A. "Approaches to Developmental Causation." In Gabriel A. Almond, Scott C. Flanagan, and Robert J. Mundt, eds., *Crisis, Choice, and Change: Historical Studies of Political Development.* Boston: Little, Brown, 1973.

Almond, Gabriel A., and G. Bingham Powell, Jr. *Comparative Politics: System, Process, and Policy.* Boston: Little, Brown, 1978.

Almond, Gabriel A., and James S. Coleman. *The Politics of the Developing Areas.* Princeton, NJ: Princeton University Press, 1960.

Almond, Gabriel A., Scott C. Flanagan, and Robert J. Mundt. *Crisis, Choice, and Change: Historical Studies of Political Development.* Boston: Little, Brown, 1973.

Almond, Gabriel A., and Sidney Verba. *The Civic Culture: Political Attitudes and Democracy in Five Nations.* Princeton, NJ: Princeton University Press, 1963.

Amnesty International Report 1983. London: Amnesty International Publications, 1983.

Anderson, Benedict. *Imagined Communities: Reflections on the Origin and Spread of Nationalism.* London: Verso, 1991.

Anderson, Charles W. *Politics and Economic Change in Latin America: The Governing of Restless Nations.* Princeton, NJ: D. Van Nostrand, 1967.

Anderson, Jon W. "Sentimental Ambivalence and the Exegesis of 'Self' in Afghanistan." *Anthropological Quarterly* 58 (October 1985).

Anderson, Perry. *Lineages of the Absolutist State.* London: NLB, 1974.

Apter, David E. *The Politics of Modernization.* Chicago: Chicago University Press, 1965.

Arato, Andrew. "Empire vs. Civil Society: Poland 1981–2." *Telos* (1981–2): 19–48.

Archer, Margaret S. "The Myth of Cultural Unity." *British Journal of Sociology* 36 (September 1985).

Azarya, Victor, and Naomi Chazan. "Disengagement from the State in Africa: Reflections on the Experience of Ghana and Guinea." *Comparative Studies in Society and History* 29 (January 1987).

Bailey, F. G. "The Peasant View of the Bad Life." *The Advancement of Science* 23 (December 1966): 399–409.

Baldwin, David A. "Power Analysis and World Politics: New Trends Versus Old Tendencies." *World Politics* 31 (January 1979): 162–3.

Bardach, Eugene. *The Implementation Game: What Happens After a Bill Becomes a Law*. Cambridge, MA: MIT Press, 1977.

Barker, Rodney. *Political Legitimacy and the State*. New York: Oxford University Press, 1990.

Barnett, Michael N. *Dialogues in Arab Politics: Negotiations in Regional Order*. New York: Columbia University Press, 1998.

Batatu, Hanna. "Some Observations on the Social Roots of Syria's Ruling, Military Group and the Causes for Its Dominance," *Middle East Journal* 35 (Summer 1981): 331–44.

Bates, Robert H. *Beyond the Miracle of the Market: The Political Economy of Agrarian Development in Kenya*. New York: Cambridge University Press, 1989.

   Markets and States in Tropical Africa: The Political Basis of Agricultural Policies. Berkeley: University of California Press, 1981.

Bayart, Jean-François, Stephen Ellis, and Béatrice Hibou. *The Criminalization of the State in Africa*. Bloomington: Indiana University Press, 1999.

Beillin, Yossi. Israel's Minister of Justice, to the Association of Israel Studies Annual Meeting, Tel Aviv, June 26, 2000.

Beloff, Max. *The Age of Absolutism, 1660–1815*. New York: Harper and Row, 1962.

Bendix, Reinhard, John Bendix, and Norman Furniss. "Reflections on Modern Western States and Civil Societies." *Research in Political Sociology* 3 (1987).

Benhabib, Seyla. *Situating the Self: Gender, Community and Postmodernism in Contemporary Ethics*. New York: Routledge, 1992.

Bennett, Douglas, and Kenneth Sharpe. "The State as Banker and Entrepreneur: The Last Resort Character of the Mexican State's Economic Intervention 1917–1970." In Sylvia Ann Hewlett and Richard S. Weinert, eds., *Brazil and Mexico: Patterns in Late Development*. Philadelphia: Institute for the Study of Human Issues, 1982.

Berger, Suzanne. *Peasants Against Politics: Rural Organization in Brittany 1911–1967*. Cambridge, MA: Harvard University Press, 1972.

Berger, Suzanne, and Michael J. Piore. *Dualism and Discontinuity in Industrial Societies*. Cambridge, MA: Cambridge University Press, 1980.

Berlant, Lauren. *The Anatomy of National Fantasy: Hawthorne, Utopia and Everyday Life*. Chicago: University of Chicago Press, 1991.

Bill, James Alban. *The Politics of Iran: Groups, Classes and Modernization*. Columbus, OH: Charles E. Merrill, 1972.

Binder, Leonard. "Crises of Political Development." In Binder, Pye, Coleman, Verba, Sidney, LaPalombra, Joseph, Weiner, and Myron, eds., *Crises and Sequences of Political Development*. Princeton, NJ: Princeton University Press, 1971.

Black, C. E. *The Dynamics of Modernization: A Study in Comparative History*. New York: Harper & Row, 1966.

Boone, Catherine. *Merchant Capital and the Roots of State Power in Senegal*. New York: Cambridge University Press, 1992.

Bibliography

"States and Ruling Classes in Postcolonial Africa: The Enduring Contradictions of Power." In Joel S. Migdal, Atul Kohli, and Vivienne Shue, eds., *State Power and Social Forces*. New York: Cambridge University Press, 1994.

Bourdieu, Pierre. "The Social Space and the Genesis of Groups." *Theory and Society* 14 (November 1985): 723–44.

Brandenburg, Frank. *The Making of Modern Mexico*. Englewood Cliffs, NJ: Prentice-Hall, 1964.

Bratton, Michael. "Peasant-State Relations in Postcolonial Africa: Patterns of Engagement and Disengagement." In Joel S. Migdal, Atul Kohli, and Vivienne Shue, eds., *State Power and Social Forces*. New York: Cambridge University Press, 1994.

Breuilly, John. *Nationalism and the State*. Chicago: University of Chicago Press, 1994.

Brigham, John. *The Constitution of Interests: Beyond the Politics of Rights*. New York: New York University Press, 1996.

Bryson, Scott S. *The Chastised Stage: Bourgeois Drama and the Exercise of Power*. Saratoga, CA: Anma Libri, 1991.

Burchell, Graham, Colin Gordon, and Peter Miller, eds., *The Foucault Effect: Studies in Governmentality*. Chicago: University of Chicago Press, 1991.

Burke, Edmund. *Reflections on the Revolution in France*. Edited by C. C. O'Brien. London: Penguin, 1969.

Calhoun, Craig. *Habermas and the Public Sphere*. Cambridge, MA: MIT Press, 1996.

Camilleri, Joseph A., and Jim Falk. *The End of Sovereignty? The Politics of a Shrinking and Fragmenting World*. Brookfield, VT: E. Elgar, 1992.

Caporaso, James A. "Introduction to the Special Issues of International Organization on Dependence and Dependency in the Global System." *International Organization* 32 (1978): 1–12.

Cardoso, Fernando Henrique, and Enzo Faletto. "Associated-Dependent Development: Theoretical Practical Implications." In Alfred Stepen, ed., *Authoritarian Brazil: Origins, Policies and Future*. New Haven, CT: Yale University Press, 1973.

Dependency and Development in Latin America. Berkeley: University of California Press, 1979.

Cederman, Lars-Erik. *Emergent Actors in World Politics: How States and Nations Develop and Dissolve*. Princeton, NJ: Princeton University Press, 1997.

Certeau, Michel de. *The Practice of Everyday Life*. Berkeley: University of California Press, 1984.

Chanock, Martin. *Law, Custom, and Social Order*. New York: Cambridge University Press, 1985.

Chazan, Naomi. "Engaging the State: Associational Life in Sub-Saharan Africa." In Joel S. Migdal, Atul Kohli, and Vivienne Shue, eds., *State Power and Social Forces*. New York: Cambridge University Press, 1994.

Chirot, Daniel. "The Corporatist Model and Socialism." *Theory and Society Journal* 9 (1980): 363–81.

Social Change in a Periphery Society: The Creation of a Balkan Colony. New York: Academic Press, 1976.

Social Change in the Twentieth Century. New York: Harcourt Brace Jovanovich, 1977.

Clapham, Christopher. *Third World Politics: An Introduction.* Madison: University of Wisconsin Press, 1985.

Collier, David, ed. *The New Authoritarianism in Latin America.* Princeton, NJ: Princeton University Press, 1979.

Collier, Gershon. *Sierre Leone: Experiment in Democracy in an African Nation.* New York: New York University Press, 1970.

Collier, Ruth B., and David Collier. "Inducements Versus Constraints: 'Disaggregating Corporatism.'" *American Political Science Review* 73 (1979): 978–9.

Shaping the Political Arena: Critical Junctures, the Labor Movement, and Regime Dynamics in Latin America. Princeton, NJ: Princeton University Press, 1991.

Combs, James E. *Dimensions of Political Drama.* Santa Monica, CA: Goodyear Publishing, 1980.

Connor, Walter D. "Revolution, Modernization, and Communism: A Review Article." *Studies in Comparative Communism* 8 (1975): 389–96.

Cover, Robert. "The Folktales of Justice: Tales of Jurisdiction." In Martha Minow, Michael Ryan, and Austin Sarat, eds., *Narrative, Violence, and the Law: The Essays of Robert Cover.* Ann Arbor: University of Michigan Press, 1993.

"Nomos and Narrative." In Martha Minow, Michael Ryan, and Austin Sarat, eds., *Narrative, Violence, and the Law: The Essays of Robert Cover.* Ann Arbor: University of Michigan Press, 1993.

Cumings, Bruce. "Corporatism in North Korea." Working paper presented at the annual meeting of the American Political Association. New York, 1981.

Cumings, Meredith Woo. *Race to the Swift: State and Finance in Korean Industrialization.* New York: Columbia University Press, 1991.

Dahl, Robert A. *Polyarchy: Participation and Opposition.* New Haven, CT: Yale University Press, 1971.

Dauvergne, Peter. "Weak states and the environment in Indonesia and the Solomon Islands." Working paper presented at Australian National Univesity. Canberra: Department of International Relations, 1997.

Dauvergne, Peter, ed. *Weak and Strong States in Asia-Pacific Societies.* Australia: Allen & Unwin, 1998.

Deutsch, Karl W. "Social Mobilization and Political Development." *American Political Science Review* 55 (1961): 493–514.

Dewey, John. *Human Nature and Conduct: An Introduction to Social Psychology.* New York: Henry Holt, 1922.

The Public and Its Problems. New York: Henry Holt, 1927.

DiMaggio, Paul. "Foreword." In Marshall W. Meyer and Lynne G. Zucker, eds., *Permanently Failing Organizations.* Newbury Park, CA: Sage, 1989.

Dirks, Nicholas B. "Rituals and Resistance: Subversions as a Social Fact." In Nicholas B. Dirks, Geoffrey Eley, and Sherry B. Ortner, eds., *Reader in Contemporary Social Theory.* Princeton, NJ: Princeton University Press, 1994.

Dominguez, Jorge I. *Insurrection or Loyalty: The Breakdown of the Spanish American Empire.* Cambridge, MA: Harvard University Press, 1980.

Bibliography

Downs, Anthony. *Inside Bureaucracy*. Boston: Little, Brown, 1967.
Duchacek, Ivo D., Daniel Latouche, and Garth Stevenson. *Perforated Sovereignties and International Relations: Trans-Sovereign Contacts of Subnational Governments*. New York: Greenwood Press, 1988.
Dunn, John. *Contemporary Crisis of the Nation State?* Cambridge, MA: Blackwell, 1995.
Durkheim, Emile. *The Elementary Forms of the Religious Life*. London: Allen & Unwin, 1915.
Duska, Ronald, and Mariellen Whelen. *Moral Development*. New York: Paulist Press, 1975.
Easton, David. *A Systems Analysis of Political Life*. New York: Wiley, 1965.
   The Political System: An Inquiry into the State of Political Science. Chicago: University of Chicago Press, 1981.
Easton, David, and Robert Hess. "Youth and Political System." In Seymour Martin Lipset and Leo Lowenthal, eds., *Culture and Social Character*. Glencoe, IL: Free Press, 1961.
Eckstein, Harry. "The Idea of Political Development: From Dignity to Efficiency." *World Politics* 34 (1982): 451–86.
Edelman, Murray. *Constructing the Political Spectacle*. Chicago: University of Chicago Press, 1988.
   Politics as Symbolic Action: Mass Arousal and Quiescence. Chicago: Markham, 1971.
Edgell, Stephen, Sandra Walklate, and Gareth Williams, eds. *Debating the Future of the Public Sphere*. Brookfield, VT: Avebury, 1995.
Eisenstadt, S. N. *Modernization: Protest and Change*. Englewood Cliffs, NJ: Prentice-Hall, 1966.
   Traditional Patrimonialism and Modern Neopatrimonialism. Vol. 1 of *Sage Research Papers in the Social Sciences, Studies in Comparative Modernization Series*. Beverly Hills, CA: Sage, 1973.
Eley, Geoffrey, and David Blackburn. *Reshaping the German Right: Radical Nationalism and Political Change after Bismarck*. New Haven, CT: Yale University Press, 1980.
Elkins, David J. *Beyond Sovereignty: Territory and Political Economy in the Twenty-First Century*. Toronto: University of Toronto Press, 1995.
Endo, Todd Isao. "The Relevance of Kohlberg's Stages of Moral Development to Research in Political Socialization." Ph.D. dissertation, Harvard University, 1973.
Engelstein, Laura. "Gender and the Juridical Subject: Prostitution and Rape in Nineteenth-Century Russian Criminal Codes." *Journal of Modern History* 60 (September 1988): 458–95.
Enloe, Cynthia H. *Police, Military and Ethnicity: Foundations of State Power*. New Brunswick, NJ: Transaction Books, 1980.
Entessar, Nader. *Kurdish Ethnonationalism*. Boulder, CD: Lynne Rienner, 1992.
Erfani, Julie A. *The Paradox of the Mexican State: Rereading Sovereignty from Independence to NAFTA*. Boulder, CO: L. Rienner, 1995.
Erikson, Erik H. *Childhood and Society* (second edition). New York: W. W. Norton, 1963.

Esherick, Joseph W., and Jeffrey N. Wasserstrom. "Acting Out Democracy: Political Theater in Modern China." *Journal of Asian Studies* 49 (November 1990): 835–65.

Evans, Peter B. *Dependent Development: The Alliance of Multinational, State, and Local Capital in Brazil.* Princeton, NJ: Princeton University Press, 1979.

Embedded Autonomy: States and Industrial Transformation. Princeton, NJ: Princeton University Press, 1995.

Evans, Peter B., Dietrich Reuschemeyer, and Theda Skocpol, eds. *Bringing the State Back In.* New York: Cambridge University Press, 1985.

Evans, Peter B., and John D. Stephens. "Studying Development Since the Sixties: The Emergence of a New Comparative Political Economy." *Theory and Society* 17 (1988).

Fagen, Richard R. "A Funny Thing Happened on the Way to the Market: Thoughts on Extending Dependency Ideas." *International Organization* 32 (1978): 287–300.

Fahim, Hussein M. "Change in Religion in a Resettled Nubian Community, Upper Egypt." *International Journal of Middle East Studies* 4 (1973): 163–77.

Fernandes, Lela. *Producing Workers: The Politics of Gender, Class, and Culture in the Calcutta Jute Mills.* Philadelphia: University of Pennsylvania Press, 1997.

Festinger, Leon. *A Theory of Cognitive Dissonance.* Stanford, CA: Stanford University Press, 1957.

Finkel, Norman J. *Commonsense Justice: Jurors' Notions of the Law.* Cambridge, MA: Harvard University Press, 1995.

Finnemore, Martha. *National Interests in International Society.* Ithaca, NY: Cornell University Press, 1996.

Foster, George M. "Peasant Society and the Image of Limited Good." *American Anthropologist* 67 (April 1965): 293–315.

Frank, Andre G. *Capitalism and Underdevelopment in Latin America.* New York: Monthly Review Press, 1967.

Crisis: In the Third World. New York: Holmes & Meier, 1981.

Frankel, Francine R. *India's Political Economy, 1947–1977: The Gradual Revolution.* Princeton, NJ: Princeton University Press, 1978.

Friedman, Lawrence M. *The Republic of Choice: Law, Authority, and Culture.* Cambridge, MA: Harvard University Press, 1990.

Galanter, Mark. "Justice in Many Rooms: Courts, Private Ordering, and Indigenous Law." *Journal of Legal Pluralism (and Unofficial Law)* 19 (1981): 56–72.

Geddes, Barbara. *Politician's Dilemma: Building State Capacity in Latin America.* Berkeley: University of California Press, 1994.

Geertz, Clifford. *The Interpretation of Cultures: Selected Essays.* New York: Basic Books, 1973.

Local Knowledge: Further Essays in Interpretive Anthropology. New York: Basic Books, 1983.

Negara: The Theatre State in Nineteenth-Century Bali. Princeton, NJ: Princeton University Press, 1980.

Gerschenkron, Alexander. *Economic Backwardness in Historical Perspective: A Book of Essays.* Cambridge, MA: Harvard University Press, 1962.

Bibliography

Goldberg, Ellis, Joel S. Migdal, and Resat Kaşaba, eds. *Rules and Rights in the Middle East.* Seattle: University of Washington Press, 1993.

Goldfrank, Walter L. *The World System of Capitalism: Past and Present.* Beverly Hills, CA: Sage, 1979.

Goldstein, Rebecca. *The Mind-Body Problem: A Novel.* New York: Random House, 1983.

Goldstone, Jack A. *Revolution and Rebellion in the Early Modern World.* Berkeley: University of California Press, 1991.

Gottlieb, Gidon. *Nation against State: A New Approach to Ethnic Conflicts and the Decline of Sovereignty.* New York: Council on Foreign Relations Press, 1971.

Goudsblom, Johan, and Stephen Mennell, eds. *The Norbert Elias Reader.* Oxford: Blackwell, 1998.

Gourevitch, Peter. "The Second Image Reversed: The International Sources of Domestic Politics." *International Organization* 32 (1978): 881–912.

Graham, Douglass H. "Mexican and Brazilian Economic Development: Legacies, Patterns, and Performance." In Sylvia Ann Hewlett and Richard S. Weinert, eds., *Brazil and Mexico: Patterns in Late Development.* Philadelphia: Institute for the Study of Human Issues, 1982.

Gramsci, Antonio. *Selections from the Prison Notebooks.* Edited by Quitin Hoare and Geoffrey N. Smith. New York: International Publishers, 1971.

Grew, Raymond, ed. *Crisis of Political Development in Europe and the United States.* Princeton, NJ: Princeton University Press, 1978.

Grindle, Merilee S. *Bureaucrats, Politicians, and Peasants in Mexico: A Case Study in Public Policy.* Berkeley: University of California Press, 1977.

"The Implementor: Political Constraints on Rural Development in Mexico." In Merilee Grindle, ed., *Politics and Policy Implementation in the Third World.* Princeton, NJ: Princeton University Press, 1980.

Guehenno, Jean-Marie. *The End of the Nation-State.* Minneapolis: University of Minnesota Press, 1995.

Guibernau, Berdun, and Maria Montserrat. *Nationalisms: The Nation-State and Nationalism in the Twentieth Century.* Cambridge, MA: Harvard University Press, 1996.

Gulbrandsen, Ornulf. "Living Their Lives in Courts: The Counter-Hegemonic Force of the Tsawana *Kgotla* in a Colonial Context." In Olivia Harris, ed., *Inside and Outside the Law.* New York: Routledge, 1996.

Gupta, Akhil. "Blurred Boundaries: The Discourse of Corruption, the Culture of Politics, and the Imagined State." *American Ethnologist* 22 (May 1995): 375–402.

Gusfield, Joseph R. "Tradition and Modernity: Misplaced Polarities in the Study of Social Change." *American Journal of Sociology* 72 (January 1967): 351–62.

Habermas, Jürgen. *Legitimation Crisis.* Boston: Beacon Press, 1975.

The Structural Transformation of the Public Sphere: An Inquiry into a Category of Bourgeois Society. Cambridge, MA: MIT Press, 1991.

Haggard, Stephen. *Pathways from the Periphery: The Politics of Growth in the Newly Industrializing Countries.* Ithaca, NY: Cornell University Press, 1990.

Hagopian, Frances. "Traditional Politics against State Transformation in Brazil." In Joel S. Migdal, Atul Kohli, and Vivienne Shue, eds., *State Power and Social Forces*. New York: Cambridge University Press, 1994.

Traditional Politics and Regime Change in Brazil. New York: Cambridge University Press, 1996.

Hall, John A., and G. John Ikenberry. *The State*. Minneapolis: University of Minnesota Press, 1989.

Halperin, Morton H. *Bureaucratic Politics and Foreign Policy*. Washington, DC: Brookings Institutions, 1974.

Hamilton, Gary C., and John R. Sutton. "The Problem of Control in the Weak State." *Theory and Society* 18 (January 1989): 15–16.

Hamilton, Nora. *The Limits of State Autonomy: Post-Revolutionary Mexico*. Princeton, NJ: Princeton University Press, 1982.

Hammergren, Linn A. "Corporatism in Latin American Polities: A Reexamination of the 'Unique' Tradition." *Comparative Politics* 9 (July 1977): 443–61.

Hannan, Michael T., and John Freeman. "The Population Ecology of Organizations." *American Journal of Sociology* 82 (1994): 929–64.

Hansen, Roger D. *The Politics of Mexican Development*. Baltimore, MD: John Hopkins University Press, 1973.

Harvey, O. J., David E. Hunt, and Harold M. Schroder. "Stages of Conceptual Development." In Edward E. Sampson, ed., *Approaches, Contexts, and Problems of Social Psychology*. Englewood Cliffs, NJ: Prentice-Hall, 1964.

Heeger, Gerald A. *The Politics of Underdevelopment*. New York: St. Martin's Press, 1974.

Hegel, Georg Wilhelm Friedrich. *Hegel's Philosophy of Right*. Oxford: The Clarendon Press, 1942.

Hernes, Gudmond, and Arnie Selvik. "Local Corporatism." In Suzanne Berger, ed., *Organizing Interests in Western Europe: Pluralism, Corporatism, and the Transformation of Politics*. New York: Cambridge University Press, 1981.

Hewlett, Sylvia Ann, and Richard S. Weinert. *Brazil and Mexico: Patterns in Late Development*. Philadelphia: Institute for the Study of Human Issues, 1982.

Higgott, Richard. "Competing Theoretical Perspectives on Development and Underdevelopment: A Recent History." *Politics* 13 (1978): 26–41.

Hindson, Paul, and Tim Gray. *Burke's Dramatic Theory of Politics*. Brookfield, VT: Avebury, 1988.

Hintze, Otto. "The Formation of States and Constitutional Development: A Study in History and Politics." In Felix Gilbert, ed., *The Historical Essays of Otto Hintze*. New York: Oxford University Press, 1975.

Hirschman, Albert O. "The Political Economy of Import-Substituting Industrialization in Latin America." *The Quarterly Journal of Economics* 82 (1968): 2–32.

Huet, Marie-Hélène. *Rehearsing the Revolution: The Staging of Marat's Death 1793–1797*. Berkeley: University of California Press, 1982.

Hunt, Lynn Avery. *The Family Romance of the French Revolution*. Berkeley: University of California Press, 1992.

Bibliography

Huntington, Samuel P. "Political Development and Political Decay." *World Politics* 17 (April 1965): 386–430.

Political Order in Changing Societies. New Haven, CT: Yale University Press, 1968.

"The Change to Change: Modernization, Development and Politics." In *Comparative Politics* 3 (1971): 282–322.

The Third Wave: Democratization in the Late Twentieth Century. Norman: University of Oklahoma Press, 1991.

Hyden, Goran. *Beyond Ujamaa in Tanzania: Underdevelopment and an Uncaptured Peasantry.* Berkeley: University of California Press, 1980.

Ingebritsen, Christine. *The Nordic States and European Unity.* Ithaca, NY: Cornell University Press, 1998.

Inglehart, Ronald. "Cognitive Mobilization and European Identity." *Comparative Politics* 3 (1970): 45–70.

Inkeles, Alex, and David H. Smith. *Becoming Modern.* Cambridge, MA: Harvard University Press, 1974.

Jackman, Robert H. *Power Without Force: The Political Capacities of Nation-States.* Ann Arbor: University of Michigan Press, 1993.

Jackson, Robert H. *Quasi-States: Sovereignty, International Relations, and the Third World.* New York: Cambridge University Press, 1990.

Jackson, Robert H., and Alan James, eds. *States in a Changing World: A Contemporary Analysis.* Oxford: Clarendon Press, 1993.

Jackson, Robert H., and Carl G. Rosberg. "Why Africa's Weak States Persist: The Empirical and the Juridical in Statehood." *World Politics* 35 (October 1982): 1–24.

Jessop, Bob. "Corporatism, Parliamentarism, and Social Democracy." In Philippe Schmitter and Gerhard Lehmbruch, eds., *Trends Towards Corporatist Intermediation.* Beverly Hills, CA: Sage, 1979.

Jones, Gareth Stedman. *Languages of Class: Studies in English Working Class History, 1832–1982.* New York: Cambridge University Press, 1983.

Joseph, Gilbert M., and Daniel Nugent. "Popular Culture and State Formation." In Gilbert M. Joseph and Daniel Nugent, eds., *Everyday Forms of State Formation: Revolution and the Negotiation of Rule in Modern Mexico.* Durham, NC: Duke University Press, 1994.

Jowitt, Kenneth. *New World Disorder: The Leninist Extinction.* Berkeley: University of California Press, 1992.

Revolutionary Breakthroughs and National Development: The Case of Romania, 1944–1965. Berkeley: University of California Press, 1971.

Kaplan, Barbara H. *Social Change in the Capitalist World Economy.* Beverly Hills, CA: Sage, 1978.

Kaplan, Robert. *The Ends of the Earth: From Togo to Turkmenistan, from Iran to Cambodia, A Journey to the Frontiers of Anarchy.* New York: Knopf, 1997.

Kasaba, Reşat. "A Time and Place for the Nonstate: Social Change in the Ottoman Empire during the 'Long Nineteenth Century.'" In Joel S. Migdal, Atul Kohli, and Vivienne Shue, eds., *State Power and Social Forces.* New York: Cambridge University Press, 1994.

Katznelson, Ira. "Structure and Configuration in Comparative Politics." In Mark Lichbach and Alan Zuckerman, eds., *Comparative Politics: Rationality, Culture, and Structure*. New York: Cambridge University Press, 1997.

Katzenstein, Peter J., *Between Power and Plenty: Foreign Economic Policies of Advanced Industrial States*. Madison: University of Wisconsin Press, 1978.

———. "Conclusion: Domestic Structures and Strategies of Foreign Economic Policy." In Peter J. Katzenstein, ed., *Between Power and Plenty: Foreign Economic Policies of Advanced Industrial States*. Madison: University of Wisconsin Press, 1978.

———. *Corporatism and Change*. Ithaca, NY: Cornell University Press, 1984.

———. *Culture of National Security: Norms and Identity in World Politics*. New York: Columbia University Press, 1996.

———. *Tamed Power*. Ithaca, NY: Cornell University Press, 1997.

Keane, John. *Democracy and Civil Society: On the Predicaments of European Socialism, the Prospects for Democracy, and the Problem of Controlling Social and of Political Power*. New York: Verso, 1988.

Keeler, John T. S. "Corporatism and Official Union Hegemony: The Case of French Agricultural Syndicalism." In Suzanne Berger, ed., *Organizing Interests in Western Europe: Pluralism, Corporatism, and the Transformation of Politics*. New York: Combridge University Press, 1981.

Keller, Edmond J., and Donald Rothchild. *Africa in the New International Order: Rethinking State Sovereignty and Regional Security*. Boulder, CO: Lynne Rienner, 1996.

Keohane, Robert O., and Joseph S. Nye, Jr. *Transnational Relations and World Politics*. Cambridge, MA: Harvard University Press, 1970.

Kertzer, David. *Ritual, Politics and Power*. New Haven: Yale University Press, 1988.

Kesselman, Mark. "Over-institutionalization and Political Constraint: The Case of France." *Comparative Politics* 3 (1970): 21–44.

Kilson, Martin. *Political Change in a West African State: A Study of the Modernization Process in Sierra Leone*. Cambridge, MA: Harvard University Press, 1966.

King, Roger. *The State in Modern Society: New Directions in Political Sociology*. Chatham, NJ: Chatham House, 1986.

Kling, Merle. "Toward a Theory of Power and Political Instability in Latin America." In James Petras and Maurice Zeitlin, eds., *Latin America: Reform or Revolution*. New York: Fawcett, 1968.

Klotz, Audie. *Norms in International Relations: The Struggle against Apartheid*. Ithaca, NY: Cornell University Press, 1995.

Koelble, Thomas A. "The New Institutionalism in Political Science and Sociology." *Comparative Politics* 27 (January 1995): 231–43.

Kohli, Atul. "Centralization and Powerlessness: India's Democracy in a Comparative Perspective." In Joel S. Migdal, Atul Kohli, and Vivienne Shue, eds., *State Power and Social Forces*. New York: Cambridge University Press, 1994.

———. *Democracy and Discontent: India's Growing Crisis of Governability*. New York: Cambridge University Press, 1990.

Bibliography

Kohlberg, Lawrence. "Education for Justice: A Modern Statement of the Platonic View." In James M. Gustafson, ed., *Moral Education*. Cambridge, MA: Harvard University Press, 1970.

"Stage and Sequence: The Cognitive Developmental Approach to Socialization." In David A. Groslin, ed., *Handbook of Socialization Theory and Research*. Chicago: Rand McNally, 1969.

Kondratieff, N. D. "The Long Waves in Economic Life." *The Review of Economic Statistics* 17 (1935): 105–15.

Krasner, Stephen D. "Approaches to the State: Alternative Conceptions and Historical Dynamics." *Comparative Politics* 16 (January 1984): 223–52.

Defending the National Interest: Raw Materials Investments and U.S. Foreign Policy. Princeton, NJ: Princeton University Press, 1978.

"Domestic Constraints on International Economic Leverage." In Klaus Knorr and Frank N. Trager, eds., *Economic Issues and National Security*. Kansas City: Regents Press of Kansas, 1977.

"Regimes and the Limits of Realism: Regimes as Autonomous." *International Organization* 36 (1982): 497–510.

"Sovereignty: An Institutionalist Perspective." *Comparative Political Studies* 21 (April 1988): 66–94.

Kuehls, Thom. *Beyond Sovereign Territory: The Space of Ecopolitics*. Minneapolis: University of Minnesota Press, 1996.

Kurth, James R. "Industrial Change and Political Change: A European Perspective." In David Collier, ed., *The New Authoritarianism in Latin America*. Princeton, NJ: Princeton University Press, 1979.

Laitin, David D. *Hegemony and Culture: Politics and Religious Change Among the Yoruba*. Chicago: University of Chicago Press, 1986.

Lamborn, Alan C. "Power and the Politics of Extraction." *International Studies Quarterly* 27 (June 1983): 120–45.

Lane, Ruth. *The Art of Comparative Politics*. Boston: Allyn and Bacon, 1997.

LaPalombara, Joseph. "Political Science and Engineering of National Development." In Monte Palmer and Larry Sterns, eds., *Political Development in Changing Societies*. Lexington, MA: D. C. Heath, 1971.

Lawson, Kenneth Gregory. *"War at the Grassroots: The Great War and the Nationalization of Civic Life."* Ph.D. dissertation, University of Washington, 2000.

Lehmbruch, Gerhard. "Liberal Corporatism and Party Government," In Philippe Schmitter and Gerhard Lehmbruch, eds., *Trends Towards Corporatist Intermediation*. Beverly Hills, CA: Sage, 1979.

Lerner, Daniel. *The Passing of Traditional Society: Modernizing the Middle East*. New York: Free Press, 1958.

"Some Comments on Center-Periphery Relations." In Richard L. Merritt and Stein Rokkan, eds., *Comparing Nations*. New Haven, CT: Yale University Press, 1966.

Levi, Margaret. "A Model, a Method, and a Map: Rational Choice in Comparative and Historical Analysis." In Mark Lichbach and Alan Zuckerman, eds., *Comparative Politics: Rationality, Culture, and Structure*. New York: Cambridge University Press, 1997.

Of Rule and Revenue. Berkeley: University of California Press, 1988.

Levy, Marian J. Jr. *Modernization and the Structure of Societies: A Setting for International Affairs*. Princeton, NJ: Princeton University Press, 1966.

Lichbach, Mark, and Alan Zuckerman, eds. *Comparative Politics: Rationality, Culture, and Structure*. New York: Cambridge University Press, 1997.

Lipton, Michael. *Why Poor People Stay Poor: Urban Bias in World Development*. Cambridge, MA: Harvard University Press, 1977.

Lowi, Theodore J. *At the Pleasure of the Mayor: Patronage and Power in New York City, 1898–1958*. New York: The Free Press, 1964.

Lustick, Ian. *Unsettled States, Disputed Lands: Britain and Ireland, France and Algeria, Israel and the West Bank–Gaza*. Ithaca, NY: Cornell University Press, 1993.

Lyons, Gene M., and Michael Mastanduno, eds. *Beyond Westphalia? State Sovereignty and International Intervention*. Baltimore, MD: John Hopkins University Press, 1995.

Malloy, James M. "Authoritarianism and Corporatism in Latin America: The Modal Pattern," In James M. Malloy, ed., *Authoritarianism and Corporatism in Latin America*. Pittsburgh, PA: University of Pittsburgh Press, 1977.

Mann, Michael. "The Autonomous Power of the State: Its Origins, Mechanisms and Results." In John A. Hall, ed., *States in History*. Oxford: Basil Blackwell, 1986.

The Sources of Social Power. New York: Cambridge University Press, 1986.

March, James G., and Johan P. Olsen. *Rediscovering Institutions: The Organizational Basis of Politics*. New York: Free Press, 1989.

Marty, Martin E. *The One and the Many: America's Struggle for the Common Good*. Cambridge, MA: Harvard University Press, 1997.

Maslow, Abraham H. *Motivation and Personality*. New York: Harper, 1954.

McClelland, David C. *The Achieving Society*. New York: Free Press, 1961.

McLellan, David. *Karl Marx: Early Texts*. Oxford: Basil Blackwell, 1979.

Mehta, Vrajanda Raj. *Beyond Marxism: Towards an Alternative Perspective*. New Delhi: Manohar, 1978.

Merkel, Peter H. "The Study of European Political Development." *World Politics* 29 (1977).

Meyer, John W., and Michael T. Hannan. *National Development in the World System: Educational, Economic, and Political Change, 1950–1970*. Chicago: University of Chicago Press, 1979.

Meyer, John W., and Brian Rowan. "Institutionalized Organizations: Formal Structure as Myth and Ceremony." *American Journal of Sociology* 83 (1977): 340–63.

Meyer, Marshall W., and Lynne G. Zucker. *Permanently Failing Organizations*. Newbury Park: Sage, 1989.

Migdal, Joel S. "Capitalist Penetration in the Nineteenth Century: Creating Conditions for New Patterns of Social Control." In Robert Wheeler and Scott Guggenheim, eds., *Power and Protest in the Countryside: Studies of Rural Unrest*. Durham, NC: Duke University Press, 1982.

Peasants, Politics, and Revolution: Pressures Towards Political and Social Change in the Third World. Princeton, NJ: Princeton University Press, 1974.

Bibliography

"Civil Society in Israel." In Ellis Goldberg, Reşat Kasaba, and Joel S. Migdal, eds., *Rules and Rights in the Middle East*. Seattle: University of Washington Press, 1993.

Strong Societies and Weak States: State–Society Relations and State Capabilities in the Third World. Princeton, NJ: Princeton University Press, 1988.

"Studying the State." In Mark I. Lichbach and Alan S. Zuckerman, eds., *Comparative Politics: Rationality, Culture, and Structure*. New York: Cambridge University Press, 1997.

Through the Lens of Israel: Explorations in State and Society. Albany: State University of New York Press, 2001.

"Why Change? Toward a New Theory of Change Among Individuals in the Process of Modernization," *World Politics* 26 (1974): 189–206.

Migdal, Joel S., Atul Kohli, and Vivienne Shue, eds. *State Power and Social Forces: Domination and Transformation in the Third World*. New York: Cambridge University Press, 1994.

Migdal, Joel S., et al. *Palestinian Society and Politics*. Princeton, NJ: Princeton University Press, 1980.

Millikan, Max F., and W. W. Rostow. *A Proposal: Key to an Effective Foreign Policy*. New York: Harper, 1957.

Minow, Martha, Michael Ryan, and Austan Sarat, eds. *Narrative Violence and the Law: The Essays of Robert Cover*. Ann Arbor: University of Michigan Press, 1993.

Mishal, Shaul. "Conflictual Pressures and Cooperative Interests: Observations on West Bank – Amman Political Relations, 1949–1967." In Joel S. Migdal, et al. *Palestinian Society and Politics*. Princeton, NJ: Princeton University Press, 1980.

Mitchell, J. Clyde. *The Kalela Dance*. Rhodes-Livingstone Papers No. 27. New York: Humanities Press, 1956.

Mitchell, Timothy. "The Effect of the State." Working paper presented at the workshop on state creation and transformation of the Social Science Research Council's Committee on the Near and Middle East. Istanbul, September 1–3, 1989.

"The Limits of the State: Beyond Statist Approaches and Their Critics." *American Political Science Review* 85 (March 1991): 82.

Modelski, George, "The Long Cycle of Global Politics and the Nation-State." *Comparative Studies in Society and History* 20 (1978): 214–35.

"Long Cycles of World Leadership." Working paper presented at the annual meeting of the American Political Science Association. New York, 1981.

Transnational Corporations and World Order: Readings in International Political Economy. San Francisco: W. H. Freeman, 1979.

Molteno, Robert. "Cleavage and Conflict in Zambian Politics: A Study in Sectionalism." In William Tordoff, ed., *Politics in Zambia*. Manchester: Manchester University Press, 1974.

Montgomery, John D. "The Quest for Political Development." *Comparative Politics* 1 (1969): 285–95.

Moore, Barrington, Jr. *Social Origins of Dictatorship and Democracy: Lord and Peasant in the Making of the Modern World*. Boston: Beacon Press, 1966.

Moore, Dahlia, and Baruch Kimmerling. "Individual Strategies of Adopting Collective Identities: The Israeli Case." *International Sociology* 10 (December 1995).

Mosca, Gaetano. *The Ruling Class*. New York: McGraw-Hill, 1939.

Nash, Manning. *The Cauldron of Ethnicity in the Modern World*. Chicago: University of Chicago Press, 1989.

Nettl, J. P. *Political Mobilization: A Sociological Analysis of Methods and Concepts*. New York: Basic Books, 1967.

"The State as a Conceptual Variable." *World Politics* 20 (1968): 559–92.

Neuberger, Benjamin. "State and Nation in African Thought." *Journal of African Studies* 4 (Summer 1977): 198–205.

"The Western Nation-State in African Perceptions of Nation-Building." *Asian and African Studies* 11 (1976): 241–61.

Newberg, Paula R. *Judging the State: Courts and Constitutional Politics in Pakistan*. New York: Cambridge University Press, 1995.

Newton, Ronald C. "Natural Corporatism and the Passing of Populism in Spanish America." In Federick B. Pike and Thomas Stritch, eds., *The New Corporatism: Social-Political Structures in the Iberian World*. Notre Dame, IN: University of Notre Dame Press, 1974.

Nisbet, Robert A. *Social Change and History: Aspects of the Western Theory of Development*. London: Oxford University Press, 1969.

Nordlinger, Eric A. *On the Autonomy of the Democratic State*. Cambridge, MA: Harvard University Press, 1981.

North, Douglass C. *Structure and Change in Economic History*. New York: W. W. Norton, 1981.

"The Western Nation-State in African Perceptions of Nation-Building." *Asian and African Studies* 11 (1976): 241–61.

O'Donnell, Guillermo. "Tensions in the Bureaucratic-Authoritarian State and the Question of Democracy." In David Collier, ed., *The New Authoritarianism in Latin America*. Princeton, NJ: Princeton University Press, 1979.

and Philippe C. Schmitter. *Transitions from Authoritarian Rule*. Baltimore, MD: John Hopkins University Press, 1986.

Offe, Claus. "The Attribution of Public Status to Interest Groups: Observation of the West German Case." In Suzanne Berger, ed., *Organizing Interests in Western Europe: Pluralism, Corporatism, and the Transformation Politics*. New York: Cambridge University Press, 1981.

Modernity and the State: East, West. Cambridge, MA: MIT Press, 1996.

Ohmae, Kenichi. *The End of the Nation-State: The Rise of Regional Economies*. New York: Free Press, 1995.

Oldenburg, Ray. *The Great Good Place: Cafés, Coffee Shops, Community Centers, Beauty Parlors, General Stores, Bars, Hangouts and How They Get You Through the Day*. New York: Paragon House, 1989.

Ó Múrchu, Niall. "Labor, the State, and Ethnic Conflict: A Comparative Study of British Rule in Palestine (1920–1939) and Northern Ireland (1973–1994)." Ph.D. dissertation, University of Washington, 2000.

Bibliography

Osiel, Mark J. "Dialogue with Dictators: Judicial Resistance in Argentina and Brazil." *Law and Social Inquiry* 20 (Spring 1995): 481–560.

Panitch, Leo. "The Development of Corporatism in Liberal Democracies." In Philippe Schmitter and Gerhard Lehmbruch, eds., *Trends Towards Corporatist Intermediation.* Beverly Hills, CA: Sage, 1979.

"Recent Theorization of Corporatism: Reflections on a Growth Industry." *British Journal of Sociology* 31 (1980): 159–82.

Parpart, Jane L., and Kathleen A. Staudt. "Women and the State in Africa." In Jane L. Parpart and Kathleen Staudt, eds., *Women and the State in Africa.* Boulder, CO: Lynne Rienner, 1989.

Parsons, Talcott. "The Political Aspect of Social Structure and Process." In David Easton, ed., *Varieties of Political Theory.* Englewood Cliffs, NJ: Prentice-Hall, 1966.

The Social System. Glencoe, IL: Free Press, 1951.

Societies: Evolutionary and Comparative Perspectives. Englewood Cliffs, NJ: Prentice-Hall, 1966.

Parsons, Talcott, and Edward Shils. *Toward a General Theory of Action.* Cambridge, MA: Harvard University Press, 1951.

Paul, David W. *The Cultural Limits of Revolutionary Politics: Change and Continuity in Socialist Czechoslovakia.* Boulder, CO: East European Quarterly and Columbia University Press, 1979.

Peled, Yoav, and Gershon Shafir. "The Roots of Peacemaking: The Dynamics of Citizenship in Israel, 1948–93." *International Journal of Middle East Studies* 28 (1996): 391–413.

Pempel, T. J. "Japanese Foreign Economic Policy: The Domestic Bases for International Behavior." In Peter J. Katzenstein, ed., *Between Power and Plenty: Foreign Economic Policies of Advanced Industrial States.* Madison: University of Wisconsin Press, 1978.

Pempel, T. J., and Keiichi Tsunekawa. "Corporatism Without Labor? The Japanese Anomaly." In Philippe Schmitter and Gerhard Lehmbruch, eds., *Trends Toward Corporatist Intermediation.* Beverly Hills, CA: Sage, 1979.

Perry, Elizabeth J. "Labor Divided: Sources of State Formation in Modern China." In Joel S. Migdal, Atul Kohli, and Vivienne Shue, eds., *State Power and Social Forces.* New York: Cambridge University Press, 1994.

Rebels and Revolutionaries in North China 1845–1945. Stanford, CA: Stanford University Press, 1980.

Pike, Frederick B., and Thomas Stritch, eds. *The New Corporatism: Social-Political Structures in the Iberian World.* Notre Dame, IN: University of Notre Dame Press, 1974.

Polanyi, Karl. *The Great Transformation: The Political and Economic Origins of Our Time.* Boston: Beacon Press, 1944.

Popkin, Samuel L. *The Rational Peasant.* Berkeley: University of California Press, 1979.

Poulantzas, Nicos. *Political Power and Social Class.* London: NLB, 1975.

Putnam, Robert D. "Bowling Alone: America's Declining Social Capital." *Current* 373 (June 1995): 3–10.

"Tuning in, Tuning Out: The Strange Disappearance of Social Capital in America." *PS: Political Science and Politics* 27 (December 1995): 664–83.

"What Makes Democracy Work?" *National Civic Review* 82 (Spring 1993): 101–7.

Pye, Lucian W. "The Concept of Political Development." *Annals of the American Academy* 358 (1965): 1–13.

Politics, Personality, and Nation-Building. New Haven, CT: Yale University Press, 1962.

Rau, Zbigniew. "Some Thoughts on Civil Society in Eastern Europe and the Lockean Contractarian Approach." *Political Studies* 35 (1987): 573–92.

Razik, Gasser Abdel. *The New York Times.* July 10, 2000, p. A10.

Redfield, Robert. *Peasant Society and Culture.* Chicago: University of Chicago Press, 1960.

Reitsma, Hendenrik-Jan A. "Development, Geography, Dependency Relations, and the Capitalist Scapegoat." *The Professional Geographer* 34 (1982): 125–30.

Reuschemeyer, Dietrich, and Peter B. Evans. "The State and Economic Transformation: Toward an Analysis of the Conditions Underlying Effective Intervention." In Evans, et al., *Bringing the State Back In.* New York: Cambridge University Press, 1985.

Richards, A. I. "Authority Patterns in Traditional Buganda." In L. A. Fallers and A. I. Richards, eds., *The King's Men: Leadership and Status in Buganda on the Eve of Independence.* New York: Oxford University Press, 1964.

Riggs, Fred W. *Administration in Developing Countries: The Theory of Prismatic Society.* Boston: Houghton Mifflin, 1964.

Rogowski, Ronald, and Lois Wasserspring. "Does Political Development Exist? Corporatism in Old and New Societies." *Comparative Politics Series 2.* Beverly Hills, CA: Sage, 1971.

Rokkan, Stein. "Cities, States, and Nations: A Dimensional Model of the Study of Contrasts in Development." In S. N. Eisenstadt and Stein Rokkan, eds., *Building States and Nations.* Beverly Hills, CA: Sage, 1973.

Roseberry, William. "Hegemony and the Language of Contention." In Gilbert Joseph and Daniel Nugent, eds., *Everyday Forms of State Formation: Revolution and the Negotiation of the Rule in Modern Mexico.* Durham, NC: Duke University Press, 1994.

Rosenau, James N. "The State in an Era of Cascading Politics: Wavering Concept, Widening Competence, Withering Colossus, or Weathering Change?" *Comparative Political Studies* 21 (April 1988): 13–44.

Ross, Marc. "Culture and Identity in Comparative Political Analysis." In Mark Lichbach and Alan Zuckerman, eds., *Comparative Politics: Rationality, Culture, and Structure.* New York: Cambridge University Press, 1997.

Rostow, Dankwart A. "Modernization and Comparative Politics: Prospects in Research and Theory." *Comparative Politics* 1 (1968): 37–51.

Rudolph, Lloyd I., and Suzanne H. Rudolph. *The Modernity of Tradition.* Chicago: University of Chicago Press, 1967.

Runciman, David. *Pluralism and the Personality of the State.* New York: Cambridge University Press, 1997.

Russell, Bertrand. *Sceptical Essays.* New York: W. W. Norton, 1928.

Bibliography

Sadat, Anwar el-. *In Search of Identity: An Autobiography*. New York: Harper & Row, 1977.

Sandbrock, Richard. "The Crisis in Political Development Theory." *Journal of Development Studies* 12 (1975): 163–85.

Sanders, John T., and Jan Narveson, eds. *For and Against the State: New Philosophical Readings*. Lanham, MD: Rowman and Littlefield, 1996.

Schlichte, Klaus. "Why States Decay: A Preliminary Assessment." Mimeograph, 1997.

Schmitter, Phillippe C. "Interest Intermediation and Regime Governability in Contemporary Western Europe and North America." In Suzanne Berger, ed., *Organizing Interests in Western Europe: Pluralism, Corporatism and the Transformation of Politics*. New York: Cambridge University Press, 1981.

Schudson, Michael. "Culture and Integration of National Societies." *International Social Science Journal* 46 (February 1994): 63–82.

Schumpeter, Joseph. *Business Cycles*. New York: McGraw Hill, 1939.

Schwartz, Benjamin. "The Limits of 'Tradition Versus Modernity' as Categories of Explanation: The Case of the Chinese Intellectuals." *Daedalus* 101 (1972): 71–88.

Scott, James C. *The Moral Economy of the Peasants: Rebellion and Subsistence in Southeast Asia*. New Haven, CT: Yale University Press, 1976.

Seeing Like a State: How Certain Schemes to Improve the Human Condition Have Failed. New Haven, CT: Yale University Press, 1998.

Sennett, Richard. *The Fall of Public Man*. New York: Knopf, 1977.

Shapiro, Martin, and Alec Stone. "The New Constitutional Politics of Europe." *Comparative Political Studies* 26 (January 1994): 397–420.

Shapiro, Michael J., and Hayward R. Alker. *Challenging Boundaries: Global Flows, Territorial Identities*. Minneapolis: University of Minnesota Press, 1996.

Shils, Edward. *Center and Periphery: Essays in Macrosociology*. Chicago: University of Chicago Press, 1975.

The Constitution of Society. Chicago: University of Chicago Press, 1972.

Political Development in the New States. Paris: Mouton, 1962.

"Political Development in the New States." *Comparative Studies in Society and History* 2 (1960): 265–92.

Shue, Vivienne. *The Reach of the State: Sketches of the Chinese Body Politic*. Stanford, CA: Stanford University Press, 1988.

"State Power and Social Organization in China." In Joel S. Migdal, Atul Kohli, and Vivienne Shue, eds., *State Power and Social Forces*. New York: Cambridge University Press, 1994.

Singh, Jitendra V., David J. Tucker, and Robert J. House. "Organizational Legitimacy and the Liability of Newness." In W. Richard Scott, ed., *Organizational Sociology*. Brookfield, VT: Dartmouth, 1994.

Siu, Helen. "Recycling Rituals: Politics and Popular Culture in Contemporary China." In Perry Link, Richard Madsen, and Paul G. Pickowiez, eds., *Unofficial China: Popular Culture and Thought in the People's Republic*. Boulder, CO: Westview Press, 1989.

Sjoberg, Gideon. *The Pre-industrial City*. New York: Free Press, 1960.

Skinner, G. William. "Chinese Peasants and the Closed Community: An Open and Shut Case." *Comparative Studies in Society and History* 13 (July 1971): 270–81.
Skocpol, Theda. "Bringing the State Back In." *Social Science Research Council Items* 36 (June 1982): 1–8.
States and Social Revolutions: A Comparative Analysis of France, Russia and China. New York: Cambridge: Cambridge University Press, 1979.
Smith, Anthony D. "Myth of the 'Modern Nation' and the Myths of Nations." *Racial Studies* 11 (January 1988): 1–26
"State-Making and Nation-Building." In Hall, ed., *States in History*. New York: B. Blackwell, 1986.
Smith, Thomas B. "The Policy Implementation Process." *Policy Sciences* 4 (June 1973): 172–98.
Springbong, Robert. *Family Power and Politics in Egypt: Sayed Bey Marei – His Clan, Clients and Cohorts.* Philadelphia: University of Pennsylvania Press, 1982.
Spruyt, Hendrik. *The Sovereign State and Its Competitors: An Analysis of Systems Change.* Princeton, NJ: Princeton University Press, 1994.
Srinivas, M. N. *Caste in Modern India and Other Essays.* Bombay: Asia Publishing House, 1962.
Social Change in Modern India. Berkeley: University of California Press, 1966.
Stepan, Alfred. *Authoritarian Brazil: Origins, Policies, and Future.* New Haven, CT: Yale University Press, 1973.
Rethinking Military Politics: Brazil and the Southern Cone. Princeton, NJ: Princeton University Press, 1988.
The State and Society: Peru in Comparative Perspective. Princeton, NJ: Princeton University Press, 1978.
Stern, Paul C. "Why do People Sacrifice for Their Nations?" *Political Psychology* 16 (1985): 217–35.
Stinchcombe, Arthur L. "Organizations and Social Structure." In James G. March, ed., *Handbook of Organizations*. Chicago: Rand-McNally, 1965.
Strang, David. "Anamoly and Commonplace in European Political Expansion: Realist and Institutional Accounts." *International Organization* 45 (Spring 1991): 143–62.
Swann, William B., John J. Griffin, Jr., Steven C. Predmore, and Bebe Gines. "The Cognitive-Affective Crossfire: When Self-Consistency Confronts Self-Enhancement." *Journal of Personality and Social Psychology* 52 (May 1987).
Swidler, Ann. "Culture in Action: Symbols and Strategies." *American Sociological Review* 51 (April 1986).
"Reflections on the History of European State-Making." In Charles Tilly, ed., *The Formation of National States in Western Europe*. Princeton, NJ: Princeton University Press, 1975.
"Western State-Making and Theories of Political Transformation." In Charles Tilly, ed., *The Formation of National States in Western Europe*. Princeton, NJ: Princeton University Press, 1978.
Tarrow, Sidney. *Territorial Politics in Industrial Nations.* New York: Praeger, 1978.
Thelen, Kathleen, and Sven Steinmo. "Historical Institutionalism in Comparative Politics." In Sven Steinmo, Kathleen Thelen, and Frank Longstreth, eds.,

Bibliography

Historical Institutionalism in Comparative Analysis. New York: Cambridge University Press, 1992.

Thompson, E. P. "Eighteenth-Century English Society: Class Struggle without Class?" *Social History* 3 (May 1978).

"Patrician Society, Plebian Culture." *Journal of Social History* 7 (Summer 1974): 382–405.

The Poverty of Theory and Other Essays. New York: Monthly Review Press, 1978.

Tilly, Charles. "Reflections on the History of European State-Making." In Charles Tilly, ed., *The Formation of National States in Western Europe.* Princeton, NJ: Princeton University Press, 1975.

The Vendée. New York: John Wiley & Sons, 1967.

"War Making and State Making as Organized Crime." In Peter B. Evans, Dietrich Rueschemeyer, and Theda Skocpol, eds., *Bringing the State Back In.* New York: Cambridge University Press, 1985.

"Western State-Making and Theories of Political Transformation." In Charles Tilly, ed., *The Formation of National States in Western Europe.* Princeton, NJ: Princeton University Press, 1975.

ed. *The Formation of National States in Western Europe.* Princeton, NJ: Princeton University Press, 1975.

Tipps, Dean C. "Modernization Theory and the Comparative Study of Societies." *Comparative Studies and Societies and History* 15 (1973): 199–240.

Triska, Jan F., and Paul M. Cocks, eds. *Political Development in Eastern Europe.* New York: Praeger, 1977.

Triska, Jan F., and Paul M. Johnson. "Political Development and Political Change in Eastern Europe: A Comparative Study." *University of Denver Monograph Series in World Affairs* 13, Book 2, 1975.

Ugalde, Antonio. *Power and Conflict in a Mexican Community: A Study of Political Integration.* Albuquerque: University of New Mexico Press, 1970.

United Nations. *The Economic Development of Latin America and Its Principal Problems.* New York: United Nations, 1950.

U.S. Department of State. *Country Reports on Human Rights Practices for 1981.* Washington, D.C., 1981.

Van Meter, Donald S., and Carl E. Van Horn. "The Policy Implementation Process: A Conceptual Framework." *Administration and Society* 6 (February 1975).

Verba, Sidney. "Sequences and Development." In Binder, et al., eds., *Crises and Sequences of Political Development.* Princeton, NJ: Princeton University Press, 1971.

Viliz, Claudio. *The Centralist Tradition in Latin America.* Princeton, NJ: Princeton University Press, 1980.

Vincent, Andrew. *Theories of the State.* Oxford: Basil Blackwell, 1987.

Vital, David. *The Origins of Zionism.* Oxford: Clarendon Press, 1975.

Zionism: The Formative Years. Oxford: Clarendon Press, 1982.

Vitalis, Robert. "Business Conflict, Collaboration, and Privilege in Interwar Europe." In Joel S. Migdal, Atul Kohli, and Vivienne Shue, eds., *State Power and Social Forces.* New York: Cambridge University Press, 1994.

When Capitalists Collide: Business Conflict and the End of Empire in Egypt. Berkeley: University of California Press, 1995.

Waldner, David. *State Building and Late Development.* Ithaca, NY: Cornell University Press, 1999.

Wallerstein, Immanuel. *The Modern World-System: Capitalist Agriculture and the Origins of the European World Economy in the Sixteenth Century.* New York: Academic Press, 1974.

The Modern World System II: Mercantilism and the Consolidation of the European World Economy, 1600–1750. New York: Academic Press, 1974.

"A World System Perspective of the Social Sciences." *British Journal of Sociology* 27 (1976): 343–52.

Waltz, Kenneth. *Theory of International Politics.* Reading, MA: Addison-Wesley, 1979.

Waterbury, John. *The Egypt of Nasser and Sadat: The Political Economy of Two Regimes.* Princeton, NJ: Princeton University Press, 1983.

Exposed to Innumerable Delusions: Public Enterprise and State Power in Egypt, India, Mexico and Turkey. New York: Cambridge University Press, 1993.

Watts, Nicole. "Kurdish Rights, Human Rights: Boundaries of Transnational Activism," Paper presented to the Workshop on Boundaries and Belonging. Seattle, July 1999.

"Virtual Kurdistan West: States and Supra-territorial Communities in the Late 20th and Early 21st Centuries." Ph.D. dissertation, University of Washington, forthcoming, 2001.

Weber, Max. *Economy and Society.* New York: Bedmister Press, 1968.

From Max Weber: Essays in Sociology, translated and edited by H. H. Gerth and C. Wright Mills. New York: Oxford University Press, 1958.

Max Weber on Law in Economy and Society, edited by Max Rheinstein. Cambridge, MA: Harvard University Press, 1954.

"Politics as a Vocation." In H. H. Gerth and C. Wright Mills, trans. and eds., *From Max Weber: Essays in Sociology.* New York: Oxford University Press, 1946.

Theory of Social and Economic Organization. New York: Free Press, 1964.

Weiner, Myron. "Motilal, Jawaharlal, Indira, and Sanjay in India's Political Transformation." In Richard J. Samuels, ed., *Political Generations and Political Development.* Lexington, MA: Lexington Books, 1977.

Weingrod, Alex. *Reluctant Pioneers.* Ithaca, NY: Cornell University Press, 1966.

Wendt, Alexander. "Constructing International Politics." *International Security* 20 (1995): 71–81.

Whitaker, C. S. Jr. "A Dysrhythmic Process of Political Change." *World Politics* 19 (January 1967): 190–217.

The Politics of Tradition: Continuity and Change in Northern Nigeria 1946–1966. Princeton, NJ: Princeton University Press, 1970.

White, Stephen K. *Edmund Burke: Modernity, Politics, and Aesthetics.* Thousand Oaks, CA: Sage, 1994.

Wiarda, Howard J. *Corporatism and Development: The Portuguese Experience.* Amherst: University of Massachusetts Press, 1977.

Bibliography

"Toward a Non-Ethnocentric Theory of Development: Alternative Conceptions from the Third World." Working paper presented to the American Political Science Association, 1981.

"Transcending Corporatism? The Portuguese Cooperative System and the Revolution of 1974." *Institute of International Studies Essay Series 3*. Columbia: University of South Carolina Press, 1976.

Wilentz, Sean. *Rites of Power: Symbolism, Ritual and Politics Since the Middle Ages*. Philadelphia: University of Philadelphia Press, 1985.

Wolf, Eric R. *Europe and the People Without History*. Berkeley: University of California Press, 1982.

Peasant Wars of the Twentieth Century. New York: Harper & Row, 1969.

Woods, Patricia. "Courting the Court: Social Visions, State Authority, and the Religious Law Debates in Israel," Ph.D. dissertation, University of Washington, forthcoming, 2001.

Zingman, Ben. "Lawrence Kohlberg: Morality *sans* Community." Unpublished paper.

Zolberg, Aristide R. *One-Party Government in the Ivory Coast* (revised edition). Princeton, NJ: Princeton University Press, 1969.

"Origins of the Modern System: A Missing Link," *World Politics* 33 (1981): 253–81.

Zubaida, Sami. *Islam, the People and the State: Essays on Political Ideas and Movements in the Middle East*. New York: Routledge, 1989.

Index

Index

Index

Continued from p. iii

Ellen Immergut, *Health Politics: Interests and Institutions in Western Europe*
Torben Iversen, *Contested Economic Institutions*
Torben Iversen, Jonas Pontusson, and David Soskice, eds., *Unions, Employers, and Central Banks: Macroeconomic Coordination and Institutional Change in Social Market Economies*
Thomas Janoski and Alexander M. Hicks, eds., *The Comparative Political Economy of the Welfare State*
Robert O. Keohane and Helen B. Milner, eds., *Internationalization and Domestic Politics*
Herbert Kitschelt, *The Transformation of European Social Democracy*
Herbert Kitschelt, Peter Lange, Gary Marks, and John D. Stephens, eds., *Continuity and Change in Contemporary Capitalism*
Herbert Kitschelt, Zdenka Mansfeldova, Radek Markowski, and Gabor Toka, *Post-Communist Party Systems*
David Knoke, Franz Urban Pappi, Jeffrey Broadbent, and Yutaka Tsujinaka, eds., *Comparing Policy Networks*
Allan Kornberg and Harold D. Clarke, *Citizens and Community: Political Support in a Representative Democracy*
David D. Laitin, *Language Repertoires and State Construction in Africa*
Mark Irving Lichbach and Alan S. Zuckerman, eds., *Comparative Politics: Rationality, Culture, and Structure*
Doug McAdam, John McCarthy, and Mayer Zald, eds., *Comparative Perspectives on Social Movements*
Scott Mainwaring and Matthew Soberg Shugart, eds., *Presidentialism and Democracy in Latin America*
Anthony W. Marx, *Making Race, Making Nations: A Comparison of South Africa, the United States and Brazil*
Joel S. Migdal, Atul Kohli, and Vivienne Shue, eds., *State Power and Social Forces: Domination and Transformation in the Third World*
Wolfgang C. Muller and Kaare Strom, *Policy, Office, or Votes?*
Ton Notermans, *Money, Markets, and the State: Social Democratic Economic Policies since 1918*
Paul Pierson, *Dismantling the Welfare State?: Reagan, Thatcher and the Politics of Retrenchment*
Marino Regini, *Uncertain Boundaries: The Social and Political Construction of European Economies*
Yossi Shain and Juan Linz, eds., *Interim Governments and Democratic Transitions*
Theda Skocpol, *Social Revolutions in the Modern World*
David Stark and László Bruszt, *Postsocialist Pathways: Transforming Politics and Property in East Central Europe*
Sven Steinmo, Kathleen Thelen, and Frank Longstreth, eds., *Structuring Politics: Historical Institutionalism in Comparative Analysis*
Sidney Tarrow, *Power in Movement: Social Movements and Contentious Politics*
Ashutosh Varshney, *Democracy, Development, and the Countryside*